कुमारसम्भवम्
KUMĀRASAMBHAVA

KUMĀRA-SAMBHAVA
OF
KĀLIDĀSA

Edited with introduction and English translation.

Edited by
C.R. DEVADHAR

MOTILAL BANARSIDASS PUBLISHERS
PRIVATE LIMITED • DELHI

First Edition: Delhi, 1985
Reprint: Delhi, 1993, 1997

ISBN: 81-208-0012-5

Also available at:

MOTILAL BANARSIDASS
41 U.A. Bungalow Road, Jawahar Nagar, Delhi 110 007
8, Mahalaxmi Chamber, Warden Road, Mumbai 400 026
120 Royapettah High Road, Mylapore, Madras 600 004
Sanas Plaza, Subhash Nagar, Pune 411 002
16 St. Mark's Road, Bangalore 560 001
8 Camac Street, Calcutta 700 017
Ashok Rajpath, Patna 800 004
Chowk, Varanasi 221 001

PRINTED IN INDIA

BY JAINENDRA PRAKASH JAIN AT SHRI JAINENDRA PRESS,
A-45 NARAINA, PHASE I, NEW DELHI 110 028
AND PUBLISHED BY NARENDRA PRAKASH JAIN FOR
MOTILAL BANARSIDASS PUBLISHERS PRIVATE LIMITED,
BUNGALOW ROAD, DELHI 110 007

INTRODUCTION

The Kumārasambhava of Kālidāsa is a tour-de-force of literary effort of a very high order, and is in fact the oriflamme of Indian poetic genius. It is a gem among Kālidāsa's poetic works. It sings of divine love and of the strife between Tāraka's demon hosts and godly hosts led by Kumāra, in which ultimately Asura Tāraka is worsted. It is based on a legend of the Śivapurāṇa.

Canto—I :—

There to the north is the mountain Himālaya. It stretches itself like a measuring rod dipping in the oceans eastern and western, a miracle of beauty astounding, a mine of mineral dyes wherewith heaven's nymphs embellish their limbs.

Dark and white rows of clouds scud across its spoors, to shed numberless weary travellers. The lion's pug-marks, the Kirātas notice; the winds the bamboo hollows fill, sweet music to make, the mind to enchant; there the phospherous plants illumine the mouths of caves, dark and wide, to light Sabara's love play. He protects darkness murky in his caverns, like owls scurrying swiftly to hide their faces being afraid of day's light.

He (Himālaya) married Menā and as the winged days flew on, she was with child. In due time she gave birth to Maināka, the husband of Nāga damsels, and Satī who was Siva's spouse. And the king of mountains begot on her the auspicious Satī; she, who was chaste after she was born, waxed day by day, like the digit of the moon, and developed a beauty of a kind ineffable.

Her relations, to whom she was dear, named her Pārvatī; to her came learning of a previous birth. She came of an age, which comes after childhood. Nārada, while wandering at will, saw his (Himālaya's) daughter by his side. The mountain could not prevail upon Śiva to accept the hand of his daughter, because he did not sue for it.

Lord Śiva performed penance, with some desire in his mind; and the lord of mountains welcomed him asking his daughter to wait upon him, with her friends. Gathering flowers for offering, and sweeping the floor of the altar, and bringing Kuśa grass she waited upon Giriśa every day.

Canto—II :—

At that time, the gods, troubled by the demon Tāraka, went to the creator and praised him. Having heard their praises, the god answered "O ye gods ! Why are you afraid ?" The gods replied "The great demon Tāraka growing impudent, through a boon you granted, has risen like a comet to devastate the world. The creator said, "So you try to attract the heart of Śiva; only two are able to bear his seed—Umā and my watery form."

Canto—III :—

The thousand eyes of Indra fell upon Kāma, who stood before him with folded hands, and said, 'What do you seek to accomplish in the world ?" Indra replied, 'The gods desire a commander-in-chief to be born out of the seed of Bhava, for victory. I have heard from heavenly nymph that the daughter of the mountain, at the behest of her father, is waiting upon Lord Śiva, who is practising penance upon the upper reaches of the mountain. Try that the self-restrained daughter of Himādri is liked by him. Kāma, accompanied by Rati, went to Śiva's Āśrama. He was also accompanied by his friend Spring, who appeared in the forest. Then approached Pārvatī, accompanied by her friends in the forest, and offered to Śiva a rosary of lotus-seeds. He was about to accept it when the god of love placed a shaft powerful upon his bow. Then Śaṁkara curbed the agitation of his senses with strong will, and looking for its cause, directed his gaze to the ends of the quarters and saw Kāma; Then all at once, a flame of fire shot from his third eye, and consumed Kāma to ashes. Pārvatī felt that her heart's desire was of no availand she was led homewards by Himādri.

Canto—IV :—

Then Rati fell into a swoon and when she opened her eyes, she lamented wildly at the sight of her husband's ashes. She said, "Thou didst leave me without cause; I shall smear these lovely ashes of my husband to my breasts, and lay myself on the funeral pyre. Oh fie upon the transience of human life !" A voice from the sky comforted her, saying, "O wife of Kusumāyudha ! preserve this thy body; for you are destined to be united with thy husband." Thus Rati, wilted by that calamity, awaited the end of that calamity.

Canto—V :—

Pārvatī told her noble father her will to stay in the forest, to observe the vow of penance till she reaped her heart's desire. A handsome hermit, who came to the forest, asked Umā, if what her friends told was mere chaffing. Then Pārvatī said that she longed to marry Śiva. The hermit said that he could not commend her choice and spoke in derogatory terms about Śiva. This Pārvatī resented bitterly. "Do thou stop this brat," said Pārvatī to her friend, and moved away from that place. Now Śiva revealed himself, and said, "O beautiful lady ! from now on, I am thy slave, won by thy penance." The momen Candraśekhara spoke thus, she gave up her fatigue born of her penance; for labour renovates one when its fruit is reaped.

Canto—VI :—

Then Gaurī sent her friend to Lord Śiva, requesting him to honour the Lord of mountains. Śiva then went to the Saptarṣis with Arundhatī in their midst. They said, 'Blessed were they in that they had a direct vision of the lord." Śiva then told them that they should request the mountain to bestow his daughter in marriage upon him. The sages then went to Himālaya's capital, and requested him to bestow his daughter on Śiva in marriage. Himālaya consented to the match and Pārvatī was joined in wedlock to Śiva.

Canto—VII :—

After elaborate preparations of marriage, Hara and his bride were joined in wedlock, and received the blessings of their relations, Arundhatī and the seven mothers amongst them. And then Śiva and Pārvatī entered their palace, where they enjoyed marital happiness.

Canto—VIII :—

They went to Gandhamādana, where they indulged in various sexual pleasures; but they were not surfeited with those pleasures like the submarine fire with the flood of waters.

Canto--IX :—

Thus while he was savouring the pleasures of love, a pigeon, who was no other than Agni, entered the chamber and sought on behalf of Indra and the gods, a commander to lead the godly hosts against the demon Tāraka. Śiva deposited his infallible semen in Fire. The moon-crested god, dwelling on Kailāsa, pleased with various kinds of enjoyments with Pārvatī, rejoiced in the company of his submissive Gaṇas.

Canto—X :—

Then Agni bearing Śiva's semen approached Indra, and was advised to cast it in the Ganges, who would receive it. The seed of Hara passed from Agni to the Ganges, and it emerged pure from her. The Kṛttikās went to the Ganges for bathing, and received from her (i.e. Ganges) Hara's semen. The wise Kṛttikās, unable to bear it, cast it in a forest of reeds, and from it was born, with immeasurable splendour, a child with six mouths.

Canto—XI :—

There was a great dispute between the Ganges, the Kṛttikās and Agni, to take the divine child. Śiva and Pārvatī came to that place and Pārvatī asked Hara, whose child it was. She was told by Śiva that it was her son, the delight of the world. Pārvatī took hold of the child and caressed it.

A great festival was held to celebrate the birth of the child. The child indulged in most graceful childish games, and attained on the sixth day fresh youth and talents; and he became a master of all the weapons and all the lores.

Canto—XII :—

Indra came with all the gods to Śiva's palace; and Śiva said "On being requested by the gods to give them a leader, I appoint my son Kumāra to the command of your army." Kumāra accepted the command of his father and Indra was overjoyed.

Canto—XIII :—

Kumāra took leave of Śiva, his father, and followed by the gods, traversed the path of stars, and reached heaven. Kāśyapa and the mother of the gods blessed him, and the gods and Kumāra marched forth to fight against Tāraka.

Canto—XIV :—

Egged on by the son of Andhaka, all together girded up their loins to kill forcibly their enemy, the great demon Tāraka. The dust, raised by the army from the ground, as it was hanging in the sky, was tawny owing to the glow of untimely twilight. And so the army marched on, and rent the skies with their war-cries.

Canto—XV :—

The great demons heard that Kumāra was leading the godly hosts against them, and they trembled with fear. And evil portents appeared before them and they felt more uneasy. Although fearing disaster, they marched forth. The two armies sought to annihilate each other in battle; and a great outcry was raised by them, that filled the hollows of space.

Canto—XVI :—

A great battle was fought, in which the two armies clashed violently together. While thus they clashed, Tāraka advanced to Indra and the other gods to fight against them.

Canto—XVII :—

The Asura said to the child warrior, "Thou art fighting against odds; wisely retreat from battle". The son of Īśa released his Śaktī against the sovereign lord of the Asuras, and brought his head to his heels. There fell upon the head of Kumāra a shower of Kalpa flowers. Indra and the gods congratulated the might of the arms of Tāraka's foe.

कुमारसम्भवम् ।

अस्त्युत्तरस्यां दिशि देवतात्मा हिमालयो नाम नगाधिराजः ।
पूर्वापरौ तोयनिधी वगाह्य स्थितः पृथिव्या इव मानदण्डः ॥१॥

There is to the North, a mountain, named Himālaya, whose soul is a deity, with his spurs diving into the Eastern and Western ocean; he stands as the measuring rod of the earth. (1).

यं सर्वशैलाः परिकल्प्य वत्सं मेरौ स्थिते दोग्धरि दोहदक्षे ।
भास्वन्ति रत्नानि महौषधीश्च पृथूपदिष्टां दुदुहुर्धरित्रीम् ॥२॥

All the mountains looked upon him as their calf, while Meru stood as the milk-man, intent on milking; they milked sparkling gems and herbs of great potency, of the earth, who had assumed the form of a cow, while Pṛthu directed the operation. (2).

अनन्तरत्नप्रभवस्य यस्य हिमं न सौभाग्यविलोपि जातम् ।
एको हि दोषो गुणसन्निपाते निमज्जतीन्दोः किरणेष्विवाङ्कः ॥३॥

And of him, of countless gems the source : he was not shorn of his beauty by snow; for, one flaw is easily lost in a conglomeration of virtues, as the Moon's spot blemishes not the moon, as it is sunk in the bright beams, whose gloam is divided between strips of clouds. (3).

यश्चाप्सरोविभ्रममण्डनानां सम्पादयित्रीं शिखरैर्बिभर्ति ।
बलाहकच्छेदविभक्तरागामकालसन्ध्यामिव धातुमत्ताम् ॥४॥

He bears on his peaks, rich minerals, like untimely twilight, which help the nymphs of heaven, to fashion their amorous decorations. (4).

आमेखलं सञ्चरतां घनानां छायामधःसानुगतां निषेव्य ।
उद्वेजिता वृष्टिभिराश्रयन्ते शृङ्गाणि यस्यातपवन्ति सिद्धाः ॥५॥

Persons on the way to salvation, having enjoyed the shadows of the clouds fallen below its peaks, while these clouds scurry over the slopes, being frightened by showers, resort to its sun-lit peaks. (5).

पदं तुषारस्रुतिधौतरक्तं यस्मिन्नदृष्ट्वाऽपि हतद्विपानाम् ।
विदन्ति मार्गं नखरन्ध्रमुक्तैर्मुक्ताफलैः केसरिणां किराताः ॥६॥

Where the Kirātas notice the lion's pug-marked, blood-stained trail, which has the blood washed by snow,—(lions) who have killed the elephants,—by the pearls dropped from the hollows of their claws, without seeing it. (6).

न्यस्ताक्षरा धातुरसेन यत्र भूर्जत्वचः कुञ्जरबिन्दुशोणाः ।
व्रजन्ति विद्याधरसुन्दरीणामनङ्गलेखक्रिययोपयोगम् ॥७॥

Where the Bhūrja-barks, red like spots on the elephant's body, whereon are written letters in mineral ink, serve the purpose of Vidyādhara ladies, as love-letters. (7).

यः पूरयन् कीचकरन्ध्रभागान् दरीमुखोत्थेन समीरणेन ।
उद्गास्यतामिच्छति किन्नराणां तानप्रदायित्वमिवोपगन्तुम् ॥८॥

Who, filling the hollows of the bamboos, by wind rising from the mouth of the valley, as if to add melody to the song of Kinnaras, are about to start singing. (8).

कपोलकण्डूः करिभिर्विनेतुं विघट्टितानां सरलद्रुमाणाम् ।
यत्र स्रुतक्षीरतया प्रसूतः सानूनि गन्धः सुरभीकरोति ॥९॥

Where, the odour of milky juice of Sarala trees, whose barks are rubbed away by elephants, who scratch their temples to allay the itching of them, makes the peaks fragrant. (9).

वनेचराणां वनितासखानां दरीगृहोत्सङ्गनिषक्तभासः ।
भवन्ति यत्रौषधयो रजन्यामतैलपूराः सुरतप्रदीपाः ॥१०॥

Where the phospherous herbs serve as lamps, burning without oil, illumining the broad mouths of the valleys to light the love-play of the foresters, accompanied by their wives. (10).

उद्वेजयत्यङ्गुलिपार्ष्णिभागान् मार्गे शिलीभूतहिमेऽपि यत्र ।
न दुर्वहश्रोणिपयोधरार्त्ता भिन्दन्ति मन्दां गतिमश्वमुख्यः ॥११॥

Though the frozen snow distressed the heels and toes, of the Kinnara women, yet they did not give up their slow gait, afflicted as they were, by the unbearable weight of their hips. (11).

दिवाकराद्रक्षति यो गुहासु लीनं दिवाभीतमिवाऽन्धकारम् ।
क्षुद्रेऽपि नूनं शरणं प्रपन्ने ममत्वमुच्चैःशिरसां सतीव ॥१२॥

He, who protects darkness, which like an owl, has hidden itself in his caves; for the good and the great spurn not the suppliant, however lowly his state. (12).

लाङ्गूलविक्षेपविसर्पिशोभैरितस्ततश्चन्द्रमरीचिगौरैः ।
यस्याऽर्थयुक्तं गिरिराजशब्दं कुर्वन्ति बालव्यजनैश्चमर्यः ॥१३॥

For, the Camari deer, by tossing about their tails, whose gleam is white like moon-beams, as it is dispersed in all directions, give significance to his title "the king of mountains", as if by waving over him the Cāmaras. (13).

यत्रांऽशुकाक्षेपविलज्जितानां यदृच्छया किम्पुरुषाऽङ्गनानाम् ।
दरीगृहद्वारविलम्बिबिम्बास्तिरस्करिण्यो जलदा भवन्ति ॥१४॥

Where wives of Kinnaras being sansculotte, their garments being snatched from them, are filled with shame; and the clouds, whose masses, hanging over the portals of their cave-houses, serve as screens. (14).

भागीरथीनिर्झरसीकराणां वोढा मुहुः कम्पितदेवदारुः ।
यद्वायुरन्विष्टमृगैः किरातैरासेव्यते भिन्नशिखण्डिबर्हः ॥१५॥

Whose breezes, charged with spray from the current of the Bhāgīrathī, and which make the Devadāru trees to quake, are enjoyed by the Kirātas, as they breathe in welcome freshness, over the wearied faces of these hunters, when they quit the chase, and which have scattered the peacock's plumage. (15).

सप्तर्षिहस्तावचितावशेषाण्यधो विवस्वान्परिवर्तमानः ।
पद्मानि यस्याऽग्रसरोरुहाणि प्रबोधयत्यूर्ध्वमुखैर्मयूखैः ॥१६॥

And as the sun revolves below its peaks, he breathes life into the lotuses, which bloom far aloft in the pools on the high Himālayan steeps and which remain after the Saptarṣis have culled them with their hands. (16).

यज्ञाङ्गयोनित्वमवेक्ष्य यस्य सारं धरित्रीधरणक्षमं च ।
प्रजापतिः कल्पितयज्ञभागं शैलाधिपत्यं स्वयमन्वतिष्ठत् ॥१७॥

And marking him as the source of the materials of sacrifice, and marking his strength, as well able to support the earth, the creator bade him share in the sacrifice, and himself attended his installation as king of the mountains. (17).

स मानसीं मेरुसखः पितॄणां कन्यां कुलस्य स्थितये स्थितिज्ञः ।
मेनां मुनीनामपि माननीयामात्माऽनुरूपां विधिनोपयेमे ॥१८॥

He, obedient to the law divine, married Menā, according to proper rites, the mind-born daughter of the manes, for the continuation of his line,—(she) who was respected by the sages and who was worthy of him in every way. (18).

कालक्रमेणाऽथ तयोः प्रवृत्ते स्वरूपयोग्ये सुरतप्रसङ्गे ।
मनोरमं यौवनमुद्वहन्त्या गर्भोऽभवद् भूधरराजपत्न्याः ॥१९॥

As the season winged with love flew on, and as they indulged in love-play, proper to their spirits, she, the wife of the king of mountains, who was so lovely, was with child. (19).

असूत सा नागवधूपभोग्यं मैनाकमम्भोनिधिबद्धसख्यम् ।
क्रुद्धेऽपि पक्षच्छिदि वृत्रशत्राववेदनाज्ञं कुलिशक्षतानाम् ॥२०॥

In due time, she gave birth to a son, Maināka, who was to be the husband of the Nāga damsels, and who had formed friendship with the ocean, and even when, Vṛtra's foe was wroth, he did not know the anguish, caused by the thunderbolt of Indra, as he clipped the wings of mountains. (20).

अथाऽवमानेन पितुः प्रयुक्ता दक्षस्य कन्या भवपूर्वपत्नी ।
सती सती योगविसृष्टदेहा तां जन्मने शैलवधूं प्रपेदे ॥२१॥

Then, the chaste Satī, Dakṣa's daughter, and the former wife of Śiva, impelled by the insult to her father, shuffled off her body by the pathway of yoga, and resorted to the spouse of the mountain for birth. (21).

सा भूधराणामधिपेन तस्यां समाधिमत्यामुदपादि भव्या ।
सम्यक्प्रयोगादपरिक्षतायां नीताविवोत्साहगुणेन सम्पत् ॥२२॥

And the king of mountains begot on her, the auspicious Satī—she—who was chaste, and was observing vows, as the power of energy produces wealth, in association with political wisdom. (22).

प्रसन्नदिक्पांसुविविक्तवातं शङ्खस्वनाऽनन्तरपुष्पवृष्टि ।
शरीरिणां स्थावरजङ्गमानां सुखाय तज्जन्मदिनं बभूव ॥२३॥

The quarters were serene, and the winds were free from specks of dust, and there was a shower of flowers, after the blare of conches; the day of her birth made for happiness, for both mobile and immobile beings. (23).

तया दुहित्रा सुतरां सवित्री स्फुरत्प्रभामण्डलया चकासे ।
विदूरभूमिर्नवमेघशब्दादुद्भिन्नया रत्नशलाकयेव ॥२४॥

The mother shone all the more, with that daughter, as the mine of turquoise, which shines, by spurting pencils of gems. (24).

दिने दिने सा परिवर्धमाना लब्धोदया चान्द्रमसीव लेखा ।
पुपोष लावण्यमयान्विशेषाञ्ज्योत्स्नान्तराणीव कलान्तराणि ॥२५॥

After she was born, as she waxed day by day, like the digit of the moon, she developed special features of beauty, as the digits of the moon, when concealed in moon-light. (25).

तां पार्वतीत्याभिजनेन नाम्ना बन्धुप्रियां बन्धुजनो जुहाव ।
उ मेति मात्रा तपसो निषिद्धा पश्चादुमाख्यां सुमुखी जगाम ॥२६॥

Her relations, to whom she was dear, named her Pārvatī; then as her mother forbade her, with the words 'U' 'Oh child' and 'Mā, Don't', from the practice of penance, she, this girl with a lovely face, came thereafter to be known by the name, 'Umā'. (26).

महीभृतः पुत्रवतोऽपि दृष्टिस्तस्मिन्नपत्ये न जगाम तृप्तिम् ।
अनन्तपुष्पस्य मधोर्हि चूते द्विरेफमाला सविशेषसङ्गा ॥२७॥

The eyes of the mountain, were not satisfied with looking at that child; for spring, albeit full of a variety of flowers yet the bee has a special attachment for the Mango-blossom. (27).

प्रभामहत्या शिखयेव दीपस्त्रिमार्गयेव त्रिदिवस्य मार्गः ।
संस्कारवत्येव गिरा मनीषी तया स पूतश्च विभूषितश्च ॥२८॥

As the lamp with a highly refulgent flame, as the savanna of the sky by the triple-streamed Bhāgirathī, as a wise man by speech is grammatically pure, so was he more embellished and purified by her. (28).

मन्दाकिनीसैकतवेदिकाभिः सा कन्दुकैः कृत्रिमपुत्रकैश्च ।
रेमे मुहुर्मध्यगता सखीनां क्रीडारसं निर्विशतीव बाल्ये ॥२९॥

She seemed to enjoy the relish of sport in her childhood, in the midst of her friends, with making platforms of sand, with balls and with dolls. (29).

तां हंसमालाः शरदीव गङ्गां महोषधिं नक्तमिवात्मभासः ।
स्थिरोपदेशामुपदेशकाले प्रपेदिरे प्राक्तनजन्मविद्याः ॥३०॥

To her came the learning of her previous birth,— (her) whose learning left a deep impression, like flights of swans in autumn to the Ganges as at night their own refulgence, to the great herbs. (30).

असम्भृतं मण्डनमङ्गयष्टेरनासवाख्यं करणं मदस्य ।
कामस्य पुष्पव्यतिरिक्तमस्त्रं बाल्यात्परं साऽथ वयः प्रपेदे ॥३१॥

She reached the age, which comes after the age of childhood, which is an inborn embellishment of the body, an agent of intoxication other than wine, a weapon of the God of love other than flowers. (31).

उन्मीलितं तूलिकयेव चित्रं सूर्यांशुभिर्भिन्नमिवाऽरविन्दम् ।
बभूव तस्याश्चतुरस्रशोभि वपुर्विभक्तं नवयौवनेन ॥३२॥

Her body, as revealed by youth, was like a painting, developed with a brush, or like a lotus, blooming into life at the touch of the rays of the sun, looked beautiful, perfect in all limbs. (32).

अभ्युन्नताङ्गुष्ठनखप्रभाभिर्निक्षेपणाद्रागमिवोद्गिरन्तौ ।
आजह्रतुस्तच्चरणौ पृथिव्यां स्थलारविन्दश्रियमव्यवस्थाम् ॥३३॥

Her feet, with the big toe and its nail raised up, oozing out the dye, by being planted on the earth, robbed the beauty of the moving land-growing lotus-plant. (33).

सा राजहंसैरिव सन्नताङ्गी गतेषु लीलाञ्चितविक्रमेषु ।
व्यनीयत प्रत्युपदेशलुब्धैरादित्सुभिर्नूपुरसिञ्जितानि ॥३४॥

She seemed to be instructed by the swans, in graceful, light tripping movement; she, of stooping limbs, who were eager to learn from her, desiring to impart to her the jingling of anklets. (34).

वृत्तानुपूर्वे च न चातिदीर्घे जङ्घे शुभे सृष्टवतस्तदीये ।
शेषाङ्गनिर्माणविधौ विधातुर्लावण्य उत्पाद्य इवास यत्नः ॥३५॥

The creator, having fashioned her legs, round and tapering from the knee down, had to make an effort in producing beauty for fashioning the remaining limbs. (35).

नागेन्द्रहस्तास्त्वचि कर्कशत्वादेकान्तशैत्यात्कदलीविशेषाः ।
लब्ध्वाऽपि लोके परिणाहि रूपं जातास्तदूर्वोरुपमानबाह्याः ॥३६॥

The trunks of elephants, because of the toughness of their skin and plantain-stalks, because of their extreme coolness, were outside the pale standards of comparison for her thighs. (36).

एतावता नन्वनुमेयशोभि काञ्चीगुणस्थानमनिन्दितायाः ।
आरोपितं यद्गिरिशेन पश्चादनन्यनारीकमनीयमङ्कम् ॥३७॥

Thus, the hips, whose loveliness was inferrable, which were clasped by the golden girdle, of this flawless damsel, were taken in his lap by Lord Śiva, an honour not shared by any other lady. (37).

तस्याः प्रविष्टा नतनाभिरन्ध्रं रराज तन्वी नवलोमराजिः ।
नीवीमतिक्रम्य सितेतरस्य तन्मेखलामध्यमणेरिवार्चिः ॥३८॥

The tiny line of soft hair crossing the knot of her

garment entered her deep navel, and shone like the sapphire, which shines at the middle of her girdle. (38).

मध्येन सा वेदिविलग्नमध्या वलित्रयं चारु बभार बाला ।
आरोहणार्थं नवयौवनेन कामस्य सोपानमिव प्रयुक्तम् ॥३९॥

She, whose waist was thin as an altar, bore on it three folds of skin, which were designed as a stairway by fresh youth, to enable love to ascend. (39).

अन्योन्यमुत्पीडयदुत्पलाक्ष्याः स्तनद्वयं पाण्डु तथा प्रवृद्धम् ।
मध्ये यथा श्याममुखस्य तस्य मृणालसूत्रान्तरमप्यलभ्यम् ॥४०॥

Her twin breasts grew in such a manner that they pressed against each other, so that between them, whose nipples were dark, even a slender thread of a lotus-stalk could not find a way. (40).

शिरीषपुष्पाऽधिकसौकुमार्यौ बाहू तदीयाविति मे वितर्कः ।
पराजितेनाऽपि कृतौ हरस्य यौ कण्ठपाशौ मकरध्वजेन ॥४१॥

I surmise that her arms were more delicate than Śirīṣa flowers; for vain was Madana's strife with Śiva, till he chose those chains to bind his conqueror, Hara, fast. (41).

कण्ठस्य तस्याः स्तनबन्धुरस्य मुक्ताकलापस्य च निस्तलस्य ।
अन्योन्यशोभाजननाद् बभूव साधारणो भूषणभूष्यभावः ॥४२॥

Her neck, uplifted owing to her breasts, and the round pearls in her necklace, by producing beauty each in the other, shared in common the relation of the embellisher and the embellished. (42).

चन्द्रं गता पद्मगुणान्न भुङ्क्ते पद्माश्रिता चान्द्रमसीमभिख्याम् ।
उमामुखं तु प्रतिपद्य लोला द्विसंश्रयां प्रीतिमवाप लक्ष्मीः ॥४३॥

The Goddess of beauty, when with the moon, does not enjoy the virtues of the lotus, and, when with the lotus, the lustre of the moon; but by resorting to the face of Umā, had the satisfaction of resorting to both. (43).

पुष्पं प्रवालोपहितं यदि स्यान्मुक्ताफलं वा स्फुटविद्रुमस्थम् ।
ततोऽनुकुर्याद्विशदस्य तस्यास्ताम्रोष्ठपर्यस्तरुचः स्मितस्य ॥४४॥

If a flower were to nestle snugly in tender leaves, or a fair pearl were to be set in fair coral, then would either of them imitate the beauty of her smile, which flasheth on her red lips. (44).

स्वरेण तस्याममृतस्रुतेव प्रजल्पितायामभिजातवाचि ।
अप्यन्यपुष्टा प्रतिकूलशब्दा श्रोतुर्वितन्त्रीरिव ताड्यमाना ॥४५॥

On hearing voice, which seemed to drip nectar, when she spoke sweetly, the koil's voice was repugnant to the ear of the hearer tuneless as the jarring note on a lute. (45).

प्रवातनीलोत्पलनिर्विशेषमधीरविप्रेक्षितमायताक्ष्या ।
तया गृहीतं नु मृगाङ्गनाभ्यस्ततो गृहीतं नु मृगाङ्गनाभिः ॥४६॥

The glances of the long-eyed one, tremulous as a blue lotus in a blast of wind,—did she borrow them from the does, or did they borrow them from her ? (46).

तस्याः शलाकाञ्जननिर्मितेव कान्तिर्भ्रुवोरायतलेखयोर्या ।
तां वीक्ष्य लीलाचतुरामनङ्गः स्वचापसौन्दर्यमदं मुमोच ॥४७॥

The charm of her long eye-brows, lovely through their graceful play, seemed to be produced by pencils of collyrium; on observing that, the God of love, so adept in graces, gave up his pride for the beauty of his bow. (47).

लज्जा तिरश्चां यदि चेतसि स्यादसंशयं पर्वतराजपुत्र्याः ।
तं केशपाशं प्रसमीक्ष्य कुर्युर्वालप्रियत्वं शिथिलं चमर्यः ॥४८॥

If, the sense of shame ever touched the hearts of lower animals, undoubtedly on seeing that braid of hair of the daughter of the mountain, the Camarī deer would relax their pride in their bushy tails. (48).

सर्वोपमाद्रव्यसमुच्चयेन यथाप्रदेशं विनिवेशितेन ।
सा निर्मिता विश्वसृजा प्रयत्नादेकस्थसौन्दर्यदिदृक्षयेव ॥४९॥

She was created by the creator, with great effort, from all materials of standards of comparison moulding each limb, as if the world's creator would behold all beauty centred in a single mould. (49).

तां नारदः कामचरः कदाचित्कन्यां किल प्रेक्ष्य पितुः समीपे ।
समादिदेशैकवधूं भवित्रीं प्रेम्णा शरीरार्धहरां हरस्य ॥५०॥

Nārada, while wandering at will, saw her near her father and prophesied that she would be the bride-to-be of Śiva, sharing through love half his body. (50).

गुरुः प्रगल्भेऽपि वयस्यतोऽस्यास्तस्थौ निवृत्तान्यवराभिलाषः ।
ऋते कृशानोर्न हि मन्त्रपूतमर्हन्ति तेजांस्यपराणि हव्यम् ॥५१॥

The father albeit, she was of an age, ripe for marriage, withdrew his desire for any other bridegroom; for except fire, no other lustre deserves an oblation, consecrated by Mantras. (51).

अयाचितारं न हि देवदेवमद्रिः सुतां ग्राहयितुं शशाक ।
अभ्यर्थनाभङ्गभयेन साधुर्माध्यस्थ्यमिष्टेऽप्यवलम्बतेऽर्थे ॥५२॥

The mountain could not prevail upon Śiva, the God of Gods, to accept his daughter, since he did not sue for her hand; a good man, for fear that his request may be repulsed, assumes an attitude of indifference, towards even a highly desired object. (52).

यदैव पूर्वे जनने शरीरं सा दक्षरोषात्सुदती ससर्ज ।
तदा प्रभृत्येव विमुक्तसङ्गः पतिः पशूनामपरिग्रहोऽभूत् ॥५३॥

When through Dakṣa's wrath, the beautiful lady shuffled off her mortal coil, in her previous birth, since that time on, the Lord of beings indifferent to worldly pleasure, remained unmarried. (53).

स कृत्तिवासास्तपसे यतात्मा गङ्गाप्रवाहोक्षितदेवदारु ।
प्रस्थं हिमाद्रेर्मृगनाभिगन्धि किञ्चित्क्वणत्किन्नरमध्युवास ॥५४॥

That God of the elephant-hide, controlling his senses for the performance of penances, resorted to a certain peak of the Himālayas, where the Devadāru trees were washed by the current of the Ganges, which was odorous, with the scent of musk, where the Kinnaras were singing in a low voice. (54).

गणा नमेरुप्रसवावतंसा भूर्जत्वचः स्पर्शवतीर्दधानाः ।
मनःशिलाविच्छुरिता निषेदुः शैलेयनद्धेषु शिलातलेषु ॥५५॥

The followers of Śiva, wearing as ear-ornaments the blossom of the Namerū, and wearing Bhūrja barks pleasant to touch and smearing Manasśila to their bodies sat on moss-covered blocks of stone. (55).

तुषारसङ्घातशिलाः खुराग्रैः समुल्लिखन्दर्पकलः ककुद्मान् ।
दृष्टः कथञ्चिद् गवयैर्विविग्नैरसोढसिंहध्वनिरुन्ननाद ॥५६॥

The humped bull (of Śiva) making a soft bellow through intoxication scratched blocks of snow with the points of his hooves, and not putting up with the lion's roar, bellowed aloud, and was looked at with difficulty, by the Gavayas (Bos gavaious). (56).

तत्राऽग्निमाधाय समित्समिद्धं स्वमेव मूर्त्यन्तरमष्टमूर्तिः ।
स्वयं विधाता तपसः फलानां केनाऽपि कामेन तपश्चचार ॥५७॥

There God Śiva who has eight forms, kindled the sacred fire, which is one of his own forms, which was blazing with the proffered oblations, performed penance, with some desire in mind, though himself, the creator of the fruit of penance. (57).

अनर्घ्यमर्घ्येण तमद्रिनाथः स्वर्गौकसामर्चितमर्चयित्वा ।
आराधनायाऽस्य सखीसमेतां समादिदेश प्रयतां तनूजाम् ॥५८॥

The Lord of Mountains received that invaluable one, with welcome offerings,—he who was worshipped by the gods, detailed his self-controlled daughter, along with her friends, to wait upon him. (58).

प्रत्यर्थिभूतामपि तां समाधेः शुश्रूषमाणां गिरिशोऽनुमेने ।
विकारहेतौ सति विक्रियन्ते येषां न चेतांसि त एव धीराः ॥५९॥

The Lord Śiva, allowed her to wait upon him, though she was an obstacle to the concentration of the mind; they alone are self-controlled, whose minds are not affected, when the cause thereof is present. (59).

अवचितबलिपुष्पा वेदिसम्मार्गदक्षा
नियमविधिजलानां बर्हिषां चोपनेत्री ।
गिरिशमुपचचार प्रत्यहं सा सुकेशी
नियमितपरिखेदा तच्छिरश्चन्द्रपादैः ॥६०॥

Gathering flowers for offering, and diligent in sweeping the altar, and fetching water for the performance of vows, and fetching Kuśa grass, thus she waited upon Girīśa every day, her fatigue being removed by the rays of the moon on his head. (60).

द्वितीयः सर्गः

तस्मिन् विप्रकृताः काले तारकेण दिवौकसः ।
तुरासाहं पुरोधाय धाम स्वायम्भुवं ययुः ॥१॥

At that time, the gods, troubled by the demon Tāraka, went to the abode of the self-created, (the creator), putting Indra at their head. (1).

तेषामाविरभूद्ब्रह्मा परिम्लानमुखश्रियाम् ।
सरसां सुप्तपद्मानां प्रातर्दीधितिमानिव ॥२॥

To them with their looks of woe, appeared the creator, as at the hour of the morn, does the sun, to a lake wherein lotuses are closed. (2).

अथ सर्वस्य धातारं ते सर्वे सर्वतोमुखम् ।
वागीशं वाग्भिरर्थ्याभिः प्रणिपत्योपतस्थिरे ॥३॥

Then all those Gods, waited upon the creator of all things, who has his mouths in four directions, and besought this Lord of speech, with truthful prayers. (3).

नमस्त्रिमूर्तये तुभ्यं प्राक्सृष्टेः केवलात्मने ।
गुणत्रयविभागाय पश्चाद्भेदमुपेयुषे ॥४॥

"Glory to thee, triple in form, who was of one uniform nature before creation, and who later underwent transformation into forms of triple quality. (4).

यदमोघमपामन्तरुप्तं बीजमज ! त्वया ।
अतश्चराचरं विश्वं प्रभवस्तस्य गीयसे ॥५॥

You are sung as the source of the world of mobile and immobile forms, which sprung into existence, from the germ you cast upon quickening waters. (5).

तिसृभिस्त्वमवस्थाभिर्महिमानमुदीरयन् ।
प्रलयस्थितिसर्गाणामेकः कारणतां गतः ॥६॥

You were the sole cause of the creation, dissolution, maintenance of the world, manifesting your greatness in triple form. (6).

स्त्रीपुंसावात्मभागौ ते भिन्नमूर्तेः सिसृक्षया ।
प्रसूतिभाजः सर्गस्य तावेव पितरौ स्मृतौ ॥७॥

Of thee, whose form is the universe, male and female were the parts, desiring to create; they were the parents of the creation that sprang into existence. (7).

स्वकालपरिमाणेन व्यस्तरात्रिन्दिवस्य ते ।
यौ तु स्वप्नावबोधौ तौ भूतानां प्रलयोदयौ ॥८॥

Of thee, night and day that thou hast divided according to thy measure, are thy sleep and waking, are the rise and the dissolution of beings. (8).

जगद्योनिरयोनिस्त्वं जगदन्तो निरन्तकः ।
जगदादिरनादिस्त्वं जगदीशो निरीश्वरः ॥९॥

Thou art the cause of the universe, thyself causeless, the death of the universe, thyself deathless though; the beginning of the world, though thyself beginningless; the destroyer of the world, thyself without destruction. Thou, the master of the universe, thyself without a master. (9).

आत्मानमात्मना वेत्सि सृजस्यात्मानमात्मना ।
आत्मना कृतिना च त्वमात्मन्येव प्रलीयसे ॥१०॥

Thou art thyself capable of creating thyself by thyself, thou knowest thyself and thou art dissolved in thyself. (10).

द्रवः सङ्घातकठिनः स्थूलः सूक्ष्मो लघुर्गुरुः ।
व्यक्तो व्यक्तेतरश्चासि प्राकाम्यं ते विभूतिषु ॥११॥

Thou art of liquid form, and hard by mass, gross subtle, light and heavy, manifest and unmanifest, and thou actest according to thy will, towards the elements. (11).

उद्घातः प्रणवो यासां न्यायैस्त्रिभिरुदीरणम् ।
कर्म यज्ञः फलं स्वर्गस्तासां त्वं प्रभवो गिराम् ॥१२॥

Thou art the source of speech, that begins with the sacred syllable 'Om', which is uttered with the three accents, which results in action viz. sacrifice whose fruit is heaven. (12).

त्वामामनन्ति प्रकृतिं पुरुषार्थप्रवर्तिनीम् ।
तद्दर्शिनमुदासीनं त्वामेव पुरुषं विदुः ॥१३॥

Thou art regarded as the primordial cause, which acts so as to accomplish the three ends of human existence, thou art known as the seer of that, thyself being indifferent. (13).

त्वं पितृणामपि पिता देवानामपि देवता ।
परतोऽपि परश्चासि विधाता वेधसामपि ॥१४॥

Thou art the father even of the fathers, the God of gods, greater than the great, the creator of creators. (14).

त्वमेव हव्यं होता च भोज्यं भोक्ता च शाश्वतः ।
वेद्यं च वेदिता चासि ध्याता ध्येयं च यत्परम् ॥१५॥

Thou art the oblation and the sacrificer, the object of enjoyment and the enjoyer, thou art the perceiver, and the object to be perceived, the meditator, and the highest object of meditation." (15).

इति तेभ्यः स्तुतीः श्रुत्वा यथार्था हृदयङ्गमाः ।
प्रसादाभिमुखो वेधाः प्रत्युवाच दिवौकसः ॥१६॥

Having heard their praises, that were true in their import, and that touched the heart, the creator who was disposed to favour, answered the gods, thus— (16).

पुराणस्य कवेस्तस्य चतुर्मुखसमीरिता ।
प्रवृत्तिरासीच्छब्दानां चरितार्था चतुष्टयी ॥१७॥

"The words, uttered by the four mouths of that ancient wise sage, had four functions, which were true in their import. (17).

स्वागतं स्वानधीकारान् प्रभावैरवलम्ब्य वः ।
युगपद् युगबाहुभ्यः प्राप्तेभ्यः प्राज्यविक्रमाः ॥१८॥

Welcome to you, ye gods, who fulfil your offices, with your great prowess, which is due to your arms, which are long as a yoke and which you have obtained simultaneously. (18).

किमिदं द्युतिमात्मीयां न बिभ्रति यथा पुरा ।
हिमक्लिष्टप्रकाशानि ज्योतींषीव मुखानि वः ॥१९॥

How is it, your mouths do not shine with their own lustre, as before, like the luminaries, dimmed by snow? (19).

प्रशमादर्चिषामेतदनुद्गीर्णसुरायुधम् ।
वृत्रस्य हन्तुः कुलिशं कुण्ठिताश्रीव लक्ष्यते ॥२०॥

This thunderbolt of Indra, the slayer of Vṛtra by the extinction of its flaming lustre, is not shining with its usual lustre and appears as if its edges are blunted. (20).

किं चायमरिदुर्वारः पाणौ पाशः प्रचेतसः ।
मन्त्रेण हतवीर्यस्य फणिनो दैन्यमाश्रितः ॥२१॥

And this noose in the hands of Varuṇa, so irresistible

to his foes, has been reduced to a lamentable state of a serpent whose power is stultified by spells. (21).

कुबेरस्य मनःशल्यं शंसतीव पराभवम् ।
अपविद्धगदो बाहुर्भग्नशाख इव द्रुमः ॥२२॥

The dart that rankles in the heart of Kubera, seems to announce his discomfiture, by his arm which has divested itself of its club, and is like a tree whose branch is lopped off. (22).

यमोऽपि विलिखन् भूमि दण्डेनास्तमितत्विषा ।
कुरुतेऽस्मिन्नमोघेऽपि निर्वाणालातलाघवम् ॥२३॥

Yama, too, scratching the ground, with his staff which has lost its lustre, shows it to be as powerless as an extinguished fire-brand. (23).

अमी च कथमादित्याः प्रतापक्षतिशीतलाः ।
चित्रन्यस्ता इव गताः प्रकामालोकनीयताम् ॥२४॥

How do the suns, cool as they have lost their refulgence, have become mostly to be admired, as if they are painted figures? (24).

पर्याकुलत्वान्मरुतां वेगभङ्गोऽनुमीयते ।
अम्भसामोघसंरोधः प्रतीपगमनादिव ॥२५॥

As the winds are checked in their flow, they seem to be arrested in their speed, as the flow of waters is checked by going in an inverse direction. (25).

आवर्जितजटामौलिविलम्बिशशिकोटयः ।
रुद्राणामपि मूर्धानः क्षतहुङ्कारशंसिनः ॥२६॥

The heads of the Rudras, with their matted crowns, bent low and with the crescents of the moon dangling from them, speak of their "Hum" sounds as being stilled. (26).

लब्धप्रतिष्ठाः प्रथमं यूयं किं बलवत्तरैः ।
अपवादैरिवोत्सर्गाः कृतव्यावृत्तयः परैः ॥२७॥

Being firmly established, have you been displaced from your positions, by your enemies, as rules by exceptions ? (27)

तद्ब्रूत वत्साः ! किमितः प्रार्थयध्वं समागताः ।
मयि सृष्टिर्हि लोकानां रक्षा युष्मास्ववस्थिता ॥२८॥

So say my children, why have you all come together, and what do you seek of me; with me rests the creation of the world, while its protection is your office." (28).

ततो मन्दानिलोद्धूतकमलाकरशोभिना ।
गुरुं नेत्रसहस्रेण नोदयामास वासवः ॥२९॥

Then Indra, with his thousand eyes, which flashed like a lotus-lake, swirled up by a gentle breeze, urged the preceptor thus. (29).

स द्विनेत्रं हरेश्चक्षुः सहस्रनयनाधिकम् ।
वाचस्पतिरुवाचेदं प्राञ्जलिर्जलजासनम् ॥३०॥

Then the preceptor, the Lord of Speech, with his two eyes, exceeding in sight the thousand eyes of Indra, with folded hand spoke to the creator- (30).

एवं यदात्थ भगवन्नामृष्टं नः परैः पदम् ।
प्रत्येकं विनियुक्तात्मा कथं न ज्ञास्यसि प्रभो ! ॥३१॥

'Oh, Holy one, just as you say, our office has been sacrileged by our enemies, how mayest thou not know, thou our Lord, that art present in everybody's heart. (31).

भवल्लब्धवरोदीर्णस्तारकाख्यो महासुरः ।
उपप्लवाय लोकानां धूमकेतुरिवोत्थितः ॥३२॥

The great demon Tāraka, growing impudent through the boon thou hast granted him, has risen like a comet to devastate the worlds. (32).

पुरे तावन्तमेवास्य तनोति रविरातपम् ।
दीर्घिकाकमलोन्मेषो यावन्मात्रेण साध्यते ॥३३॥

In his city, the sun gives as much light as is sufficient to make the lotuses in his pleasure-ponds, bloom. (33).

सर्वाभिः सर्वदा चन्द्रस्तं कलाभिर्निषेवते ।
नादत्ते केवलां लेखां हरचूडामणीकृताम् ॥३४॥

The moon, serves him with all his digits, save the one that is in the crest of Hara. (34).

व्यावृत्तगतिरुद्याने कुसुमस्तेयसाध्वसात् ।
न वाति वायुस्तत्पार्श्वे तालवृन्तानिलाधिकम् ॥३५॥

The wind does not blow in his garden more than the wind coming from a fan for fear of punishment, for thieving the flowers in the Garden. (35).

पर्यायसेवामुत्सृज्य पुष्पसम्भारतत्पराः ।
उद्यानपालसामान्यमृतवस्तमुपासते ॥३६॥

The seasons serve him simultaneously, giving up their sequence, intent upon serving him, with a wealth of flowers, in common with the keepers of Gardens. (36).

तस्योपायनयोग्यानि रत्नानि सरितां पतिः ।
कथमप्यम्भसामन्तरानिष्पत्तेः प्रतीक्षते ॥३७॥

The ocean somehow waits for the gems in its waters, to be ready for use fit for making a present unto him. (37).

ज्वलन्मणिशिखाश्चैनं वासुकिप्रमुखा निशि ।
स्थिरप्रदीपतामेत्य भुजङ्गाः पर्युपासते ॥३८॥

The serpents led by Vāsuki, serve him with steadily burning lamps, in the form of their flashing crest-gems. (38).

तत्कृतानुग्रहापेक्षी तं मुहुर्दूतहारितैः ।
अनुकूलयतीन्द्रोऽपि कल्पद्रुमविभूषणैः ॥३९॥

Indra, expecting to be favoured by him, ingratiates himself into his favour, by often sending him ornaments, yielded by the Kalpadrumas, (the wishyielding trees), sent through his emissaries. (39).

इत्थमाराध्यमानोऽपि क्लिश्नाति भुवनत्रयम् ।
शाम्येत्प्रत्यपकारेण नोपकारेण दुर्जनः ॥४०॥

Though propitiated thus, he harasses the three worlds; a wicked person is pacified by opposition, and not by conferring obligations. (40).

तेनामरवधूहस्तैः सदयालूनपल्लवाः ।
अभिज्ञाश्छेदपातानां क्रियन्ते नन्दनद्रुमाः ॥४१॥

By him, the trees in the (paradisal garden) Nandana, whose tender sprouts are culled by the wives of the gods, with their own hands, for making ear-ornaments, are made cognizant of lopping and falling (of leaves). (41).

वीज्यते स हि संसुप्तः श्वाससाधारणानिलैः ।
चामरैः सुरबन्दीनां बाष्पसीकरवर्षिभिः ॥४२॥

When he is asleep, he is fanned with wind, as gentle and soft as their breath, with chowries, by the female prisoners from the god's camp, which are dripping with drops of tears. (42).

उत्पाट्य मेरुशृङ्गाणि क्षुण्णानि हरितां खुरैः ।
आक्रीडपर्वतास्तेन कल्पिताः स्वेषु वेश्मसु ॥४३॥

Tearing up the peaks of Meru, pulverised by the hooves of the horses of the sun, he has devised them as pleasure-mounds in his own palaces. (43).

मन्दाकिन्याः पयः शेषं दिग्वारणमदाविलम् ।
हेमाम्भोरुहसस्यानां तद्वाप्यो धाम साम्प्रतम् ॥४४॥

Only the waters of the Mandākinī, soiled by the ichor of the quarter-elephants remain, while the crop of golden lotuses finds a home in his pleasure-ponds. (44).

भुवनालोकनप्रीतिः स्वर्गिभिर्नानुभूयते ।
खिलीभूते विमानानां तदापातभयात्पथि ॥४५॥

The gods no more enjoy the pleasure of watching the world, the path of the aerial cars in the sky being blocked through fear of his attack. (45).

यज्वभिः सम्भृतं हव्यं विततेष्वध्वरेषु सः ।
जातवेदोमुखान्मायी मिषतामाच्छिनत्ति नः ॥४६॥

He, the wily one, snatches from fire, the mouth of the gods, the oblations proffered by the sacrificer, while we are simply looking on. (46).

उच्चैरुच्चैःश्रवास्तेन हयरत्नमहारि च ।
देहबद्धमिवेन्द्रस्य चिरकालार्जितं यशः ॥४७॥

He robbed the lofty horse, Uccaiśravas, a gem among horses, the embodiment of Indra's glory, accumulated during a long time. (47).

तस्मिन्नुपायाः सर्वे नः क्रूरे प्रतिहतक्रियाः ।
वीर्यवन्त्योषधानीव विकारे सान्निपातिके ॥४८॥

All our devices against him come to nought, as potent herbs do, against a distemper caused by the inflammation of the three biles. (48).

जयाशा यत्र चास्माकं प्रतिघातोत्थितार्चिषा ।
हरिचक्रेण तेनास्य कण्ठे निष्कमिवार्पितम् ॥४९॥

The quoit of Viṣṇu, whereon rested our hopes of victory, from which sparks of fire rose, on account of a flow, seemed to offer him a golden necklace in his neck. (49).

तवीयास्तोयदेष्वद्य पुष्करावर्तकादिषु ।
अभ्यस्यन्ति तटाघातं निर्जितैरावता गजाः ॥५०॥

His elephants, which have to-day vanquished Airāvata, practise the sport of butting, against the clouds, Puṣkara and Āvartaka. (50).

तदिच्छामो विभो ! स्रष्टुं सेनान्यं तस्य शान्तये ।
कर्मबन्धच्छिदं धर्मं भवस्येव मुमुक्षवः ॥५१॥

So, for his destruction, we desire to create some leader of the army : those who wish to snap the bonds of Saṁsāra, desire religious practice, for breaking the bonds of Karma. (51).

गोप्तारं सुरसैन्यानां यं पुरस्कृत्य गोत्रभित् ।
प्रत्यानेष्यति शत्रुभ्यो बन्दीमिव जयश्रियम् ॥५२॥

Making him the leader of the armies of the gods, Indra will wrest back the glory of victory, like a female prisoner." (52).

वचस्यवसिते तस्मिन् ससर्ज गिरमात्मभूः ।
गर्जितानन्तरां वृष्टिं सौभाग्येन जिगाय सा ॥५३॥

When he had finished speaking, the self-born creator spoke and that speech was far superior in beauty to a shower after thunder. (53).

सम्पत्स्यते वः कामोऽयं कालः कश्चित्प्रतीक्ष्यताम् ।
न त्वस्य सिद्धौ यास्यामि सर्गव्यापारमात्मना ॥५४॥

"This your desire will be accomplished; waitf or some time, but to enable him to attain success, I shall cease from the act of creation. (54).

इतः स दैत्यः प्राप्तश्रीर्नेत एवार्हति क्षयम् ।
विषवृक्षोऽपि संवर्ध्य स्वयं छेत्तुमसाम्प्रतम् ।।५५।।

To me the demon owes his rise, and he deserves not to be destroyed by me; having grown a tree of poison, it is improper to cut it oneself. (55).

वृतं तेनेदमेव प्राङ् मया चास्मै प्रतिश्रुतम् ।
वरेण शमितं लोकानलं दग्धुं हि तत्तपः ।।५६।।

He has already chosen this, and I have promised him that; his penance, well capable of consuming the world, has been allayed by me, by granting him a boon. (56).

संयुगे सांयुगीनं तमुद्यतं प्रसहेत कः ।
अंशादृते निषिक्तस्य नीललोहितरेतसः ।।५७।।

Who would be able to bear him, so adept in fighting, except a portion of the seed of Śiva, cast (in some womb). (57).

स हि देवः परं ज्योतिस्तमःपारे व्यवस्थितम् ।
परिच्छिन्नप्रभावर्द्धिर्न मया न च विष्णुना ।।५८।।

That God is the highest light, established beyond Darkness, the greatness of his prowess being beyond mine or Viṣṇu's conception. (58).

उमारूपेण ते यूयं संयमस्तिमितं मनः ।
शम्भोर्यतध्वमाक्रष्टुमयस्कान्तेन लोहवत् ॥५९॥

So you try to attract the heart of Śiva, checked by self-control, like an iron rod, by a piece of magnet. (59).

उभे एव क्षमे वोढुमुभयोर्बीजमाहितम् ।
सा वा शम्भोस्तदीया वा मूर्तिर्जलमयी मम ॥६०॥

Only two are able to bear the seed of Śiva, She (Umā) or my watery form. (60).

तस्यात्मा शितिकण्ठस्य सैनापत्यमुपेत्य वः ।
मोक्ष्यते सुरबन्दीनां वेणीर्वीर्यविभूतिभिः ॥६१॥

His soul (his son) assuming the office of your commander, will loosen the braids of female prisoners, through the excess of his prowess." (61).

इति व्याहृत्य विबुधान् विश्वयोनिस्तिरोदधे ।
मनस्याहितकर्तव्यास्तेऽपि देवा दिवं ययुः ॥६२॥

Having addressed the gods thus, the source of the universe (i.e. Brahman) disappeared; and the gods, too, laying their duties to their hearts, went to heaven. (62).

तत्र निश्चित्य कन्दर्पमगमत्पाकशासनः ।
मनसा कार्यसंसिद्धौ त्वराद्विगुणरंहसा ॥६३॥

Fixing upon Kāma as one, who would achieve that end, Indra remembered him in his mind, whose speed was doubled by eagerness. (63).

अथ स ललितयोषिद्भ्रूलताचारुशृङ्गं
रतिवलयपदाङ्के चापमासज्य कण्ठे ।
सहचरमधुहस्तन्यस्तचूताङ्कुरास्त्रः
शतमखमुपतस्थे प्राञ्जलिः पुष्पधन्वा ॥६४॥

Then the flower-bowed Kāma, fixing his bow to his neck, (the bow) whose ends looked lovely as the creeper-like brow of graceful ladies and marked by Rati's anklet-bearing foot, and placing his missile of mango-blossoms into the hands of his companion, Spring, presented himself before Śatamakha (i.e. Indra). (64.)

तृतीयः सर्गः

तस्मिन्मघोनस्त्रिदशान्विहाय सहस्रमक्ष्णां युगपत्पपात ।
प्रयोजनापेक्षितया प्रभूणां प्रायश्चलं गौरवमाश्रितेषु ॥१॥

The thousand eyes of Indra fell upon Kāma simultaneously; generally, the regard, the masters feel for their servants, is unsteady depending as it does, on their desire to gain their purpose. (1).

स वासवेनासनसन्निकृष्टमितो निषीदेति विसृष्टभूमिः ।
भर्तुः प्रसादं प्रतिनन्द्य मूर्ध्ना वक्तुं मिथः प्राक्रमतैवमेनम् ॥२॥

He was asked by Indra to take his seat near his throne, which Indra pointed out to him; and greeting the favour of his master, (Kāma) proceeded to talk mutually in secret. (2).

आज्ञापय ज्ञातविशेष पुंसां लोकेषु यत्ते करणीयमस्ति ।
अनुग्रहं संस्मरणप्रवृत्तमिच्छामि संवर्द्धितमाज्ञया ते ॥३॥

"Command me, O thou ! that knowest the special merit of men, what thou seekest in the world to accomplish. The favour thou hast shown me by remembering me I desire it to be augmented. (3).

केनाभ्यसूया पदकाङ्क्षिणा ते नितान्तदीर्घैर्जनिता तपोभिः ।
यावद्भवत्याहितसायकस्य मत्कार्मुकस्याऽस्य निदेशवर्ती ॥४॥

Who has inflamed thy wrath by seeking to attain thy position by performing protracted penances ? For he will be soon the target of my bow upon which an arrow is placed. (4).

असंमतः कस्तव मुक्तिमार्गं पुनर्भवक्लेशभयात्प्रपन्नः ।
बद्धश्चिरं तिष्ठतु सुन्दरीणामारेचितभ्रूचतुरैः कटाक्षैः ॥५॥

Whom dost thou abhor ? Who, fearing the agony of rebirth, has taken to the path of salvation ? Let him stand transfixed by the glances of beautiful women, accompanied by the dance of the eye-brow. (5).

अध्यापितस्योशनसापि नीतिं प्रयुक्तरागप्रणिधिर्द्विषस्ते ।
कस्यार्थधर्मौ वद पीडयामि सिन्धोस्तटावोघ इव प्रवृद्धः ॥६॥

Although taught statecraft by Śukra himself, whose worldly goods (Artha) and Dharma shall I block by sending as my emissary, desire for worldly pleasures, as erodes river's bank, its overflooded currents. (6).

कामेकपत्नीव्रतदुःखशीलां लोलं मनश्चारुतया प्रविष्टाम् ।
नितम्बिनीमिच्छसि मुक्तलज्जां कण्ठे स्वयंग्राहनिषक्तबाहुम् ॥७॥

What chaste wife, who suffers pain on account of keeping her vow, who has entered thy fickle heart on account of her beauty, dost thou desire to clasp thy neck in her arms shamelessly, of her own accord? (7).

कयासि कामिन् ! सुरतापराधात्पादानतः कोपनयाऽवधूतः ।
तस्याः करिष्यामि दृढानुतापं प्रवालशय्याशरणं शरीरम् ॥८॥

O thou, love-lorn, by what lady, hast thou been spurned, on account of your faithlessness in love, when fallen prostrate before her, whom I should cause to betake herself to a bed of tender leaves, being full of deep remorse? (8).

प्रसीद विश्राम्यतु वीर ! वज्रं शरैर्मदीयैः कतमः सुरारिः ।
बिभेतु मोघीकृतबाहुवीर्यः स्त्रीभ्योऽपि कोपस्फुरिताधराभ्यः ॥९॥

Be pleased, O hero; let thy thunderbolt rest; what of the enemy of the gods shall I make by my arrow fear women, whose brows are wrinkled in anger, the power of their arms being frustrated? (9).

तव प्रसादात्कुसुमायुधोऽपि सहायमेकं मधुमेव लब्ध्वा ।
कुर्यां हरस्यापि पिनाकपाणेर्धैर्यच्युतिं के मम धन्विनोऽन्ये ॥१०॥

Through thy favour, I even the flower-armed Kāma, with Spring as my only ally, shall make even Pinākin (Śiva) lose courage; other bowmen are nothing before me." (10).

अथोरुदेशादवतार्य पादमाक्रान्तिसम्भावितपादपीठम् ।
सङ्कल्पितार्थे विवृतात्मशक्तिमाखण्डलः काममिदं बभाषे ॥११॥

Then Indra, lowering his foot from a wide region, honoured the foot-stool by planting his foot on it and spoke to Kāma, who had revealed his power in the accomplishment of the desired object, thus :—(11).

सर्वं सखे ! त्वय्युपपन्नमेतदुभे ममाऽस्त्रे कुलिशं भवांश्च ।
वज्रं तपोवीर्यमहत्सु कुण्ठं त्वं सर्वतोगामि च साधकं च ॥१२॥

"Friend, all this is possible for thee; both you and my thunderbolt are my missiles; my thunderbolt is powerless against those who are rich in penance, but thou art ubiquitous and accomplisheth the end. (12).

अवैमि ते सारमतः खलु त्वां कार्ये गुरुण्यात्मसमं नियोक्ष्ये ।
व्यादिश्यते भूधरतामवेक्ष्य कृष्णेन देहोद्वहनाय शेषः ॥१३॥

I know thy strength, and so I appoint thee, my equal, to accomplish a weighty task; Kṛṣṇa, seeing his power to hold the earth makes use of Śeṣa to hold his body. (13).

आशंसता बाणगतिं वृषाङ्के कार्यं त्वया नः प्रतिपन्नकल्पम् ।
निबोध यज्ञांशभुजामिदानीमुच्चैर्द्विषामीप्सितमेतदेव ॥१४॥

Saying that you will direct your arrow's flight towards Śiva, you have almost accomplished our task; know that the gods who have powerful enemies desire nothing else (14).

अमी हि वीर्यप्रभवं भवस्य जयाय सेनान्यमुशन्ति देवाः ।
स च त्वदेकेषुनिपातसाध्यो ब्रह्माङ्गभूर्ब्रह्मणि योजितात्मा ॥१५॥

These gods desire a commander sprung from Hara's seed; he who has concentrated his mind on Brahma, by duly reciting mantra is to be subdued by the fall of only one arrow of yours. (15).

तस्मै हिमाद्रेः प्रयतां तनूजां यतात्मने रोचयितुं यतस्व ।
योषित्सु तद्वीर्यनिषेकभूमिः सैव क्षमेत्यात्मभुवोपदिष्टम् ॥१६॥

Try to induce him whose mind is self-controlled, to be predisposed towards Himādri's self-controlled daughter; for she alone, among women, is capable of bearing his seed; so Brahmā has told. (16).

गुरोर्नियोगाच्च नगेन्द्रकन्या स्थाणुं तपस्यन्तमधित्यकायाम् ।
अन्वास्त इत्यप्सरसां मुखेभ्यः श्रुतं मया मत्प्रणिधिः स वर्गः ॥१७॥

For through her father's command, Pārvati (Nagendra's daughter) is waiting upon Lord Śiva, who is practising penance upon an upper ridge of Himādri; so have I heard from apsarasas' mouth; for they are my emissaries. (17).

तद् गच्छ सिद्ध्यै कुरु देवकार्यमर्थोऽयमर्थान्तरभाव्य एव ।
अपेक्षते प्रत्ययमुत्तमं त्वां बीजाङ्कुरः प्रागुदयादिवाम्भः ॥१८॥

Then proceed, accomplish gods' business; for this business is to be accomplishes through another; for as a sprout from a seed requires water before it appears, so does it expect thee as the best cause. (18).

तस्मिन्सुराणां विजयाभ्युपाये तवैव नामास्त्रगतिः कृती त्वम् ।
अप्यप्रसिद्धं यशसे हि पुंसामनन्यसाधारणमेव कर्म ॥१९॥

For, the only means for subduing Hara is your arrow's

flight; for you are, indeed, blest; an extraordinary deed, though obscure, leads to man's success. (19).

सुराः समभ्यर्थयितार एते कार्यं त्रयाणामपि विष्टपानाम् ।
चापेन ते कर्म न चातिहिंस्रमहो बतासि स्पृहणीयवीर्यः ॥२०॥

For these gods are the snppliants; this business belongs to the three worlds, the deed wrought by thy bow is not very cruel. (20).

मधुश्च ते मन्मथ साहचर्यादसावनुक्तोऽपि सहाय एव ।
समीरणो नोदयिता भवेति व्यादिश्यते केन हुताशनस्य ॥२१॥

Spring, O Madana, thy ally is, though unbespoken; who ever doth command wind to help fire to blaze up?" (21).

तथेति शेषामिव भर्तुराज्ञामादाय मूर्ध्ना मदनः प्रतस्थे ।
ऐरावतास्फालनकर्कशेन हस्तेन पस्पर्श तदङ्गमिन्द्रः ॥२२॥

"So be it", said Madana, and started and honoured his master's command by receiving it on his head as a garland of favour. And Indra patted him with his hand, hardened by striking Airāvata. (22).

स माधवेनाभिमतेन सख्या रत्या च साशङ्कमनुप्रयातः ।
अङ्गव्ययप्रार्थितकार्यसिद्धिः स्थाण्वाश्रमं हैमवतं जगाम ॥२३॥

Accompanied by Spring, his esteemed friend, and by Rati in fear of peril, he wended his way to Śiva's Himavata Abode, by himself immolating. (23).

तस्मिन्वने संयमिनां मुनीनां तपःसमाधेः प्रतिकूलवर्ती ।
सङ्कल्पयोनेरभिमानभूतमात्मानमाधाय मधुर्जजृम्भे ॥२४॥

In that forest, Spring, opposed to the concentration for penances of the self-restrained sages, manifested himself, having taken the form which became the pride of the self-born. (24).

कुबेरगुप्तां दिशमुष्णरश्मौ गन्तुं प्रवृत्ते समयं विलङ्घ्य ।
दिग्दक्षिणा गन्धवहं मुखेन व्यलीकनिश्वासमिवोत्ससर्ज ॥२५॥

When the sun transited out of time, towards the quarter protected by Kubera, the Southern quarter experited from her mouth wind—the breath, as it were, of grief unbearable. (25).

असूत सद्यः कुसुमान्यशोकः स्कन्धात्प्रभृत्येव सपल्लवानि ।
पादेन नापैक्षत सुन्दरीणां सम्पर्कमासिञ्जितनूपुरेण ॥२६॥

Aśoka forthwith burgeoned forth flowers from the trunk onwards, in leaves encased, and did not expect contact of beautiful ladies' feet, with tinkling anklets dight. (26).

सद्यः प्रवालोद्गमचारुपत्रे नीते समाप्तिं नवचूतबाणे ।
निवेशयामास मधुर्द्विरेफान् नामाक्षराणीव मनोभवस्य ॥२७॥

When Spring had fashioned for Kāma, a new shaft with tender leaves for feathers, he forthwith incised upon it the letters as if of Madana's name in the form of bees. (27).

वर्णप्रकर्षे सति कर्णिकारं दुनोति निर्गन्धतया स्म चेतः ।
प्रायेण सामग्र्यविधौ गुणानां पराङ्मुखी विश्वसृजः प्रवृत्तिः ॥२८॥

Spite of richness of colour, from absence of fragrance, the Karṇikāra pains the mind. Averse is the Creator's activity from creating a totality of good qualities. (28).

बालेन्दुवक्राण्यविकासभावाद्बभुः पलाशान्यतिलोहितानि ।
सद्यो वसन्तेन समागतानां नखक्षतानीव वनस्थलीनाम् ॥२९॥

The very red Palāśa flowers shone like moon's curved crescent for want of blooming, as if they were the nail-marks by Vasanta, made on wood-land spots when he was united with them. (29).

लग्नद्विरेफाञ्जनभक्तिचित्रं मुखे मधुश्रीस्तिलकं प्रकाश्य ।
रागेण बालारुणकोमलेन चूतप्रवालोष्ठमलञ्चकार ॥३०॥

Spring's glory, manifesting on its forehead a tilaka-mark charming, with collyrium of bees thereto clinging with twilight's colour delicate, embellished her lips in the form of tender mango-sprouts. (30).

मृगाः प्रियालद्रुममञ्जरीणां रजःकणैर्विघ्नितदृष्टिपाताः ।
मदोद्धताः प्रत्यनिलं विचेरुर्वनस्थलीर्मर्मरपत्रमोक्षाः ॥३१॥

The deer, their glances obstructed by Priyāla's pollen yellow, wandered with intoxication swollen windwards, towards the woodland spots, treading the leaves so as to make murmuring sounds. (31).

चूताङ्कुरास्वादकषायकण्ठः पुंस्कोकिलो यन्मधुरं चुकूज ।
मनस्विनीमानविघातदक्षं तदेव जातं वचनं स्मरस्य ॥३२॥

The male Koil with its throat hoarse with fresh mango blossom tasted, sweetly cooed, so that it bespake Cupid's mind. (32).

हिमव्यपायाद्विशदाधराणामापाण्डुरीभूतमुखच्छवीनाम् ।
स्वेदोद्गमः किम्पुरुषाङ्गनानां चक्रे पदं पत्रविशेषकेषु ॥३३॥

Sweat appeared on ornamental paintings of Kimpuruṣa ladies; pallid was their complexion from the snow being rubbed away. (33).

तपस्विनः स्थाणुवनौकसस्तामाकालिकीं वीक्ष्य मधुप्रवृत्तिम् ।
प्रयत्नसंस्तम्भितविक्रियाणां कथञ्चिदीशा मनसां बभूवुः ॥३४॥

The hermits dwelling in the forest, seeing Spring's untimely onset, were somehow able to control their minds, with effort curbing their passions. (34).

तं देशमारोपितपुष्पचापे रतिद्वितीये मदने प्रपन्ने ।
काष्ठागतस्नेहरसानुविद्धं द्वन्द्वानि भावं क्रियया विवव्रुः ॥३५॥

When Cupid with his bow strung, appeared in the forest, accompanied by Rati, several couples exhibited their love by various appropriate actions—(love), which was mingled with heightened affection. (35).

मधु द्विरेफः कुसुमैकपात्रे पपौ प्रियां स्वामनुवर्तमानः ।
शृङ्गेण च स्पर्शनिमीलिताक्षीं मृगीमकण्डूयत कृष्णसारः ॥३६॥

The bee, following his mate, drank wine from the same flower-cup; and the black antelope scratched with his horns his mate who had her eyes closed by the pleasure of the touch. (36)

ददौ रसात्पङ्कजरेणुगन्धि गजाय गण्डूषजलं करेणुः ।
अर्धोपभुक्तेन बिसेन जायां सम्भावयामास रथाङ्गनामा ॥३७॥

The female elephant gave to its mate a mouthful of water, flavoured with the scent of the pollen of lotuses; and the cakravāka honoured his mate with a half-chewed lotus-stalk. (37).

गीतान्तरेषु श्रमवारिलेशैः किञ्चित्समुच्छ्वासितपत्रलेखम् ।
पुष्पासवाघूर्णितनेत्रशोभि प्रियामुखं किम्पुरुषश्चुचुम्बे ॥३८॥

A kinnara kissed the mouth of his beloved, which looked beautiful, as it whirled in consequence of her having guzzled floral wine and which had its ornamental paintings disfigured by drops of sweat caused by fatigue in the midst of a song. (38).

पर्याप्तपुष्पस्तबकस्तनाभ्यः स्फुरत्प्रवालोष्ठमनोहराभ्यः ।
लतावधूभ्यस्तरवोऽप्यवापुर्विनम्रशाखाभुजबन्धनानि ॥३९॥

The trees, too, were embraced by the bent branches, as if they were the arms of bride-like creepers, who possessed fully round breasts in the form of their big bunches of flowers, and whose lips in the form of their shining leaves looked lovely. (39).

श्रुताप्सरोगीतिरपि क्षणेऽस्मिन् हरः प्रसंख्यानपरो बभूव ।
आत्मेश्वराणां न हि जातु विघ्नाः समाधिभेदप्रभवो भवन्ति ॥४०॥

Śiva, although he heard the song of heavenly nymphs, set himself upon concentrating his mind upon himself, at this moment; obstacles impede not the mind's concentration of those who are Captains of their souls. (40).

लतागृहद्वारगतोऽथ नन्दी वामप्रकोष्ठार्पितहेमवेत्रः ।
मुखार्पितैकाङ्गुलिसंज्ञयैव मा चापलायेति गणान् व्यनैषीत् ॥४१॥

Nandī who was at the entrance of the arbour, and who held a cane-staff in his left wrist, restrained the Gaṇas by making a sign to them by putting a finger in his mouth; thus commanding them to refrain from his chief. (41).

निष्कम्पवृक्षं निभृतद्विरेफं मूकाण्डजं शान्तमृगप्रचारम् ।
तच्छासनात्काननमेव सर्वं चित्रार्पितारम्भमिवावतस्थे ॥४२॥

By the command of Īśvara, the trees in the forest were not trembling, the birds were mute and the deer quiescent; the whole forest seemed to have all its activity drawn in a picture. (42).

दृष्टिप्रपातं परिहृत्य तस्य कामः पुरःशुक्रमिव प्रयाणे ।
प्रान्तेषु संसक्तनमेरुशाखं ध्यानास्पदं भूतपतेर्विवेश ॥४३॥

Kāma, avoiding his gaze like a king from the direction which has Śukra in its frontal part, dived into the place, where the lord of the goblin-hosts practised meditation, and on whose borders were branches of nameru trees interlacing one another. (43).

स देवदारुद्रुमवेदिकायां शार्दूलचर्मव्यवधानवत्याम् ।
आसीनमासन्नशरीरपातस्त्रियम्बकं संयमिनं ददर्श ॥४४॥

And Kāma, who was near shuffling off his mortal coil saw the self-restrained Hara who was squatting on an altar of Devadāru covered with tiger skin. (44).

पर्यङ्कबन्धस्थिरपूर्वकायमृज्वायतं सन्नमितोभयांसम् ।
उत्तानपाणिद्वयसन्निवेशात् प्रफुल्लराजीवमिवाङ्कमध्ये ॥४५॥

His body was steady owing to Paryaṅka posture; his shoulders were drooping and both his upturned hands rested in his lap, like blooming lotuses. (45).

भुजङ्गमोनद्धजटाकलापं कर्णावसक्तद्विगुणाक्षसूत्रम् ।
कण्ठप्रभासङ्गविशेषनीलां कृष्णत्वचं ग्रन्थिमतीं दधानम् ॥४६॥

God Śiva, whose matted locks were bound by a serpent and to whose ears was tied a rosary of Akṣa beads and who was wearing a knotted black antelope-skin, which was extremely blue owing to its contact with the blue colour of the neck of Śiva. (46).

किञ्चित्प्रकाशस्तिमितोग्रतारैर्भ्रूविक्रियायां विरतप्रसङ्गैः ।
नेत्रैरविस्पन्दितपक्ष्ममालैर्लक्ष्यीकृतघ्राणमधोमयूखैः ॥४७॥

His eyes, with their severe-looking pupils, were shining a little; his eyebrows ceased to dance; his eyelashes did not flicker and his eyes with their downward gaze, he rested on the tip of his nose. (47).

अवृष्टिसंरम्भमिवाम्बुवाहमपामिवाधारमनुत्तरङ्गम् ।
अन्तश्चराणां मरुतां निरोधान्निवातनिष्कम्पमिव प्रदीपम् ॥४८॥

He was like a cloud, not spilling down showers; like a lake without ripples; by controlling the inner winds, he was like a lamp unflickering in a windless place. (48).

कपालनेत्रान्तरलब्धमार्गैर्ज्योतिःप्ररोहैरुदितैः शिरस्तः ।
मृणालसूत्राधिकसौकुमार्यां बालस्य लक्ष्मीं ग्लपयन्तमिन्दोः ॥४९॥

He obscured the light of the crescent moon, more delicate than a lotus fibre, by rays of light upshooting from his head, making their way from the eye in his forehead. (49).

मनो नवद्वारनिषिद्धवृत्ति हृदि व्यवस्थाप्य समाधिवश्यम् ।
यमक्षरं क्षेत्रविदो विदुस्तमात्मानमात्मन्यवलोकयन्तम् ॥५०॥

Restraining his mind's activity in the nine outlets of the body, curbing his mind, which was controlled by concentration in his heart, he, who was known to the knowers of the Vedas as the eternal immutable, looking upon his soul in his own soul. (50).

स्मरस्तथाभूतमयुग्मनेत्रं पश्यन्नदूरान्मनसाऽप्यधृष्यम् ।
नालक्षयत्साध्वससन्नहस्तः स्रस्तं शरं चापमपि स्वहस्तात् ॥५१॥

Smara (the god of love) seeing the god (above described) Śiva, not from afar, who had odd eyes and who was unassailable even by the mind, did not mark that his bow and arrow dropped from his hand drooping through fright. (51).

निर्वाणभूयिष्ठमथास्य वीर्यं सन्धुक्षयन्तीव वपुर्गुणेन ।
अनुप्रयाता वनदेवताभ्यामदृश्यत स्थावरराजकन्या ॥५२॥

Then appeared Pārvatī, accompanied by sylvan deities who revived his valour almost lost by the beauty of her body. (52).

अशोकनिर्भत्सितपद्मरागमाकृष्टहेमद्युतिकर्णिकारम् ।
मुक्ताकलापीकृतसिन्धुवारं वसन्तपुष्पाभरणं वहन्ती ॥५३॥

Adorning herself with the flowers of spring in which the Aśoka flower spurned the Padmarāga gem, the karnikāra cried down the sheen of gold, and in which the Sinduvāra stood for clusters of pearls. (53).

आवर्जिता किञ्चिदिव स्तनाभ्यां वासो वसाना तरुणार्करागम् ।
पर्याप्तपुष्पस्तबकावनम्रा सञ्चारिणी पल्लविनी लतेव ॥५४॥

She was bent beneath the burden of her breasts and, draped in a garment crimson like the young Sun; she was like a moving plant covered with leaves, but beneath abundant bunches of flowers; (54).

स्रस्तां नितम्बादवलम्बमाना पुनः पुनः केसरदामकाञ्चीम् ।
न्यासीकृतां स्थानविदा स्मरेण मौर्वीं द्वितीयामिव कार्मुकस्य ॥५५॥

Frequently holding the girdle of Bakul-wreaths, slipping down from her lips, and deposited there as a second string of his bow, by the god of love, who knew the proper place for it; (55).

सुगन्धिनिश्वासविवृद्धतृष्णं बिम्बाधरासन्नचरं द्विरेफम् ।
प्रतिक्षणं सम्भ्रमलोलदृष्टिर्लीलारविन्देन निवारयन्ती ॥५६॥

Warding off the bee that hovered around her bimba-like lip whose thirst grew by her breath smelling sweat by the lotus, that adorned her hand, her eye rolling every moment through confusion; (56).

तां वीक्ष्य सर्वावयवानवद्यां रतेरपि ह्रीपदमादधानाम् ।
जितेन्द्रिये शूलिनि पुष्पचापः स्वकार्यसिद्धिं पुनराशशंसे ॥५७॥

On seeing her who was blameless in all her limbs, and

put to shame even Rati, Kāma once again, built up hopes of success in his venture in regard to the self-controlled Śiva. (57).

भविष्यतः पत्युरुमा च शम्भोः समाससाद प्रतिहारभूमिम् ।
योगात्स चान्तः परमात्मसंज्ञं दृष्ट्वा परं ज्योतिरुपारराम ॥५८॥

Umā came to the portal of the palace of Hara who was to be her future husband; and he ceased from Yaugic contemplation on perceiving within the light which is the highest soul. (58).

ततो भुजङ्गाधिपतेः फणाग्रैरधः कथञ्चिद्धृतभूमिभागः ।
शनैःकृतप्राणविमुक्तिरीशः पर्यङ्कबन्धं निबिडं बिभेद ॥५९॥

Then he, whose seat was somehow held by Śeṣa, gradually releasing his vital breath, broke his fast Paryaṅka-posture. (59).

तस्मै शशंस प्रणिपत्य नन्दी शुश्रूषया शैलसुतामुपेताम् ।
प्रवेशयामास च भर्तुरेनां भ्रूक्षेपमात्रानुमतप्रवेशाम् ॥६०॥

Then, bowing down to him, Nandī announced to him that Umā had arrived to wait upon him and on his indicating his consent by a flicker of his eyebrow, fetched her to Īśa. (60).

तस्याः सखीभ्यां प्रणिपातपूर्वं स्वहस्तलूनः शिशिरात्ययस्य ।
व्यकीर्यत त्र्यम्बकपादमूले पुष्पोच्चयः पल्लवभङ्गभिन्नः ॥६१॥

Then she, after bowing down to him, scattered at the feet of Tryambaka the flowers of spring, mixed with bits of leaves that had been gathered by her friends. (61).

उमाऽपि नीलालकमध्यशोभि विस्रंसयन्ती नवकर्णिकारम् ।
चकार कर्णच्युतपल्लवेन मूर्ध्ना प्रणामं वृषभध्वजाय ॥६२॥

Umā, too, disengaged the fresh Karṇikāra flower from her dark hair wherein it shone, and bowed down her head to Vṛṣabhadhvaja, while the leaf that adorned her ear slipped from it. (62).

अनन्यभाजं पतिमाप्नुहीति सा तथ्यमेवाभिहिता भवेन ।
नहीश्वरव्याहृतयः कदाचित्पुष्णन्ति लोके विपरीतमर्थम् ॥६३॥

And Śiva said to her, "Mayest thou obtain a husband unwavering in his love to thee; for the words of the great do not breed a sense that is false". (63).

कामस्तु बाणावसरं प्रतीक्ष्य पतङ्गवद्वह्निमुखं विविक्षुः ।
उमासमक्षं हरबद्धलक्ष्यः शरासनज्यां मुहुराममर्श ॥६४॥

Kāma, too, who was waiting for an opportunity to release his arrow, touched the string of his bow in the presence of Umā, and seemed to desire to enter the mouth of Fire, like a moth, making Hara his target. (64).

अथोपनिन्ये गिरिशाय गौरी तपस्विने ताम्ररुचा करेण ।
विशोषितां भानुमतो मयूखैर्मन्दाकिनीपुष्करबीजमालाम् ॥६५॥

Then Gaurī brought to Giriṣa, the anchorite, with her hand which had a red gleam, a rosary of lotus seeds of the lotuses that grew in the Ganges and that were dried by the rays of the sun. (65).

प्रतिग्रहीतुं प्रणयिप्रियत्वात् त्रिलोचनस्तामुपचक्रमे च ।
सम्मोहनं नाम च पुष्पधन्वा धनुष्यमोघं समधत्त बाणम् ॥६६॥

Śiva; who loved a supplicant, was about to accept the rosary, when the god of the flower-bow, placed upon his bow an unfailing shaft named Sammohana. (66).

हरस्तु किञ्चित्परिलुप्तधैर्यश्चन्द्रोदयारम्भ इवाम्बुराशिः ।
उमामुखे बिम्बफलाधरोष्ठे व्यापारयामास विलोचनानि ॥६७॥

Hara lost a little bit his firmness like the ocean at moon-rise, and directed his glance towards Umā's mouth with its Bimbalike lips. (67).

विवृण्वती शैलसुताऽपि भावमङ्गैः स्फुरद्बालकदम्बकल्पैः ।
साचीकृता चारुतरेण तस्थौ मुखेन पर्यस्तविलोचनेन ॥६८॥

Pārvatī, too, manifested her feeling with her limbs which were like flashing young Kadamba, and she stood bent sideways with bewildered eyes. (68).

अथेन्द्रियक्षोभमयुग्मनेत्रः पुनर्वशित्वाद्बलवन्निगृह्य ।
हेतुं स्वचेतोविकृतेर्दिदृक्षुर्दिशामुपान्तेषु ससर्ज दृष्टिम् ॥६९॥

Then Śaṅkara curbed the agitation of his senses with a strong will, as he was self-controlled, and looking for its cause, directed his eyes to the ends of the quarters. (69).

स दक्षिणापाङ्गनिविष्टमुष्टिं नतांसमाकुञ्चितसव्यपादम् ।
ददर्श चक्रीकृतचारुचापं प्रहर्तुमभ्युद्यतमात्मयोनिम् ॥७०॥

He saw the self-born (Kāma), resting his fist on the corner of his right eye, his shoulders bent, his left foot contracted and about to strike with an arrow placed upon his beautiful bow, fully bent. (70)

तपःपरामर्शविवृद्धमन्योर्भ्रूभङ्गदुष्प्रेक्ष्यमुखस्य तस्य ।
स्फुरन्नुदर्चिः सहसा तृतीयादक्ष्णः कृशानुः किल निष्पपात ॥७१॥

And from Śiva's third eye there shot up, all of a sudden, a flame of fire with its rays blazing up; his face, difficult to see as its eyebrow was (frightfully) wrinkled as he was greatly angered at disturbance in his penance. (71).

क्रोधं प्रभो संहर संहरेति यावद्गिरः खे मरुतां चरन्ति ।
तावत्स वह्निर्भवनेत्रजन्मा भस्मावशेषं मदनं चकार ॥७२॥

While the gods cried in heaven, "O Lord ! do curb your anger," the fire blazing from the eye of Bhava burnt Madana so that ashes were his only residue. (72).

तीव्राभिषङ्गप्रभवेण वृत्तिं मोहेन संस्तम्भयतेन्द्रियाणाम् ।
अज्ञातभर्तृव्यसना मुहूर्तं कृतोपकारेव रतिर्बभूव ॥७३॥

On Rati, the activity of whose senses was removed by the severe calamity, the swoon, that made her oblivious of her husband's death, seemed to confer an obligation for a while. (73).

तमाशु विघ्नं तपसस्तपस्वी वनस्पतिं वज्र इवावभज्य ।
स्त्रीसन्निकर्षं परिहर्तुमिच्छन्नन्तर्दधे भूतपतिः सभूतः ॥७४॥

Śiva, who was practising penance, having blasted him (i.e. Kāma) who was obstacle in his penance, like the thunderbolt a tree, wishing to avoid contact with a woman, disappeared with his hosts (Gaṇas). (74).

शैलात्मजाऽपि पितुरुच्छिरसोऽभिलाषं
व्यर्थं समर्थ्य ललितं वपुरात्मनश्च ।

सख्योः समक्षमिति चाधिकजातलज्जा
शून्या जगाम भवनाभिमुखी कथञ्चित् ॥७५॥

Pārvati, too, considering as of no avail both the heart's desire of her high-souled father and her own graceful body, felt much ashamed of herself, now that all this happened in the presence of friends, was ill at ease, and moved homeward with great difficulty. (75).

सपदि मुकुलिताक्षीं रुद्रसंरम्भभीत्या
दुहितरमनुकम्प्यामद्रिरादाय दोर्भ्याम् ।
सुरगज इव बिभ्रत्पद्मिनीं दन्तलग्नां
प्रतिपथगतिरासीद् वेगदीर्घीकृताङ्गः ॥७६॥

Then Himādri led his daughter by her hand—(she) who shut her eyes out of fear of Rudra's wrath, and was on his way (homeward), and stretching his body, appeared like the elephant of the gods (Airāvata) carrying a lotus plant clinging to his tusks. (76).

चतुर्थः सर्गः

अथ मोहपरायणा सती विवशा कामवधूर्विबोधिता ।
विधिना प्रतिपादयिष्यता नववैधव्यमसह्यवेदनम् ॥१॥

Now Rati, who was sunk in a swoon and was helpless, was roused by fate, who caused her to undergo the experience of fresh widowhood with its insufferable agony. (1).

अवधानपरे चकार सा प्रलयान्तोन्मिषिते विलोचने ।
न विवेद तयोरतृप्तयोः प्रियमत्यन्तविलुप्तदर्शनम् ॥२॥

She opened her eyes at the end of her swoon, and looked about her attentively, and was scarcely conscious that the beloved object of her insatiable eyes was not ever to be seen. (2).

अयि जीवितनाथ जीवसीत्यभिधायोत्थितया तया पुरः ।
ददृशे पुरुषाकृति क्षितौ हरकोपानलभस्म केवलम् ॥३॥

"Dost thou live, O Lord of my life!", thus she spoke and rising saw before her the ashes produced by Hara's wrath, patterned after a man's form. (3).

अथ सा पुनरेव विह्वला वसुधालिङ्गनधूसरस्तनी ।
विललाप विकीर्णमूर्धजा समदुःखामिव कुर्वती स्थलीम् ॥४॥

Then again, she was overwhelmed with grief, and sprawled on the earth, so that her bosom was grey with dust, and bemoaned (her loss), making the woodland region share her grief. (4).

उपमानमभूद्विलासिनां करणं यत्तव कान्तिमत्तया ।
तदिदं गतमीदृशीं दशां न विदीर्ये कठिनाः खलु स्त्रियः ॥५॥

Your limbs, which were a beau ideal of gallants on account of their liveliness, have been reduced to such a sad plight, and yet I am not broken down; Ah! how cruel are the hearts of women! (5).

क्व नु मां त्वदधीनजीवितां विनिकीर्य क्षणभिन्नसौहृदः ।
नलिनीं क्षतसेतुबन्धनो जलसङ्घात इवासि विद्रुतः ॥६॥

Whither, indeed, art thou gone? in a moment forgetting our kindly relations; leaving me, who depended on thee, like a lake bursting its retaining wall, the lotus plant. (6).

कृतवानसि विप्रियं न मे प्रतिकूलं न च ते मया कृतम् ।
किमकारणमेव दर्शनं विलपन्त्यै रतये न दीयते ॥७॥

Thou didst me no wrong, nor did I act in a way contrary to thee; why without any cause, dost thou not show thyself to Rati, who is lamenting? (7).

स्मरसि स्मर मेखलागुणैरुत गोत्रस्खलितेषु बन्धनम् ।
च्युतकेशरदूषितेक्षणान्यवतंसोत्पलताडनानि वा ॥८॥

Dost thou remember, Smara, how I tied thee, when thou didst blunder in speaking my name, or my striking thee with lotuses used as ear-ornaments, whose filaments escaping, pained the eyes? (8).

हृदये वससीति मत्प्रियं यदवोचस्तदवैमि कैतवम् ।
उपचारपदं न चेदिदं त्वमनङ्गः कथमक्षता रतिः ॥९॥

That thou didst say, "thou livest in my heart," words agreeable to me, I understand to be mere deceitful cunning. Had it not been merely complimentary how is it that thou art bodiless and Rati scatheless? (9).

परलोकनवप्रवासिनः प्रतिपत्स्ये पदवीमहं तव ।
विधिना जन एष वञ्चितस्त्वदधीनं खलु देहिनां सुखम् ॥१०॥

I will betake myself to the path to the other world,

thou hast taken; fate has deceived the world of men; for, on thee doth life depend. (10).

रजनीतिमिरावगुण्ठिते पुरमार्गे घनशब्दविक्लवाः ।
वसतिं प्रिय ! कामिनां प्रियास्त्वदृते प्रापयितुं क ईश्वरः ॥११॥

When the night is veiled by darkness, who, save thee, is able to lead the love-lorn lasses, distressed by the rumble of clouds, to their lovers' homes ? (11).

नयनान्यरुणानि घूर्णयन् वचनानि स्खलयन्पदे पदे ।
असति त्वयि वारुणीमदः प्रमदानामधुना विडम्बना ॥१२॥

The intoxication caused by wine to the young handsome ladies, making every word of theirs slip, and causing their red eyes to roll, will be of no avail in thy absence. (12).

अवगम्य कथीकृतं वपुः प्रियबन्धोस्तव निष्फलोदयः ।
बहुलेऽपि गते निशाकरस्तनुतां दुःखमनङ्ग मोक्ष्यति ॥१३॥

Knowing that thou, his loved brother, liveth only in legend, the moon, who shall rise to no purpose, will give up her tenuity with great grief, though the dark half of the month is past. (13).

हरितारुणचारुबन्धनः कलपुंस्कोकिलशब्दसूचितः ।
वद सम्प्रति कस्य बाणतां नवचूतप्रसवो गमिष्यति ॥१४॥

Say, whose shaft, the new mango blossom, will be, with a green and red stalk, suggested by the cry of the male koil? (14).

अलिपंक्तिरनेकशस्त्वया गुणकृत्ये धनुषो नियोजिता ।
विरुतैः करुणस्वनैरियं गुरुशोकामनुरोदितीव माम् ॥१५॥

Now and then hast thou put to use a row of bees as a string to thy bow. By its piteous cries it seems to lament after me. (15).

प्रतिपद्य मनोहरं वपुः पुनरप्यादिश तावदुत्थितः ।
रतिदूतिपदेषु कोकिलां मधुरालापनिसर्गपण्डिताम् ॥१६॥

Assuming a handsome form and again rising (from death), order the koil, adept in clever speech, to assume the role of the messenger of love. (16).

शिरसा प्रणिपत्य याचितान्युपगूढानि सवेपथूनि च ।
सुरतानि च तानि ते रहः स्मर संस्मृत्य न शान्तिरस्ति मे ॥१७॥

O Smara, the embraces accompanied by tremor, which I besought of thee and that love-play of thine in our privacy, give me no peace as I remember them. (17),

रचितं रतिपण्डित त्वया स्वयमङ्गेषु ममेदमार्तवम् ।
ध्रियते कुसुमप्रसाधनं तव तच्चारु वपुर्न दृश्यते ॥१८॥

This decoration of my limbs with the flowers of the season still holds; O adept in love-making! But that handsome form of thine is not to be seen. (18).

विबुधैरसि यस्य दारुणैरसमाप्ते परिकर्मणि स्मृतः ।
तमिमं कुरु दक्षिणेतरं चरणं निर्मितरागमेहि मे ॥१९॥

This my right foot, whose decoration was incomplete, when the cruel gods remembered thee; come and paint that foot. (19).

अहमेत्य पतङ्गवर्त्मना पुनरङ्काश्रयणी भवामि ते ।
चतुरैः सुरकामिनीजनैः प्रिय यावन्न विलोभ्यसे दिवि ॥२०॥

I shall come in manner of a moth, and shall lie in thy lap, before thou art beguiled by the wily heavenly nymphs. (20).

मदनेन विनाकृता रतिः क्षणमात्रं किल जीवितेति मे ।
वचनीयमिदं व्यवस्थितं रमण ! त्वामनुयामि यद्यपि ॥२१॥

The Rati lived, though for a moment, bereft of Madana; this censure has become a settled fact amongst men, Charm! I follow thee in death. (21).

क्रियतां कथमन्त्यमण्डनं परलोकान्तरितस्य ते मया ।
सममेव गतोऽस्यतर्कितां गतिमङ्गेन च जीवितेन च ॥२२॥

How may I arrange a funeral decoration for thee, who hast departed to the other world? Thou hast reached an uninferrable flight with thy body and life simultaneously. (22).

ऋजुतां नयतः स्मरामि ते शरमुत्सङ्गनिषण्णधन्वनः ।
मधुना सह सस्मितां कथां नयनोपान्तविलोकितं च यत् ॥२३॥

I remember how thou didst straighten thy arrow while thy bow was lying in thy lap; and those smiling words thou didst speak to Vasanta and those thy glances askance. (23).

क्व नु ते हृदयङ्गमः सखा कुसुमायोजितकार्मुको मधुः ।
न खलूग्ररुषा पिनाकिना गमितः सोऽपि सुहृद्गतां गतिम् ॥२४॥

Where, indeed, is thy handsome friend Madhu, who devised a flowery bow for thee? Not, indeed, has he been brought to the flight of thyself, his friend, by the Pināka-wielder whose wrath is severe. (24).

अथ तैः परिदेविताक्षरैर्हृदये दिग्धशरैरिवाहतः ।
रतिमभ्युपपत्तुमातुरां मधुरात्मानमदर्शयत्पुरः ॥२५॥

Struck in the heart by those words of lament, Madhu, to comfort Rati in distress, manifested himself before her. (25).

तमवेक्ष्य रुरोद सा भृशं स्तनसम्बाधमुरो जघान च ।
स्वजनस्य हि दुःखमग्रतो विवृतद्वारमिवोपजायते ॥२६॥

On seeing him, bitterly did she weep, and beat her breasts, so as to inflict pain on them; for before one's relations, the flood-gates of grief are opened wide. (26).

इति चैनमुवाच दुःखिता सुहृदः पश्य वसन्त किं स्थितम् ?
तदिदं कणशो विकीर्यते पवनैर्भस्म कपोतकर्बुरम् ॥२७॥

Then grieved at heart, she said to Vasanta, "See what remains of your friend. Here are the ashes, variegated like a dove, scattered in particles before the winds. (27).

अयि सम्प्रति देहि दर्शनं स्मर ! पर्युत्सुक एष माधवः ।
दयितास्वनवस्थितं नृणां न खलु प्रेम चलं सुहृज्जने ॥२८॥

"Ah! Show thyself to me now, O Smara! Mādhava is yearning (to see thee). Men's love, which is unsteady towards their lovers, is not so towards their friends. (28).

अमुना ननु पार्श्ववर्तिना जगदाज्ञां ससुरासुरं तव ।
बिसतन्तुगुणस्य कारितं धनुषः पेलवपुष्पपत्रिणः ॥२९॥

With Spring by thy side, together with gods and demons, the whole world was made to obey the command of thy bow, with its string of lotus fibre, and its shafts of delicate flowers. (29).

गत एव न ते निवर्तते स सखा दीप इवानिलाहतः ।
अहमस्य दशेव पश्य मामविषह्यव्यसनेन धूमिताम् ॥३०॥

Like a lamp, snuffed by wind, thy friend returns not, once gone; see me; I am like a smouldering wick of that lamp smoking through unbearable pain. (30).

विधिना कृतमर्धवैशसं ननु मां कामवधे विमुञ्चता ।
अनपायिनि संश्रयद्रुमे गजभग्ने पतनाय वल्लरी ॥३१॥

Fate, by leaving me (unscathed), while killing Kāma, has accomplished but half death; when the tree of support, which is undamaged, is smashed by an elephant, the creeper (clinging to it) falls down. (31).

तदिदं क्रियतामनन्तरं भवता बन्धुजनप्रयोजनम् ।
विधुरां ज्वलनातिसर्जनान्ननु मां प्रापय पत्युरन्तिकम् ॥३२॥

So, do immediately this office for thy friend; reach me, distressed that I am, to my husband by throwing me into fire. (32).

शशिना सह याति कौमुदी सह मेघेन तडित्प्रलीयते ।
प्रमदाः पतिवर्त्मगा इति प्रतिपन्नं हि विचेतनैरपि ॥३३॥

Moonlight goes by the way of the moon, lightning melts with the cloud; that women follow the way of their husbands is accepted even by inanimate beings. (33).

अमुनैव कषायितस्तनी सुभगेन प्रियगात्रभस्मना ।
नवपल्लवसंस्तरे यथा रचयिष्यामि तनुं विभावसौ ॥३४॥

With just these lovely ashes of my husband's limbs I shall smear my breasts, and I shall arrange myself (lay myself) on fire as on a bed of leaves. (34).

कुसुमास्तरणे सहायतां बहुशः सौम्य ! गतस्त्वमावयोः ।
कुरु सम्प्रति तावदाशु मे प्रणिपाताञ्जलियाचितश्चिताम् ॥३५॥

O gentle one; thou hast often helped us in arranging our bed of flowers; now quickly arrange for me a funeral pyre, which I beseech thee to do. (35).

तदनु ज्वलनं मदर्पितं त्वरयेर्दक्षिणवातवीजनैः ।
विदितं खलु ते यथा स्मरः क्षणमप्युत्सहते न मां विना ॥३६॥

The fire laid to my body; quicken it by wafting Malaya winds; for you know that Smara has not the heart to live without me, even for a single moment. (36).

इति चापि विधाय दीयतां सलिलस्याञ्जलिरेक एव नौ ।
अविभज्य परत्र तं मया सहितः पास्यति ते स बान्धवः ॥३७॥

Afrer doing this, make an offering of a handful of water to both of us; that friend of yours shall drink it with me, undivided in the other world. (37).

परलोकविधौ च माधव ! स्मरमुद्दिश्य विलोलपल्लवाः ।
निवपेः सहकारमञ्जरीः प्रियचूतप्रसवो हि ते सखा ॥३८॥

O Mādhava! In making obsequious offerings to Smara, offer him mango-blossoms with twirling leaves; for that friend of yours was fond of mango-blossoms." (38).

इति देहविमुक्तये स्थितां रतिमाकाशभवा सरस्वती ।
शफरीं ह्रदशोषविक्लवां प्रथमा वृष्टिरिवान्वकम्पयत् ॥३९॥

A voice from the sky took pity on Rati, prepared to throw away her life, like the first shower of the season, the fish, distressed by the lake drying up. (39).

कुसुमायुधपत्नि ! दुर्लभस्तव भर्ता न चिराद्भविष्यति ।
शृणु येन स कर्मणा गतः शलभत्वं हरलोचनार्चिषि ॥४०॥

O wife of the flower-armed! It will not take very long for thee to meet thy husband. Listen, how he flew like a moth into the flame of the eye of Hara. (40).

अभिलाषमुदीरितेन्द्रियः स्वसुतायामकरोत्प्रजापतिः ।
अथ तेन निगृह्य विक्रियामभिशप्तः फलमेतदन्वभूत् ॥४१॥

Prajāpati, when his senses were inflamed, did lust after his daughter; and then controlling his passion, he cursed Smara, so that he experienced this plight (fruit). (41).

परिणेष्यति पार्वतीं यदा तपसा तत्प्रवणीकृतो हरः ।
उपलब्धसुखस्तदा स्मरं वपुषा स्वेन नियोजयिष्यति ॥४२॥

When Hara will be favourably inclined to marry

Pārvatī, through her penance, then feeling happy, he will restore him his body. (42).

इति चाह स धर्मयाचितः स्मरशापावधिदां सरस्वतीम् ।
अशनेरमृतस्य चोभयोर्वशिनश्चाम्बुधराश्च योनयः ॥४३॥

Thus he spake, when requested by Dharma (Prajāpati); for the self-controlled and the cloud, each of these is the source of ambrosia and lightning respectively. (43).

तदिदं परिरक्ष शोभने भवितव्यप्रियसङ्गमं वपुः ।
रविपीतजला तपात्यये पुनरोघेन हि युज्यते नदी ॥४४॥

"Protect this thy body, which is destined to be united with the loved one; for a river, whose waters are drained off by the sun, is restored its current at summer's end." (44).

इत्थं रतेः किमपि भूतमदृश्यरूपं मन्दीचकार मरणव्यवसायबुद्धिम् ।
तत्प्रत्ययाच्च कुसुमायुधबन्धुरेनामाश्वासयत्सुचरितार्थपदैर्वचोभिः ।४५।

Thus an invisible being repressed Rati's determination to die; and through faith in those words, the friend of Kusumāyudha (the god of love), comforted her with words, the meaning of which was to be fully borne out. (45).

अथ मदनवधूरुपप्लवान्तं व्यसनकृशा परिपालयाम्बभूव ।
शशिन इव दिवातनस्य लेखा किरणपरिक्षयधूसरा प्रदोषम् ॥४६॥

Thus Rati, the wife of Madana, wilted by the calamity, awaited the end of that calamity; like the crescent of the moon, pale owing to loss of rays during day-time, awaiting (the approach) of the night. (46).

पञ्चमः सर्गः

तथा समक्षं दहता मनोभवं पिनाकिना भग्नमनोरथा सती।
निनिन्द रूपं हृदयेन पार्वती प्रियेषु सौभाग्यफला हि चारुता ॥१॥

Pārvatī, whose heart's desire was frustated by Pinākin (Śiva) by burning the mind-born (Kāma) before her very eyes, blamed in her heart her beauty; for beauty is that which wins the heart of the husband. (1).

इयेष सा कर्तुमवन्ध्यरूपतां समाधिमास्थाय तपोभिरात्मनः।
अवाप्यते वा कथमन्यथा द्वयं तथाविधं प्रेम पतिश्च तादृशः ॥२॥

She desired to make her beauty fruitful by penances after concentrating her mind; how could, otherwise, be won two things: love of that kind, and that kind of husband? (2).

निशम्य चैनां तपसे कृतोद्यमां सुतां गिरीशप्रतिसक्तमानसाम्।
उवाच मेना परिरभ्य वक्षसा निवारयन्ती महतो मुनिव्रतात् ॥३॥

Menā, on hearing that she had set her mind on the performance of penance as she had fixed her heart on Hara, spoke to her, forbidding her from undertaking arduous penance. (3).

मनीषिताः सन्ति गृहेषु देवतास्तपः क्व वत्से ! क्व च तावकं वपुः।
पदं सहेत भ्रमरस्य पेलवं शिरीषपुष्पं न पुनः पतत्रिणः ॥४॥

"The gods, you desire, are in our house, what disparity is there between your fresh youth and penance; the delicate Śirīṣa flower can bear the bee's tread but not that of a bird." (4).

इति ध्रुवेच्छामनुशासती सुतां शशाक मेना न नियन्तुमुद्यमात् ।
क ईप्सितार्थस्थिरनिश्चयं मनः पयश्च निम्नाभिमुखं प्रतीपयेत् ॥५॥

Menā, thus advising her daughter whose resolve was inexorable, was not able to restrain her daughter from her undertaking. Who can oppose a mind, resolutely fixed upon the desired object; and water, flowing on a downward course? (5).

कदाचिदासन्नसखीमुखेन सा मनोरथज्ञं पितरं मनस्विनी ।
अयाचतारण्यनिवासमात्मनः फलोदयान्ताय तपःसमाधये ॥६॥

Once, Pārvatī desired to convey to her father her firm resolve through a friend, who was near, and begged him to allow her to dwell in the forest for the performance of the vow of penance, till the fruit was obtained. (6).

अथानुरूपाभिनिवेशतोषिणा कृताभ्यनुज्ञा गुरुणा गरीयसा ।
प्रजासु पश्चात्प्रथितं तदाख्यया जगाम गौरीशिखरं शिखण्डिमत् ॥७॥

And permitted by her father, who was pleased at her resolve, which was quite befitting her, she went to the Gaurī-peak, the haunt of peacocks, which was later known in the world by that name. (7).

विमुच्य सा हारमहार्यनिश्चया विलोलयष्टिप्रविलुप्तचन्दनम् ।
बबन्ध बालारुणबभ्रु वल्कलं पयोधरोत्सेधविशीर्णसंहति ॥८॥

She, whose resolve was inexorable, discarded the string of pearls, which wiped out the sandal from her breast, and she covered her breast with a bark garment, shattered in the texture by her uplifted breast, tawny as the young dawn. (8).

यथा प्रसिद्धैर्मधुरं शिरोरुहैर्जटाभिरप्येवमभूत्तदाननम् ।
न षट्पदश्रेणिभिरेव पङ्कजं सशैवलासङ्गमपि प्रकाशते ॥९॥

Her face became as lovely by her matted locks, as by her well-dressed hair; for the' lotus shines as well by moss clinging to it, as by a swarm of bees. (9).

प्रतिक्षणं सा कृतरोमविक्रियां व्रताय मौञ्जीं त्रिगुणां बभार याम् ।
अकारि तत्पूर्वनिबद्धया तया सरागमस्या रसनागुणास्पदम् ॥१०॥

The thrice-folded Maunjī-girdle, which she wore for her vow, which caused horripilation every moment, and which tied before the girdle, made red her waist, the place of her girdle. (10).

विसृष्टरागादधरान्निवर्तितः स्तनाङ्गरागारुणिताच्च कन्दुकात् ।
कुशाङ्कुरादानपरिक्षताङ्गुलिः कृतोऽक्षसूत्रप्रणयी तया करः ॥११॥

Withdrawing her hand from her lip which was bereft of Ālaktaka paint, and from her ball, which was red with the paint from her breast; the hand, the fingers of which were wounded as she cut the blades of Kuśa grass, was made by her the companion of the rosary of Akṣa beads. (11).

महार्हशय्यापरिवर्तनच्युतैः स्वकेशपुष्पैरपि या स्म दूयते ।
अशेत सा बाहुलतोपधायिनी निषेदुषी स्थण्डिल एव केवले ॥१२॥

Painted by the flowers fallen from her hair, as she rolled from side to side in her costly bed, she slept pillowed on her creeper-like arm, as she occupied the altar. (12).

पुनर्ग्रहीतुं नियमस्थया तया द्वयेऽपि निक्षेप इवार्पितं द्वयम् ।
लतासु तन्वीषु विलासचेष्टितं विलोलदृष्टं हरिणाङ्गनासु च ॥१३॥

As she was observing vows for penance, she kept two things as deposits with two; her graceful movements with the lithe plants and her unsteady glances with the female deer. (13).

अतन्द्रिता सा स्वयमेव वृक्षकान् घटस्तनप्रस्रवणैर्व्यवर्धयत् ।
गुहोऽपि येषां प्रथमाप्तजन्मनां न पुत्रवात्सल्यमपाकरिष्यति ॥१४॥

Unwearied, she herself tended the trees, with water cascading from breast-like pitchers; her love for them (trees) as her children, being first-born, even Guha would not undo. (14).

अरण्यबीजाञ्जलिदानलालितास्तथा च तस्यां हरिणा विशश्वसुः ।
यथा तदीयैर्नयनैः कुतूहलात्पुरः सखीनाममिमीत लोचने ॥१५॥

The deer, reared by handfuls of grains (nīvāra) grown in the forest, so won her confidence, that she measured her eyes by comparing them with those of the deer before her friends. (15).

कृताभिषेकां हुतजातवेदसं त्वगुत्तरासङ्गवतीमधीतिनीम् ।
दिदृक्षवस्तामृषयोऽभ्युपागमन्न धर्मवृद्धेषु वयः समीक्ष्यते ॥१६॥

Now came sages to see her; she who had taken bath and made offerings to fire and had donned a deer-skin as her upper garment, and was chanting hymns; for age is no consideration in those that are rich in Dharma. (16).

विरोधिसत्त्वोज्झितपूर्वमत्सरं द्रुमैरभीष्टप्रसवार्चितातिथि ।
नवोटजाभ्यन्तरसम्भृतानलं तपोवनं तच्च बभूव पावनम् ॥१७॥

That religious domicile became hallowed; animals inimical to each other gave up their natural antipathy and the trees welcomed their guests with their fruit, inside the new cottages where the sacred fire was fed (with oblations). (17).

यदा फलं पूर्वतपःसमाधिना न तावता लभ्यममंस्त काङ्क्षितम् ।
तदानपेक्ष्य स्वशरीरमार्दवं तपो महत्सा चरितुं प्रचक्रमे ॥१८॥

When she thought her desired object could not be accomplished by her preliminary ascetic discipline, then not minding the delicate beauty of her body, she started performing more austere penances. (18).

क्लमं ययौ कन्दुकलीलयाऽपि या तया मुनीनां चरितं व्यगाह्यत ।
ध्रुवं वपुः काञ्चनपद्मनिर्मितं मृदु प्रकृत्या च ससारमेव च ॥१९॥

She, who was fatigued even by ball-play, now took to the life of ascetics. Surely her body which was fashioned out of golden lotuses, was delicate by nature and yet full of vitality. (19).

शुचौ चतुर्णां ज्वलतां हविर्भुजां शुचिस्मिता मध्यगता सुमध्यमा ।
विजित्य नेत्रप्रतिघातिनीं प्रभामनन्यदृष्टिः सवितारमैक्षत ॥२०॥

In summer, seated in the midst of four fires, she of a winning smile, and a delicate waist, conquered the dazzling blaze of fire, and not looking anywhere else, she concentrated her gaze upon the sun. (20).

तयातितप्तं सवितुर्गभस्तिभिर्मुखं तदीयं कमलश्रियं दधौ ।
अपाङ्गयोः केवलमस्य दीर्घयोः शनैः शनैः श्यामिकया कृतं पदम्

Her lovely face was so scorched by the rays of the sun, that it bore the beauty of a blooming lotus; only gradually, a dark ring formed round the long corners of her eyes. (21).

अयाचितोपस्थितमम्बु केवलं रसात्मकस्योडुपतेश्च रश्मयः ।
बभूव तस्याः किल पारणाविधिर्न वृक्षवृत्तिव्यतिरिक्तसाधनः ॥२२॥

Only water which came to her unsought, and the rays of the moon, who is watery in form, became the means of her satisfying her hunger not different from that of trees. (22).

निकामतप्ता विविधेन वह्निना नभश्चरेणेन्धनसम्भृतेन सा ।
तपात्यये वारिभिरुक्षिता नवैर्भुवा सहोष्माणममुञ्चदूर्ध्वगम् ॥२३॥

Intensely singed by various fires, and by the one that wanders in the sky (i.e. the sun) and bathed by showers of fresh water at the end of summer, she gasped out along with the earth hot vapoury breath which rose upwards. (23).

स्थिताः क्षणं पक्ष्मसु ताडिताधराः पयोधरोत्सेधनिपातचूर्णिताः ।
वलीषु तस्याः स्खलिताः प्रपेदिरे चिरेण नाभिं प्रथमोदबिन्दवः ॥२४॥

The first drops of rain stayed, for a moment, on her eye-lashes, its compactness reduced to spray on her rising bosom, then stumbled in the three folds of her skin and reached her (deep) navel after a long time. (24).

शिलाशयां तामनिकेतवासिनीं निरन्तरास्वन्तरवातवृष्टिषु ।
व्यलोकयन्नुन्मिषितैस्तडिन्मयैर्महातपःसाक्ष्य इव स्थिताः क्षपाः ॥२५॥

Under the showers, accompanied compactly with winds, she lived homeless; lying on a slab of stone, she was looked at with the eyes of lightning by nights who stood as witnesses of her austere penances. (25).

निनाय सात्यन्तहिमोत्करानिलाः सहस्यरात्रीरुदवासतत्परा ।
परस्पराक्रन्दिनि चक्रवाकयोः पुरो वियुक्ते मिथुने कृपावती ॥२६॥

Standing in water, she passed the nights of Pauṣa in which blew winds charged densely with particles of snow, taking pity on the pair of cakravākas who suffered severance from one another, and who were before her, crying to one another. (26).

मुखेन सा पद्मसुगन्धिना निशि प्रवेपमानाधरपत्रशोभिना ।
तुषारवृष्टिक्षतपद्मसम्पदां सरोजसन्धानमिवाकरोदपाम् ॥२७॥

With her mouth redolent of the odour of lotuses, and shining with her quivering lip, she seemed to provide the lotus-lakes with a lotus, whose wealth of flowers was destroyed by a shower of snow. (27).

स्वयंविशीर्णद्रुमपर्णवृत्तिता परा हि काष्ठा तपसस्तया पुनः ।
तदप्यपाकीर्णमतः प्रियंवदां वदन्त्यपर्णेति च तां पुराविदः ॥२८॥

Subsisting on leaves, fallen of themselves, is the height of penance; even that she discarded; that is why the sweet-tongued one is called Aparṇā by those who know the past. (28).

मृणालिकापेलवमेवमादिभिर्व्रतैः स्वमङ्गं ग्लपयन्त्यहर्निशम् ।
तपः शरीरैः कठिनैरुपार्जितं तपस्विनां दूरमधश्चकार सा ॥२९॥

She got her body, delicate as a lotus-stalk, attenuated by observing such austere vows as these; thus she far exceeded the penances of ascetics by her penances performed through the medium of her body. (29).

अथाजिनाषाढधरः प्रगल्भवाग् ज्वलन्निव ब्रह्ममयेन तेजसा ।
विवेश कश्चिज्जटिलस्तपोवनं शरीरबद्धः प्रथमाश्रमो यथा ॥३०॥

Then a certain bachelor with matted locks, holding an āṣāḍha staff and wearing a piece of antelope-skin, bold of speech, and as if flaming with spiritual lustre, entered the penance grove, as if, he was the first stage of life in bodily form. (30).

तमातिथेयी बहुमानपूर्वया सपर्यया प्रत्युदियाय पार्वती ।
भवन्ति साम्येऽपि निविष्टचेतसां वपुर्विशेषेष्वतिगौरवाः क्रियाः ॥३१॥

Pārvatī, offered him respectful worship and a welcome offering; the actions of those whose mind is concentrated are full of great respect, even towards their equal, who have an impressive form. (31).

विधिप्रयुक्तां परिगृह्य सत्क्रियां परिश्रमं नाम विनीय च क्षणम् ।
उमां स पश्यन्नृजुनैव चक्षुषा प्रचक्रमे वक्तुमनुज्झितक्रमः ॥३२॥

That bachelor received the welcome-offering made according to proper rites and dissipating his fatigue awhile, looked at Umā with straight eye, and began addressing her in the proper order. (32).

अपि क्रियार्थं सुलभं समित्कुशं जलान्यपि स्नानविधिक्षमाणि ते ।
अपि स्वशक्त्या तपसि प्रवर्तसे शरीरमाद्यं खलु धर्मसाधनम् ॥३३॥

"I hope samidhās and kuśa grass are available in quantities sufficient for the performance of penance. Is there water fit for ablution? I hope, you perform your penance without overstraining your strength; for our body is the prime instrument of penance. (33).

अपि त्वदावर्जितवारिसम्भृतं प्रवालमासामनुबन्धि वीरुधाम् ।
चिरोज्झितालक्तकपाटलेन ते तुलां यदारोहति दन्तवाससा ॥३४॥

I hope the leaves of the creepers watered by thee are continuously burgeoning; which leaves are equable to thy lips, which are coral-red, though they are no longer painted with the alaktaka dye. (34).

अपि प्रसन्नं हरिणेषु ते मनः करस्थदर्भप्रणयापहारिषु ।
य उत्पलाक्षि ! प्रचलैर्विलोचनैस्तवाक्षिसादृश्यमिव प्रयुञ्जते ॥३५॥

I hope, the mind is pleased with the deer, who O lotus-eyed, seem to imitate thine eyes with their tremulous eyes. (35).

यदुच्यते पार्वति ! पापवृत्तये न रूपमित्यव्यभिचारि तद्वचः ।
तथा हि ते शीलमुदारदर्शने तपस्विनामप्युपदेशतां गतम् ॥३६॥

What they say that beauty of form does not lead to sin is infallibly true; for thy character, O lady, large-eyed, is an exemplar even to the sages. (36).

विकीर्णसप्तर्षिबलिप्रहासिभिस्तथा न गाङ्गैः सलिलैर्दिवश्च्युतैः ।
यथा त्वदीयैश्चरितैरनाविलैर्महीधरः पावित एष सान्वयः ॥३७॥

This mountain is not hallowed by the waters of the Ganges, spilling down from the sky and smiling with (i.e. shining with) the Bali offerings, made by the Saptarṣis, as much as by thy pure acts (of devotion). (37).

अनेन धर्मः सविशेषमद्य मे त्रिवर्गसारः प्रतिभाति भाविनि ! ।
त्वया मनोनिर्विषयार्थकामया यदेक एव प्रतिगृह्य सेव्यते ॥३८॥

O lady of noble intentions, meseems that Dharma excels the other two ends of human existence, now that thou hast adopted Dharma only, (to the exclusion of the other two) with a mind purged of desire for worldly goods and desires. (38).

प्रयुक्तसत्कारविशेषमात्मना न मां परं सम्प्रतिपत्तुमर्हसि ।
यतः सतां सन्नतगात्रि ! सङ्गतं मनीषिभिः साप्तपदीनमुच्यते ॥३९॥

Having shown me special honour, it behoves thee n t to look upon me as a stranger; for the friendship of good, O lady with stooping limbs ! is bred by taking together seven steps only. (39).

अतोऽत्र किञ्चिद्भवतीं बहुक्षमां द्विजातिभावादुपपन्नचापलः ।
अयं जनः प्रष्टुमनास्तपोधने ! न चेद्रहस्यं प्रतिवक्तुमर्हसि ॥४०॥

Hence I wish to ask you something, O lady, rich in penance, and of a highly forgiving nature, if it be not a secret; being a brahmin my outspokenness is but just and proper. (40).

कुले प्रसूतिः प्रथमस्य वेधसस्त्रिलोकसौन्दर्यमिवोदितं वपुः ।
अमृग्यमैश्वर्यसुखं नवं वयस्तपःफलं स्यात्किमतः परं वद ॥४१॥

Thou art born in a family, descended from the primeval creator, and your body is dowered with a beauty, which represents the loveliness of the three worlds put together; the happiness which opulence gives is yours, and is not to be sought, a youthful age; say what more fruit can penance give? (41)

भवत्यनिष्टादपि नाम दुस्सहान्मनस्विनीनां प्रतिपत्तिरीदृशी ।
विचारमार्गप्रहितेन चेतसा न दृश्यते तच्च कृशोदरि त्वयि ॥४२॥

Such activity of wise ladies results from unbearable misbehaviour (on the part of husband, or some other person). But, O lady of slim waist ! I do not see that in thee, however much I think about it. (42).

अलभ्यशोकाभिभवेयमाकृतिर्विमानना सुभ्रु ! कुतः पितुर्गृहे ।
पराभिमर्शो न तवास्ति कः करं प्रसारयेत्पन्नगरत्नसूचये ॥४३॥

Your body is incapable of suffering pain from insult by your husband or any other person; whence can there be any affront in your father's house? How can a stranger dare to insult thee? Who shall stretch his hand to grasp the pencil-like gem from the serpent's hood? (43).

किमित्यपास्याभरणानि यौवने धृतं त्वया वार्धकशोभि वल्कलम् ।
वद प्रदोषे स्फुटचन्द्रतारका विभावरी यद्यरुणाय कल्पते ॥४४॥

Why have you set aside ornaments when so young and assumed barks befitting old age? Say whether at the beginning of the night, when the moon and the stars are so manifest, she can be ready for the break of the morning twilight? (44).

दिवं यदि प्रार्थयसे वृथा श्रमः पितुः प्रदेशास्तव देवभूमयः ।
अथोपयन्तारमलं समाधिना न रत्नमन्विष्यति मृग्यते हि तत् ॥४५॥

If you seek heaven, your efforts are vain; for your father's lands are a part of heaven; and if you seek a husband, enough of penance; for a jewel seeketh not, but is itself sought. (45).

निवेदितं निःश्वसितेन सोष्मणा मनस्तु मे संशयमेव गाहते ।
न दृश्यते प्रार्थयितव्य एव ते भविष्यति प्रार्थितदुर्लभः कथम् ॥४६॥

Your sighs have declared your mind, but my mind is in doubt; there is none, whom you need seek; how can one be difficult to obtain when sought by you? (46).

अहो स्थिरः कोऽपि तवेप्सितो युवा चिराय कर्णोत्पलशून्यतां गते ।
उपेक्षते यः श्लथलम्बिनीर्जटाः कपोलदेशे कलमाग्रपिङ्गलाः ॥४७॥

Ah ! How adamant is the young man you desire, who recks not of the matted locks tawny as rice-clustertips, spilling down on your cheeks, bereft of ear-lotus. (47).

मुनिव्रतैस्त्वामतिमात्रकर्शितां दिवाकराप्लुष्टविभूषणास्पदाम् ।
शशाङ्कलेखामिव पश्यतो दिवा सचेतसः कस्य मनो न दूयते ॥४८॥

What man, alive, does not feel pain in his heart, on seeing that you are thinned by the vows of an anchorite, and the places where ornaments are worn darkened by the heat of the sun, as on seeing the moon's crescent by day? (48).

अवैमि सौभाग्यमदेन वञ्चितं तव प्रियं यश्चतुरावलोकिनः ।
करोति लक्ष्यं चिरमस्य चक्षुषो न वक्त्रमात्मीयमरालपक्ष्मणः ॥४९॥

I understand your beloved to be deluded by the beauty of his form, that he does not make your lovely face with its straight eye-lashes the target of his eyes for a long time. (49).

कियच्चिरं श्राम्यसि गौरि ! विद्यते ममापि पूर्वाश्रमसञ्चितं तपः ।
तदर्धभागेन लभस्व काङ्क्षितं वरं तमिच्छामि च साधु वेदितुम् ॥५०॥

How long, O Gauri! will you weary yourself? I, too, have accumulated penance in the first stage of my life (Brahmacaryāśrama); by half of it may you win the desired husband; I wish to know him well." (50).

इति प्रविश्याभिहिता द्विजन्मना मनोगतं सा न शशाक शंसितुम् ।
अथो वयस्यां परिपार्श्ववर्तिनीं विवर्तितानञ्जननेत्रमैक्षत ॥५१॥

Thus, the Brahmin sought to worm the secret out of her, but she was unable to reveal to him her secret out of bashfulness; but she then turned her eye which was without collyrium, to her friend. (51).

सखी तदीया तमुवाच वर्णिनं निबोध साधो ! तव चेत्कुतूहलम् ।
यदर्थमम्भोजमिवोष्णवारणं कृतं तपःसाधनमेतया वपुः ॥५२॥

Her friend said to the bachelor, "Understand, noble sir, if you are desirous to know the reason why she has made her body, which wards off heat, like a lotus, the vehicle of her penance. (52).

इयं महेन्द्रप्रभृतीनधिश्रियश्चतुर्दिगीशानवमत्य मानिनी ।
अरूपहार्यं मदनस्य निग्रहात्पिनाकपाणिं पतिमाप्तुमिच्छति ॥५३॥

This proud lady moved by the behests of Madana,

disregarding the Guardians of Quarters, Indra and others of great eminence, desires to win Lord Siva for husband. (53)

प्रसह्यहुङ्कारनिर्वर्ततः पुरा पुरारिमप्राप्तमुखः शिलीमुखः ।
इमां हृदि व्यायतपातमक्षिणोद्विशीर्णमूर्तेरपि पुष्पधन्वनः ॥५४॥

The shaft of the flower-armed, formerly repulsed by God Śiva, by an unbearable grunt, deep in Pārvatī's tender heart lay, although the body of the flower-armed god lay, a shattered frame. (54).

तदा प्रभृत्युन्मदना पितुर्गृहे ललाटिकाचन्दनधूसरालका ।
न जातु बाला लभते स्म निर्वृतिं तुषारसङ्घातशिलातलेष्वपि ॥५५॥

From that time on, passion-smitten, in her father's house, her hair grey, with the sandal applied to her forehead, the dear girl did not find comfort in her heart, although she would lie on slabs of ice. (55).

उपात्तवर्णे चरिते पिनाकिनः सबाष्पकण्ठस्खलितैः पदैरियम् ।
अनेकशः किन्नरराजकन्यका वनान्तसङ्गीतसखीररोदयत् ॥५६॥

As she sang the deeds of Śiva in song, in words, faltering in utterance through her tear-choked throat, she often made her kinnara friends, her companions in the interior of the forest, weep. (56).

त्रिभागशेषासु निशासु च क्षणं निमील्य नेत्रे सहसा व्यबुध्यत ।
क्व नीलकण्ठ व्रजसीत्यलक्ष्यवागसत्यकण्ठार्पितबाहुबन्धना ॥५७॥

She had just a wink of sleep; while three quarters of the night yet remained, she awoke all of a sudden; "where dost thou go, Nīlakaṇṭha? "She said indistinctly, clasping his neck, which was not there. (57).

यदा बुधैः सर्वगतस्त्वमुच्यसे न वेत्सि भावस्थमिमं कथं जनम् ।
इति स्वहस्तोल्लिखितश्च मुग्धया रहस्युपालभ्यत चन्द्रशेखरः ॥५८॥

'As the wise describe thee as omnipresent, how do you not know this person who is in love with thee'? Thus did she in her privacy revile Candraśekhara, limned by her own hand. (58).

यदा च तस्याधिगमे जगत्पतेरपश्यदन्यं न विधिं विचिन्वती ।
तदा सहास्माभिरनुज्ञया गुरोरियं प्रपन्ना तपसे तपोवनम् ॥५९॥

When she did not find any means to win the lord of the World, with the consent of her father, however, she attempted to seek it. She came to this forest with us for practising penance. (59).

द्रुमेषु सख्या कृतजन्मसु स्वयं फलं तपःसाक्षिषु दृष्टमेष्वपि ।
न च प्ररोहाभिमुखोऽपि दृश्यते मनोरथोऽस्याः शशिमौलिसंश्रयः ॥६०॥

In trees planted by Pārvatī herself, although fruit has appeared, the witness of her penance, her heart's desire for Candramauli does not seem to sprout. (60).

न वेद्मि स प्रार्थितदुर्लभः कदा सखीभिरस्रोत्तरमीक्षितामिमाम् ।
तपःकृशामभ्युपपत्स्यते सखीं वृषेव सीतां तदवग्रहक्षताम् ॥६१॥

I do not know, when He (Śiva) inaccessible though besought, will favour our friend wilted by penance. "So saying her friends looked at her, after shedding tears, like Indra favouring the earth, parched by drought. (61).

अगूढसद्भावमितीङ्गितज्ञया निवेदितो नैष्ठिकसुन्दरस्तया ।
अयीदमेवं परिहास इत्युमामपृच्छदव्यञ्जितहर्षलक्षणः ॥६२॥

The handsome hermit, who had vowed celibacy for life, and was concealing her good feelings, was told by her (Pārvatī's) friend, who knew her heart; and asked Umā, without showing signs of joy on his face, if that was mere chaffing on the part of her friend. (62).

अथाग्रहस्ते मुकुलीकृताङ्गुलौ समर्पयन्ती स्फटिकाक्षमालिकाम् ।
कथञ्चिदद्रेस्तनया मिताक्षरं चिरव्यवस्थापितवागभाषत ॥६३॥

Umā, holding in the palm of her hand, the fingers of which were closed into bud, a rosary of crystal beads, somehow steadied her speech, and spake in measured words. (63).

यथा श्रुतं वेदविदां वर त्वया जनोऽयमुच्चैःपदलङ्घनोत्सुकः ।
तपः किलेदं तदवाप्तिसाधनं मनोरथानामगतिर्न विद्यते ॥६४॥

"O rich in Vedic Lore, what you have heard is true: that this person is eagerly longing to attain a high place; for nothing is inaccessible to desire." (64).

अथाह वर्णी विदितो महेश्वरस्त्वदर्थिनी त्वं पुनरेव वर्तसे ।
अमङ्गलाभ्यासरतिं विचिन्त्य तं तवानुवृत्तिं न च कर्तुमुत्सहे ॥६५॥

Then the celibate said, "I know Maheśvara; but as for you, you seek him (for husband); but as I reflect that he is given to inauspicious things, I dare not commend your choice. (65).

अवस्तुनिर्बन्धपरे कथं नु ते करोऽयमामुक्तविवाहकौतुकः ।
करेण शम्भोर्वलयीकृताहिना सहिष्यते तत्प्रथमावलम्बनम् ॥६६॥

O thou ! that hankereth after trifling objects, how could thy hand, which is divested of the marriage bracelet, bear to be clutched by Śiva's hand coiled by serpents, for the first time? (66).

त्वमेव तावत्परिचिन्तय स्वयं कदाचिदेते यदि योगमर्हतः ।
वधूदुकूलं कलहंसलक्षणं गजाजिनं शोणितबिन्दुवर्षि च ॥६७॥

Think thou, O lovely one ! if these ever deserve to be brought together : the bride's silken garment emblazoned with figures of swans, and elephant-hide dripping with drops of blood. (67).

चतुष्कपुष्पप्रकराबकीर्णयोः परोऽपि को नाम तवानुमन्यते ।
अलक्तकाङ्कानि पदानि पादयोर्विकीर्णकेशासु परेतभूमिषु ॥६८॥

Who, even your enemy, can commend your feet treading the flower-covered quadrangle of a four flanked house, treading the cemetery ground, covered with hair—your feet painted with alaktaka? (68).

अयुक्तरूपं किमतः परं वद त्रिनेत्रवक्षः सुलभं तवापि यत् ।
स्तनद्वयेऽस्मिन् हरिचन्दनास्पदे पदं चिताभस्मरजः करिष्यति ॥६९॥

What could be more improper than this, that thy breasts, fit to be plastered with haricandana, should be bespattered with funeral ashes, in thy easily available embraces by Hara. (69).

इयं च तेऽन्या पुरतो विडम्बना यदूढया वारणराजहार्यया ।
विलोक्य वृद्धोक्षमधिष्ठितं त्वया महाजनः स्मेरमुखो भविष्यति ॥७०॥

This is your another discomfiture, that big masses of men will be smiling on seeing thee, fit to ride huge elephants, riding thy mount of an old bull. (70).

द्वयं गतं सम्प्रति शोचनीयतां समागमप्रार्थनया पिनाकिनः ।
कला च सा कान्तिमती कलावतस्त्वमस्य लोकस्य च नेत्रकौमुदी ॥७१॥

Now two have become deplorable by Pināki's desire to obtain them : the shining crescent of the moon, and then, the moon-light of the world's eyes. (71).

वपुर्विरूपाक्षमलक्ष्यजन्मता दिगम्बरत्वेन निवेदितं वसु ।
वरेषु यद् बालमृगाक्षि ! मृग्यते तदस्ति किं व्यस्तमपि त्रिलोचने ॥७२॥

His body is deformed, having three eyes, his birth obscure, his wealth declared by his having the sky for garment; whatever is to be sought in a bridegroom, is that to be found even singly in Trilocana (Śiva). (72).

निवर्तयास्मादसदीप्सितान्मनः क्व तद्विधस्त्वं क्व च पुण्यलक्षणा ।
अपेक्ष्यते साधुजनेन वैदिकी श्मशानशूलस्य न यूपसत्क्रिया ॥७३॥

Turn your mind away from this unseemly desire; what disparity is there between him of that type and you of auspicious qualities ! Wise men expect not Vedic consecration of the stake in the cemetery of the sort of the sacrificial post." (73).

इति द्विजातौ प्रतिकूलवादिनि प्रवेपमानाधरलक्ष्यकोपया ।
विकुञ्चितभ्रूलतमाहिते तया विलोचने तिर्यगुपान्तलोहिते ॥७४॥

When thus the Brahmin spoke something unfavourably to her, she, whose anger was visible from her trembling lips, looked at him with eyes, red at the corners, obliquely with eyebrows knit. (74).

उवाच चैनं परमार्थतो हरं न वेत्सि नूनं यत एवमात्थ माम् ।
अलोकसामान्यमचिन्त्यहेतुकं द्विषन्ति मन्दाश्चरितं महात्मनाम् ॥७५॥

She said to him, "Thou dost not know Hara in his true nature, that thou speakest thus; the dull hate the actions of the great, which are extraordinary and inscrutable in their motive. (75).

विपत्प्रतीकारपरेण मङ्गलं निषेव्यते भूतिसमुत्सुकेन वा ।
जगच्छरण्यस्य निराशिषः सतः किमेभिराशोपहतात्मवृत्तिभिः ॥७६॥

An auspicious thing is sought by one who seeks to counteract adverse circumstances, or by one who longs for prosperity; what has one, who has no desire, and is the refuge of the world, to do with the impulses of the soul, marred by desire (for worldly objects)? (76).

अकिञ्चनः सन्प्रभवः स सम्पदां त्रिलोकनाथः पितृसद्मगोचरः ।
स भीमरूपः शिव इत्युदीर्यते न सन्ति याथार्थ्यविदः पिनाकिनः ॥७७॥

Though himself poor, he is the source of wealth—he, the Lord of the three worlds living in a cemetery; though frightful in aspect, he is called 'auspicious in nature'; no one knows Pināki in his true nature. (77).

विभूषणोद्भासि पिनद्धभोगि वा गजाजिनालम्बि दुकूलधारि वा ।
कपालि वा स्यादथवेन्दुशेखरं न विश्वमूर्तेरवधार्यते वपुः ॥७८॥

His body may be adorned by ornaments, or may be coiled round by serpents; may be draped in elephant hide, or in a silken garment; he may hold a skull, or may be adorned by the crescent of the moon; the form of one, who incorporates the whole world is inscrutable. (78).

तवङ्गसंसर्गमवाप्य कल्पते ध्रुवं चिताभस्मरजो विशुद्धये ।
तथा हि नृत्याभिनयक्रियाच्युतं विलिप्यते मौलिभिरम्बरौकसाम् ॥७९॥

The funeral ashes, coming in contact with his limbs tend to purge sin; while when it drops down in his dance, it smears the heads of the gods. (79).

असम्पदस्तस्य वृषेण गच्छतः प्रभिन्नदिग्वारणवाहनो वृषा ।
करोति पादावुपगम्य मौलिना विनिद्रमन्दाररजोऽरुणाङ्गुली ॥८०॥

Indra, approaching him on his mount of a quarter-elephant, makes the toes of the feet of Śiva, who rides his bull and is penury-ridden, red with the pollen of full-blown Mandāra flowers. (80).

विवक्षता दोषमपि च्युतात्मना त्वयैकमीशं प्रति साधु भाषितम् ।
यमामनन्त्यात्मभुवोऽपि कारणं कथं स लक्ष्यप्रभवो भविष्यति ॥८१॥

Speaking of his faults, you, of a fallen soul, have at least mentioned one good quality of his; how could he, who is the source of the self-born, be one, whose source could be noticed ? (81).

अलं विवादेन यथा श्रुतस्त्वया तथाविधस्तावदशेषमस्तु सः ।
ममात्र भावैकरसं मनः स्थितं न कामवृत्तिर्वचनीयमीक्षते ॥८२॥

Enough of argument; may he be of the nature you have heard; my heart is full of the one sentiment of love;

one who is caprice-ridden, does not care for a fault. (82).

निवार्यतामालि किमप्ययं बटुः पुनर्विवक्षुः स्फुरितोत्तराधरः ।
न केवलं यो महतोऽपभाषते शृणोति तस्मादपि यः स पापभाक् ॥८३॥

Do thou stop this brat, O friend; he seems to be desirous of speaking again. Not only he, who reviles the great is sinful, but he, who (willingly) hears the same from him is also so. (83).

इतो गमिष्याम्यथवेति वादिनी चचाल बाला स्तनभिन्नवल्कला ।
स्वरूपमास्थाय च तां कृतस्मितः समाललम्बे वृषराजकेतनः ॥८४॥

I will move from here''. So saying, the young lady, whose scarf of the bark of a tree slipped from her breasts, left. The bull-emblemed god, smiling, hung on to her. (84).

तं वीक्ष्य वेपथुमती सरसाङ्गयष्टि-
र्निक्षेपणाय पदमुद्धृतमुद्वहन्ती ।
मार्गाचलव्यतिकराकुलितेव सिन्धुः
शैलाधिराजतनया न ययौ न तस्थौ ॥८५॥

The daughter of the king of mountains, on seeing him, was full of tremor, and had sweat on her supple body; and holding her foot uplifted to step forward, like a river obstructed by a mountain she meets on the way, did neither halt nor move away. (85).

अद्य प्रभृत्यवनताङ्गि ! तवास्मि दासः
क्रीतस्तपोभिरिति वादिनि चन्द्रमौलौ ।
अह्नाय सा नियमजं क्लममुत्ससर्ज
क्लेशः फलेन हि पुनर्नवतां विधत्ते ॥८६॥

"From to-day on, I am thy slave, O maiden with stooping limbs !—won by thy penance". The moment Candraśekhara spoke thus, that very moment she gave up fatigue, born of her observance of her vow; for labour renovates one, when its fruit is reaped. (86).

———

षष्ठः सर्गः

अथ विश्वात्मने गौरी संदिदेश मिथः सखीम् ।
दाता मे भूभृतां नाथः प्रमाणीक्रियतामिति ॥१॥

The Gaurī secretly sent her friend to Lord Śiva, who is the Universe, requesting him to honour the Lord of mountains as her giver. (1).

तया व्याहृतसंदेशा सा बभौ निभृता प्रिये ।
चूतयष्टिरिवाभ्याशे मधौ परभृतोन्मुखी ॥२॥

Having sent her message through her (friend) she felt more attached to Hara than ever, like a branch of mango, favouring the koil at Spring's advent. (2).

स तथेति प्रतिज्ञाय विसृज्य कथमप्युमाम् ।
ऋषीन् ज्योतिर्मयान् सप्त सस्मार स्मरशासनः ॥३॥

Saying "so be it" he, the vanquisher of Smara, somehow, took leave of Umā and remembered the luminous Saptarṣis (the Great Bear). (3).

ते प्रभामण्डलैर्व्योम द्योतयन्तस्तपोधनाः ।
सारुन्धतीकाः सपदि प्रादुरासन् पुरः प्रभोः ॥४॥

Those sages, rich in penance, illumining the sky by their multitudes of light appeared before the Lord (Śiva) with Arundhatī. (4).

आप्लुतास्तीरमन्दारकुसुमोत्करवीचिषु ।
आकाशगङ्गास्रोतःसु दिङ्नागमदगन्धिषु ॥५॥

Bathed in the heavenly Ganges, whose waves bore scattered clusters of Mandāra flowers, and were redolent of the odour of the ichor of quarter-elephants; (5).

मुक्तायज्ञोपवीतानि बिभ्रतो हैमवल्कलाः ।
रत्नाक्षसूत्राः प्रव्रज्यां कल्पवृक्षा इवाश्रिताः ॥६॥

Wearing pearl-sacred threads and golden barks, and beads of jewels in their rosaries, betaking themselves to the life of sanyāsins; they stood as Kalpavṛkṣas (wish-yielding trees). (6).

अधःप्रस्थापिताश्वेन समावर्जितकेतुना ।
सहस्ररश्मिना शश्वत् सप्रणाममुदीक्षिताः ॥७॥

They seemed to be looked at respectfully by the Sun himself who drove his horses nether-wards, with streamers flying low. (7).

आसक्तबाहुलतया सार्धमुद्धृतया भुवा ।
महावराहदंष्ट्रायां विश्रान्ताः प्रलयापदि ॥८॥

And at the dissolution of an aeon, resting upon the tusk of the primeval boar, with their creeper-like arms, along with the earth, uplifted on it; (8).

सर्गशेषप्रणयनाद् विश्वयोनेरनन्तरम् ।
पुरातनाः पुराविद्भिर्धातार इति कीर्तिताः ॥९॥

The creators of the universe, which remained uncreated, after Brahman had fashioned it, and named the ancient creators by those who know the stories past; (9).

प्राक्तनानां विशुद्धानां परिपाकमुपेयुषाम् ।
तपसामुपभुञ्जानाः फलान्यपि तपस्विनः ॥१०॥

These anchorites, enjoyed the fruit of their pure penance come to fruition. (10).

तेषां मध्यगता साध्वी पत्युः पादार्पितेक्षणा ।
साक्षादिव तपःसिद्धिर्बभासे बह्वरुन्धती ॥११॥

Arundhatī, who stood in their midst, had bent her gaze upon her husband's feet, was as the accomplishment incarnate of their penance. (11).

तामगौरवभेदेन मुनींश्चापश्यदीश्वरः ।
स्त्रीपुमानित्यनास्थैषा वृत्तं हि महितं सताम् ॥१२॥

Īśvara looked upon those sages with equal respect; man or woman is no consideration with the great; it is actions they commend. (12).

तद्दर्शनादभूच्छंभोर्भूयान् दारार्थमादरः ।
क्रियाणां खलु धर्म्याणां दांपत्यं मूलसाधनम् ॥१३॥

At their sight, Śambhu felt considerable respect for his wife; for good religious acts depend upon good wives. (13).

धर्मेणापि पदं शर्वे कारिते पार्वतीं प्रति ।
पूर्वापराधभीतस्य कामस्योच्छ्वसितं मनः ॥१४॥

Having caused Śarva's mind to be disposed towards Pārvatī by proper marriage rites, the mind of Kāma, who had previously offended, felt an access of the hope of revival. (14).

अथ ते मुनयः सर्वे पूजयित्वा जगद्गुरुम् ।
इदमूचुरनूचानाः प्रीतिकण्टकितत्वचः ॥१५॥

Then all those sages, adepts in the knowledge of the Vedas, honoured the Lord of the world, addressed him while their limbs were thrilled with pleasure. (15).

यद् ब्रह्म सम्यगाम्नातं यदग्नौ विधिवद् धुतम् ।
यच्च तप्तं तपस्तस्य विपक्वं फलमद्य नः ॥१६॥

"To-day has come to fruition our painstaking study of the Vedas, our oblations offered to fire, according to due rites, and the penance we practised. (16).

यदध्यक्षेण जगतां वयमारोपितास्त्वया ।
मनोरथस्याप्यपथं मनोविषयमात्मनः ॥१७॥

Since you, the Lord of the world, place us in the region of your mind, beyond the region of our utmost wish. (17).

यस्य चेतसि वर्तेथाः स तावत् कृतिनां वरः ।
किं पुनर्ब्रह्मयोनेर्यस्तव चेतसि वर्तते ॥१८॥

Foremost among the blessed is he, in whose mind thou dwelleth; what need be of one, whom thou, the source of Brahman, dost remember? (18).

सत्यमर्काच्च सोमाच्च परमध्यास्महे पदम् ।
अद्य तूच्चैस्तरं तस्मात् स्मरणानुग्रहात्तव ॥१९॥

It is true, we now occupy a place higher than that of the sun and the moon; but through thy favour of remembering us we occupy a still higher place. (19).

त्वत्संभावितमात्मानं बहु मन्यामहे वयम् ।
प्रायः प्रत्ययमाधत्ते स्वगुणेषूत्तमादरः ॥२०॥

We think highly of ourselves, being honoured by thee; the respect paid to one by the great, generally creates confidence in one's good qualities. (20).

या नः प्रीतिर्विरूपाक्ष त्वदनुध्यानसंभवा ।
सा किमावेद्यते तुभ्यमन्तरात्मासि देहिनाम् ॥२१॥

The pleasure we feel in contemplating thee, O Virūpākṣa! need it be told thee? Thou art the indwelling spirit of all beings. (21).

साक्षाद् दृष्टोऽसि न पुनर्विद्मस्त्वां वयमञ्जसा ।
प्रसीद कथयात्मानं न धियां पथि वर्तसे ॥२२॥

We have direct vision of thee; we know thee not in thy true nature; be gracious, tell us; thou art beyond the reach of our mind. (22).

किं येन सृजसि व्यक्तमुत येन बिभर्षि तत् ।
अथ यस्तस्य संहर्ता भागः कतम एष ते ॥२३॥

What part is this of thine? Is it the one by which thou dost create, or the one by which thou dost dissolve the universe? (23).

अथवा सुमहत्येषा प्रार्थना देव तिष्ठतु ।
चिन्तितोपस्थितांस्तावच्छाधि नः करवाम किम् ॥२४॥

Or, O Lord, let this great request stand aside; commend us, what we should do; - we, who have presented ourselves, the moment we were thought of." (24).

अथ मौलिगतस्येन्दोर्विशदैर्दशनांशुभिः ।
उपचिन्वन् प्रभां तन्वीं प्रत्याह परमेश्वरः ॥२५॥

Then the great god answered, augmenting the dim lustre of the crescent moon on his crest by the serene rays of his teeth. (25).

विदितं वो यथा स्वार्था न मे काश्चित् प्रवृत्तयः ।
ननु मूर्तिभिरष्टाभिरित्थंभूतोऽस्मि सूचितः ॥२६॥

"You know that my actions are not for any selfish ends; the eight forms of mine suggest that I am of this nature. (26).

सोऽहं तृष्णातुरैर्वृष्टिं विद्युत्वानिव चातकैः ।
अरिविप्रकृतैर्देवैः प्रसूतिं प्रति याचितः ॥२७॥

Like the thirsty cātakas' prayer, for showers, the gods harassed by their eminence beg that I beget a son. (27).

अत आहर्तुमिच्छामि पार्वतीमात्मजन्मने ।
उत्पत्तये हविर्भोक्तुर्यजमान इवारणिम् ॥२८॥

So I desire to take Pārvatī to wife that I may beget a son; like a sacrificer, the churning wood for producing fire. (28).

तामस्मदर्थे युष्माभिर्याचितव्यो हिमालयः ।
विक्रियायै न कल्पन्ते संबन्धाः सदनुष्ठिताः ॥२९॥

You should prey to Himālaya that Pārvatī be bestowed upon us in marriage; for relationships established by the good do not prove fruitless. (29).

उन्नतेन स्थितिमता धुरमुद्वहता भुवः ।
तेन योजितसंबन्धं वित्त मामप्यवञ्चितम् ॥३०॥

By that lofty and eminent one, bearing the yoke of the earth, know that I, too, am not deceived by the marriage -tie. (30).

एवं वाच्यः स कन्यार्थमिति वो नोपदिश्यते ।
भवत्प्रणीतमाचारमामनन्ति हि साधवः ॥३१॥

It is hardly necessary that you should be advised to ask him for the hand of his daughter in marriage. The institutions promulgated by you are honoured as standard rules by the good. (31).

आर्याप्यरुन्धती तत्र व्यापारं कर्तुमर्हति ।
प्रायेणैवंविधे कार्ये पुरंध्रीणां प्रगल्भता ॥३२॥

It behoves the noble Arundhatī to help us in this marriage, for (goodly) matrons are clever in such matters, generally. (32).

तत्प्रयातौषधिप्रस्थं सिद्धये हिमवत्पुरम् ।
महाकोशीप्रपातेऽस्मिन् संगमः पुनरेव नः ॥३३॥

So proceed to Oṣadhiprastha, the capital of Himālaya for the accomplishment of this purpose; we shall meet again at Mahākośi falls." (33).

तस्मिन् संयमिनामाद्ये जाते परिणयोन्मुखे ।
जहुः परिग्रहव्रीडां प्राजापत्यास्तपस्विनः ॥३४॥

When He, the foremost of the self-restrained, was favourably disposed to marriage, the sages, the sons of Brahmā, gave up feeling of shame in respect of marrying wives. (34).

ततः परममित्युक्त्वा प्रतस्थे मुनिमण्डलम् ।
भगवानपि संप्राप्तः प्रथमोद्दिष्टमास्पदम् ॥३५॥

Then saying, 'It is all right,' the circle of sages started to leave; the holy Lord (Śiva) too reached the desired place. (35).

तेऽप्याकाशमसिश्यामुत्पत्य परमर्षयः ।
आसेदुरोषधिप्रस्थं मनसा सह मानसाः ॥३६॥

Those great sages, fleet as the mind, flew into the sky, dark as a sword, and reached Oṣadhiprastha— (36).

अलकामतिवाह्येव वसतिं वसुसंपदाम् ।
स्वर्गाभिष्यन्दवमनं कृत्वेवोपनिवेशितम् ॥३७॥

Founded by dividing Alakā, the home of riches which was as if a portion slivered out from the heaven; (37).

गङ्गास्रोतःपरिक्षिप्तं वप्रान्तर्ज्वलितौषधि ।
बृहन्मणिशिलासालं गुप्तावपि मनोहरम् ॥३८॥

Encircled by the streams of the Ganges, with medicinal herbs shining in the rampart, which was built with gems; beautiful though hidden; (38).

जितसिंहभया नागा यत्राश्वा बिलयोनयः ।
यक्षाः किंपुरुषाः पौराः योषितो वनदेवताः ॥३९॥

Where the elephants had overcome the fear of lions, and the horses were born from holes, Yakṣas and Kimpuruṣas were citizens, and the forest women were the women of that city; (39).

शिखरासक्तमेघानां व्यज्यन्ते यत्र वेश्मनाम् ।
अनुगर्जितसंदिग्धाः करणैर्मुरजस्वनाः ॥४०॥

Where are suggested by time-beats the sounds of drums,

confounded with the roar of clouds, clinging to the house-tops; (40).

यत्र कल्पद्रुमैरेव विलोलविटपांशुकैः ।
गृहयन्त्रपताकाश्रीरपौरादरनिर्मिता ॥४१॥

Where, without the citizens wishing it, were made flags of cloth, yielded by the waving branches of the Kalpataru (the wish-yielding tree) the glory of the poles raised over mansions; (41).

यत्र स्फटिकहर्म्येषु नक्तं सोपानपङ्क्तिषु ।
ज्योतिषां प्रतिबिम्बानि प्राप्नुवन्त्युपहारताम् ॥४२॥

Where at night on crystal terraces, in drinking places, the reflections of stars become flower-offerings; (42).

यत्रौषधिप्रकाशेन नक्तं दर्शितसंचराः ।
अनभिज्ञास्तमिस्राणां दुर्दिनेष्वभिसारिकाः ॥४३॥

Where on cloudy nights, the love-lorn damsels (Abhisārikās) finding their way by the light of phosphorescent herbs, know not darkness; (43).

यौवनान्तं वयो यस्मिन् नान्तकः कुसुमायुधः ।
रतिः स्वेदसमुत्थानं निद्रा संज्ञाविपर्ययः ॥४४॥

Where age ends with youth (knows not old age), where death comes from no other cause but love (Kusumāyudha), and sleep, induced by love-dalliance, is loss of consciousness; (44).

भ्रूभेदिभिः सकम्पोष्ठं ललिताङ्गुलितर्जनैः ।
यत्र कोपैः कृताः स्त्रीणामाप्रसादार्थिनः प्रियाः ॥४५॥

Where young men are made to supplicate damsels, till their favour is won, and their anger, indicated by knitted eye-brows, by throbbing lips, and by chiding by the lovely finger, is removed; (45).

संतानकतरुच्छायासुप्तविद्याधराध्वगम् ।
यस्य चोपवनं बाह्यं सुगन्धिर्गन्धमादनः ॥४६॥

Where in the park on the skirts of that city, slept Vidyādharas, who were way-farers, under Santānaka trees, and where outside it was situated the odorous Gandhamādana. (46).

तत् कान्तमृषयो दिव्याः प्रेक्ष्य हैमवतं पुरम् ।
स्वर्गाभिसंधिसुकृतं वञ्चनामिव मेनिरे ॥४७॥

Then those divine sages, on seeing that Capital town of Himālaya, considering the good deed they performed with a view to winning heaven as deceit. (47),

ते सद्मनि गिरेर्वेगादुन्मुखद्वास्थवीक्षिताः ।
अवतेरुर्जटाभारैर्लिखितानलनिश्चलैः ॥४८॥

Speedily did they alight at the palace of the mountain (Himālaya) and were looked at by the door-keepers with unturned eyes, and the mass of their matted locks glinted like fires, drawn in paintings. (48).

गगनादवतीर्णा सा यथावृद्धपुरःसरा ।
तोयान्तर्भास्करालीव रेजे मुनिपरंपरा ॥४९॥

That line of sages, alighting from the sky in the order

of precedence of age, shone like the reflections of the sun in water. (49).

तानर्घ्यानर्घ्यमादाय दूरात् प्रत्युद्ययौ गिरिः ।
नमयन् सारगुरुभिः पादन्यासैर्वसुंधराम् ॥५०॥

The mountain came to receive those worshipful sages from afar, bending the earth under his weighty steps.(50).

धातुताम्राधरः प्रांशुर्देवदारुबृहद्भुजः ।
प्रकृत्यैव शिलोरस्कः सुव्यक्तो हिमवानिति ॥५१॥

Himavān was so named because he had metal-red lips, was full and had arms long as devadāru, and was by nature stone-chested. (51).

विधिप्रयुक्तसत्कारैः स्वयं मार्गस्य देशकः ।
स तैराक्रमयामास शुद्धान्तं शुद्धवर्त्मभिः ॥५२॥

He ushered them, whose actions were pure and who were duly offered hospitality according to proper rites into his harem, himself leading the way. (52).

तत्र वेत्रासनासीनान् नीचासनपरिग्रहः ।
इत्युवाचेश्वरान् वाचं प्राञ्जलिः पृथिवीधरः ॥५३॥

The Lord of mountains, folding his hands, occupied a seat himself, and addressed them, when they had seated themselves on cane-seats. ((53).

अपमेघोदयं वर्षमदृष्टकुसुमं फलम् ।
अतर्कितोपपन्नं वो दर्शनं प्रतिभाति मे ॥५४॥

"Your sight appears to me to have come to me quite unsurmised, like a shower without clouds, like fruit without flower. (54).

मूढं बुधमिवात्मानं हैमीभूतमिवायसम् ।
भूमेर्दिवमिवारूढं मन्ये भवदनुग्रहात् ॥५५॥

Through your favour, I, a dullard, feel enlightened, or like iron turned into gold, or like one climbing from earth into heaven. (55).

अद्य प्रभृति भूतानामभिगम्योऽस्मि शुद्धये ।
यदध्यासितमर्हद्भिस्तद्धि तीर्थं प्रचक्षते ॥५६॥

From to-day on, I am approachable by beings for purification; what is occupied by the great is called a a holy place. (56).

अवैमि पूतमात्मानं द्वयेनैव द्विजोत्तमाः ।
मूर्ध्नि गङ्गाप्रपातेन धौतपादाम्भसा च वः ॥५७॥

I understand, O best of Brahmins, to be purified by two; : by the Ganges falling on my head, and by the water with which I have washed your feet. (57).

जङ्गमं प्रैष्यभावेन स्थावरं चरणाङ्कितम् ।
विभक्तानुग्रहं मन्ये द्विरूपमपि मे वपुः ॥५८॥

My two-fold body is favoured in two ways by you; my mobile body by waiting upon you, as your servant; and my immobile body by being trodden under your feet. (58).

भवत्संभावनोत्थाय परितोषाय मूर्च्छते ।
अभिव्याप्तदिगन्तानि नाङ्गानि प्रभवन्ति मे ॥५९॥

My limbs, although they cover the ends of the quarters, are unable to contain the pervading joy of contentment at the honour you have shown me. (59).

न केवलं दरीसंस्थं भास्वतां दर्शनेन वः ।
अन्तर्गतमपास्तं मे रजसोऽपि परं तमः ॥६०॥

Not only is the darkness from the valleys dissipated by the sight of shining luminaries like your good selves, but also the inner darkness in my heart, arising from the quality of ignorance. (60).

कर्तव्यं वो न पश्यामि स्याच्चेत् किं नोपदिश्यते ।
मन्ये मत्पावनायैव प्रस्थानं भवतामिह ॥६१॥

I do not see anything you seek to accomplish; and should there be one, could it not be accomplished ? I think your coming here is for the purpose of sanctifying me. (61).

तथापि तावत् कस्मिंश्चिदाज्ञां मे दातुमर्हथ ।
विनियोगप्रसादा हि किंकराः प्रभविष्णुषु ॥६२॥

Yet deign to command me to do something for you; servants are (only) favoured by the commands of their masters. (62).

एते वयममी दाराः कन्येयं कुलजीवितम् ।
ब्रूत येनार्थिनो यूयमनास्था बाह्यवस्तुषु ॥६३॥

Here are we; here is my wife, and here my daughter; say, with whom can you accomplish your purpose? We have no regard for external objects." (63).

इत्युक्तवांस्तमेवार्थं दरीमुखविसर्पिणा ।
द्विरिव प्रतिशब्देन व्याजहार हिमाचलः ॥६४॥

Having stated his purpose, he seemed to repeat the same, by his voice reverberating at the mouth of a cave. (64).

अथाङ्गिरसमग्रण्यमुदाहरणवस्तुषु ।
ऋषयः प्रेरयामासुः प्रत्युवाच स भूधरम् ॥६५॥

Then urged by the sages, Aṅgirasa, who was the foremost among the recounters of tales, answered the mountain. (65).

उपपन्नमिदं सर्वमतः परमपि त्वयि ।
मनसः शिखराणां च सदृशी ते समुन्नतिः ॥६६॥

"All this you have said, and even more, is possible for you; equal is the loftiness of your mind and your peaks. (66).

स्थाने त्वां स्थावरात्मानं विष्णुमाहुस्तथा हि ते ।
चराचराणां भूतानां कुक्षिराधारतां गतः ॥६७॥

It is proper that you, whose form is immovable, are regarded as Viṣṇu; for my belly has become the refuge of movable and immovable beings. (67).

गामधास्यत् कथं नागो मृणालमृदुभिः फणैः ।
आरसातलमूलात् त्वमवालम्बिष्यथा न चेत् ॥६८॥

How could the serpent (Śeṣa) have borne the earth upon his hoods delicate like lotus-stalks, had you not supported him with your feet from the very bottom of the nether regions? (68).

अच्छिन्नामलसंतानाः समुद्रोर्म्यनिवारिताः ।
पुनन्ति लोकान् पुण्यत्वात् कीर्तयः सरितश्च ते ॥६९॥

Thy fame and thy rivers, flowing in all, uninterrupted and limpid current, unchecked by the waves of the sea, sanctify people by their purity. (69).

यथैव श्लाघ्यते गङ्गा पादेन परमेष्ठिनः ।
प्रभवेन द्वितीयेन तथैवोच्छ्रितशिरसा त्वया ॥७०॥

As the Ganges is praised on account of her source, the foot of Hari, so also on account of her other source, thy lofty peaks. (70).

तिर्यगूर्ध्वमधस्ताच्च व्यापको महिमा हरेः ।
त्रिविक्रमोद्यतस्यासीत् स तु स्वाभाविकस्तव ॥७१॥

Hari's greatness became ubiquitous, only when he prepared himself to take the three steps, while thine is natural. (71).

यज्ञभागभुजां मध्ये पदमाक्रम्य तस्थुषा ।
उच्चैर्हिरण्मयं शृङ्गं सुमेरोर्वितथीकृतम् ॥७२॥

By thee, establishing thyself among the gods, thou

hast rendered the golden peak of Meru of no account. (72).

काठिन्यं स्थावरे काये भवता सर्वमर्पितम् ।
इदं तु ते भक्तिनम्रमर्हंदाराधनं वपुः ॥७३॥

Thou has transferred all thy hardness to thy immovable form; but this your form, humble through devotion makes for the propitiation of the good. (73).

तवागमनकार्यं नः शृणु कार्यं तवैव तत् ।
श्रेयसामुपदेशात्तु वयमप्यंशभागिनः ॥७४॥

So listen, for what purpose we come here; it is also thy purpose; by our advising thee what is good for thee, we also take a share in that good. (74).

अणिमादिगुणोपेतमस्पृष्टपुरुषान्तरम् ।
शब्दमीश्वर इत्युच्चैः सार्धचन्द्रं बिभर्ति यः ॥७५॥

He, who bears the name Iśvara, which is shared by none else, together with the crescent-moon, and who possessed the miraculous powers like Aṇimā and the rest; (75).

कल्पितान्योन्यसामर्थ्यैः पृथिव्यादिभिरात्मभिः ।
यस्येदं ध्रियते विश्वं धुर्यैर्यानमिवाध्वनि ॥७६॥

Who supported this world with his eight forms like the earth and the others that help one another, as veteran horses bear a carriage on the road; (76).

योगिनो यं विचिन्वन्ति क्षेत्राभ्यन्तरवर्तिनम् ।
अनावृत्तिभयं यस्य पदमाहुर्मनीषिणः ॥७७॥

Whom the Yogins seek, immanent in all beings and whose place the wise describe as one from which there is no fear of return; (77).

स ते दुहितरं साक्षात् साक्षी विश्वस्य कर्मणः ।
वृणुते वरदः शंभुरस्मत्संक्रामितैः पदैः ॥७८॥

Śambhu, the giver of boons, directly seeks your daughter by asking us to convey his request to you. (78).

तमर्थमिव भारत्या सुतया योक्तुमर्हसि ।
अशोच्या हि पितुः कन्या सद्भर्त्रे प्रतिपादिता ॥७९॥

Deign to wed your daughter to god Śiva, as sense is wedded to speech; a daughter is no longer a source of grief, once she is wedded to a good husband. (79).

यावन्त्येतानि भूतानि स्थावराणि चराणि च ।
मातरं कल्पयन्त्वेनामीशो हि जगतः पिता ॥८०॥

Whatever the number of beings movable and immovable, should look upon her as their mother; for Lord Īśa is the father of the whole world. (80).

प्रणम्य शितिकण्ठाय विबुधास्तदनन्तरम् ।
चरणौ रञ्जयन्त्वस्याश्चूडामणिमरीचिभिः ॥८१॥

Let the gods bow to Śiva, and let them thereafter irradiate his feet with the rays of gems in their crests. (81).

उमा वधूर्भवान् दाता याचितार इमे वयम् ।
वरः शंभुरलं ह्येष त्वत्कुलोद्भूतये विधिः ॥८२॥

A bride like Umā, a giver like your good self, and we to sue for her hand, and a bridegroom like Śambhu; all these are enough for the prosperity of your family. (82).

अस्तोतुः स्तूयमानस्य वन्द्यस्यानन्यवन्दिनः ।
सुतासंबन्धविधिना भव विश्वगुरोर्गुरुः ॥८३॥

Be thou, the father, worthy of being respected by one who bows to none, but himself bowed down to by all, praised by all, but himself praising none." (83).

एवंवादिनि देवर्षौ पार्श्वे पितुरधोमुखी ।
लीलाकमलपत्राणि गणयामास पार्वती ॥८४॥

As Nārada spoke thus, Pārvatī, standing by the side of her father, with her head hung low, counted petals of the lotus that graced her hand. (84).

शैलः संपूर्णकामोऽपि मेनामुखमुदैक्षत ।
प्रायेण गृहिणीनेत्राः कन्यार्थेषु कुटुम्बिनः ॥८५॥

The mountain, although, all his wishes were fulfilled, looked at the face of Menā; for house-holders look through the eyes of their wives, in the matter of marriage of their daughters. (85).

मेने मेनापि तत्सर्वं पत्युः कार्यं समीप्सितम् ।
भवन्त्यव्यभिचारिण्यो भर्तुरिष्टे पतिव्रताः ॥८६॥

Menā gave her consent to the object, desired by her husband; chaste wives do not invariably fail their husbands in their desire. (86).

इयमत्रोत्तरं न्याय्यमिति बुद्धया विमृश्य सः ।
आददे वचसामन्ते मङ्गलालंकृता सुताम् । ८७॥

Thinking in his mind that that was the proper thing to do, at the end of his speech he took his daughter by hand. (87).

एहि सर्वात्मना वत्से भिक्षा त्वं परिकल्पिता ।
अर्थिनो मुनयः प्राप्तं गृहमेधिफलं मया ॥८८॥

"Come, my daughter; thou hast been designed as alms to Śiva who is the soul of the universe; the sages are suing for thy hand on behalf of Lord Śiva; I have obtained the fruit of being a house-holder." (88).

एतावदुक्त्वा तनयां मुनीनाह महीधरः ।
इयं नमति वः सर्वा स्त्रिलोचनवधूरिति ॥८९॥

Having said this to his daughter, the mountain spoke to the sages, "Here is she, bowing to you all as the bride of Lord Śiva." (89).

ईप्सितार्थक्रियोदारं तेऽभिनन्द्य गिरेर्वचः ।
आशीर्भिरेधयामासुः पुरः पाकाभिरम्बिकाम् ॥९०॥

They greeted the words of the mountain, lofty through the accomplishment of the desired object; they wished Pārvatī a long life, and offered her fruit with their blessings. (90).

तां प्रणामादरस्रस्तजाम्बूनदवतंसकाम् ।
अङ्कमारोपयामास लज्जमानामरुन्धती ॥९१॥

Arundhatī, took the bashful Pārvatī in her lap, her golden ear-rings, slipping in her confusion, as she paid her respects. (91).

तन्मातरं चाश्रुमुखीं दुहितृस्नेहविक्लवाम् ।
वरस्यानन्यपूर्वस्य विशोकामकरोद् गुणैः ॥९२॥

She removed the grief of her mother, who was greatly affected by her love for her daughter, by lauding the virtues of the unique bridegroom. (92).

वैवाहिकीं तिथिं पृष्टास्तत्क्षणं हरबन्धुना ।
ते त्र्यहादूर्ध्वमाख्याय चेरुश्चीरपरिग्रहाः ॥९३॥

Asked the date of the wedding by Himālaya, the would be relatives of Hara, they who had tattered bark as their possession, said it was three days after i.e. on the fourth day, and then they left. (93).

ते हिमाचलमामन्त्र्य पुनः प्रेक्ष्य च शूलिनम् ।
सिद्धं चास्मै निवेद्यार्थं तद्विसृष्टाः खमुद्ययुः ॥९४॥

They took their leave of Himālaya, and approached the trident-armed (Śiva), and bidden leave by him, they flew to the heavens after narrating to him that his purpose was accomplished. (94).

पशुपतिरपि तान्यहानि कृच्छ्राद्
अगमयदद्रिसुतासमागमोत्कः ।
कमपरमवशं न विप्रकुर्युर्
विभुमपि तं यदमी स्पृशन्ति भावाः ॥९५॥

Paśupati, too, passed those days in great distress, earnestly longing for union with Pārvatī; who would possess himself in patience under stress of these emotions, when they affect even the self-controlled lord of all? (95).

सप्तमः सर्गः

अथौषधीनामधिपस्य वृद्धौ तिथौ च जामित्रगुणान्वितायाम् ।
समेतबन्धुर्हिमवान् सुताया विवाहदीक्षाविधिमन्वतिष्ठत् ॥१॥

At the waxing of the moon, on a day, when the aspect of the stars was favourable in Pārvatī's horoscope, accompanied by her relations, Himavān celebrated his daughter's marriage, (1).

वैवाहिकैः कौतुकसंविधानैर् गृहे गृहे व्यग्रपुरंध्रिवर्गम् ।
आसीत्पुरं सानुमतोऽनुरागाद् अन्तःपुरं चैककुलोपमेयम् ॥२॥

The ladies of the household in every house were absorbed in preparations of marriage; through love for Himavat, the whole city and the household of Himavat were as one family. (2).

संतानकाकीर्णचतुष्पथं तच् चीनांशुकैः कल्पितकेतुमालम् ।
भासा ज्वलत्काञ्चनतोरणानां स्थानान्तरं स्वर्ग इवावभासे ॥३॥

The city appeared to be heaven itself transferred to another place, where Mandāra flowers were strewn over the broad royal streets and where buntings and flags of china flaunted the air; and it appeared to be so by the blazing lustre of the golden arches. (3).

एकैव सत्यामपि पुत्रपङ्क्तौ चिरस्य दृष्टेव मृतोत्थितेव ।
उपोढपाणिग्रहणेति पित्रोर् उमा विशेषोच्छ्वसितं बभूव ॥४॥

Albeit, they had many sons and daughters, they looked upon Umā, seen after long time, as risen from the dead; and because her wedding was imminent, she was the very lifebreath of her parents. (4).

अङ्काद्ययावङ्कमुदीरिताशीः सा मण्डनान्मण्डनमन्वभुङ्क्त ।
संबन्धभिन्नोऽपि गिरेः कुलस्य स्नेहस्तवेकायतनं जगाम ॥५॥

Receiving the blessing of her relations, she went from lap to lap of her relatives, and received ornament upon ornament from them; although the family of the mountain was divided by reason of his many sons into many families, yet they became but one family by the common bond of love. (5).

मैत्रे मुहूर्ते शशलाञ्छनेन योगं गतासूत्तरफल्गुनीषु ।
तस्याः शरीरे प्रतिकर्म चक्रुर् बन्धुस्त्रियो याः पतिपुत्रवत्यः ॥६॥

At the auspicious hour of Mitra, at the conjunction of the moon with the constellation Uttaraphālguni, women with sons and husbands living, attended to her ornaments. (6).

सा गौरसिद्धार्थनिवेशवद्भिर् दूर्वाप्रवालैः प्रतिभिन्नरागम् ।
निर्नाभिकौशेयमुपात्तबाणम् अभ्यङ्गनेपथ्यमलंचकार ॥७॥

She embellished her entire person with a silken garment worn above the navel; its beauty heightened by dūrvā-blades sprinkled intermittantly by white mustard seeds; and she held an arrow in her hand. (7).

तथा च संपर्कमुपेत्य बाला विवाहदीक्षाविधिसायकेन ।
करेण भानोर्बहुलावसाने संधुक्ष्यमाणेव शशाङ्कलेखा ॥८॥

The girl, coming into contact with the arrow, in the initiation-rite of marriage, looked like the crescent of the moon which at the dark half of the moon waxes, by being filled with the rays of the sun. (8).

तां लोध्रकल्केन हृताङ्गतैलाम् आश्यानकालेयकृताङ्गरागाम् ।
वासो वसानामभिषेकयोग्यम् नार्यश्चतुष्काभिमुखीमनैषुः ॥९॥

She, with the oiliness of her person removed by lodhra powder and dry kāleya smeared to her body as unguent, and wearing a bath-towel, was led by her women to the four-pillared bath-house. (9).

विन्यस्तवैडूर्यशिलातलेऽस्मिन्न् आविद्धमुक्ताफलभक्तिचित्रे ।
आवर्जिताष्टापदकुम्भतोयैः सतूर्यमेनां स्नपयांबभूवुः ॥१०॥

Her women bathed with water poured from golden pitchers, on an emerald slab in that house where the walls were decorated with pictures drawn by the proper arrangement of pearls and to the accompaniment of music. (10).

सा मङ्गलस्नानविशुद्धगात्री गृहीतपत्युद्गमनीयवस्त्रा ।
निवृत्तपर्जन्यजलाभिषेका प्रफुल्लकाशा वसुधेव रेजे ॥११॥

She, with her limbs, pure from the auspicious bath, wearing the washed garments of her husband, and having finished her bath in open rain, shone like earth with kāsa flowers blooming. (11).

तस्मात् प्रदेशाच्च वितानवन्तं युक्तं मणिस्तम्भचतुष्टयेन ।
पतिव्रताभिः परिगृह्य निन्ये क्लृप्तासनं कौतुकवेदिमध्यम् ॥१२॥

From that region wives, devoted to their husbands, led her to seat on the marriage-altar with a canopy, supported by four jewelled columns. (12.)

तां प्राङ्मुखीं तत्र निवेश्य तन्वीं क्षणं व्यलम्बन्त पुरो निषण्णाः ।
भूतार्थशोभाह्रियमाणनेत्राः प्रसाधने संनिहितेऽपि नार्यः ॥१३॥

Seating her there, with her face turned towards the east, they lingered, seated before her, with their eyes being attracted by her genuine beauty, although her ornaments were close by. (13).

धूपोष्मणा त्याजितमार्द्रभावं केशान्तमन्तःकुसुमं तदीयम् ।
पर्याक्षिपत् काचिदुदारबन्धं दूर्वावता पाण्डुमधूकदाम्ना ॥१४॥

A certain hand-maid dried her hair with fumes of incense, entwining flowers in them, braided them into a high coiffeur and strung a chaplet of Madhūka flowers interspersed with Dūrvā in it. (14).

प्रसक्तशुक्लागुरु चक्रुरस्या गोरोचनापत्रविभङ्गमङ्गम् ।
सा चक्रवाकाङ्कितसैकतायास् त्रिस्रोतसः कान्तिमतीत्य तस्थौ ॥१५॥

They smeared to her person white sandal and decked it in ornamental designs in Gorocanā; she stood, surpassing the beauty of the triple-streamed river, on whose banks of sands, straddle Cakravākas. (15).

लग्नद्विरेफं परिभूय पद्मं समेघलेखं शशिनश्च बिम्बम् ।
तदाननश्रीरलकैः प्रसिद्धैश् चिच्छेद सादृश्यकथाप्रसङ्गम् ॥१६॥

The beauty of her face, surpassing the beauty of the lotus with bees clinging to it, and the orb of the moon, covered by clouds cut short all talk of comparison, with her well known beautiful hair. (16).

कर्णार्पितो रोध्रकषायरूक्षे गोरोचनाभेदनितान्तगौरे ।
तस्याः कपोले परभागलाभाद् बबन्ध चक्षूंषि यवप्ररोहः ॥१७॥

The Yava sprout, placed on her ear, arrested the eye, attaining the height of beauty, against the background of her forehead, conspicuous by Lodhra paste, and very red by the application of Gorocanā. (17).

रेखाविभक्तः प्रविभक्तगात्र्याः किंचिन्मधूच्छिष्टविसृष्टरागः ।
कामप्यभिख्यां स्फुरितैरपुष्यद् प्रासन्नलावण्यफलोऽधरोष्ठः ॥१८॥

The lower-lip of her, whose limbs were well-proportioned, enhanced her beauty ineffably; whose loveliness was frightened by streaks of bee-wax which marked it off from the upper-lip which quivered and which was close to the reward of its loveliness (viz. kissing, cossetting). (18).

पत्युः शिरश्चन्द्रकलामनेन स्पृशेति सख्या परिहासपूर्वम् ।
सा रञ्जयित्वा चरणौ कृताशीर् माल्येन तां निर्वचनं जघान ॥१९॥

When her friend told her chaffingly "with this your foot strike the crest of the crescent moon," she made her friend paint her feet and receiving the blessings (of elders) was silently struck by her friend with a flower-wreath. (19).

तस्याः सुजातोत्पलपत्रकान्ते प्रसाधिकाभिर्नयने समीक्ष्य ।
न चक्षुषोः कान्तिविशेषबुद्ध्या कालाञ्जनं मङ्गलमित्युपात्तम् ॥२०॥

The hand-maidens, seeing her eyes lovely as lotus-petals, put collyrium in her eye, not with a view to giving brightness to the eye but for auspiciousness. (20).

सा संभवद्भिः कुसुमैर्लतेव ज्योतिर्भिरुद्यद्भिरिव त्रियामा ।
सरिद्विहंगैरिव लीयमानैर् आमुच्यमानाभरणा चकाशे ॥२१॥

She shone, when her ornaments were removed, like a plant whose buds have yet to appear, like the night when the stars have yet to appear, or like a river where the birds have nestled. (21).

आत्मानमालोक्य च शोभमानम् आदर्शबिम्बे स्तिमितायताक्षी ।
हरोपयाने त्वरिता बभूव स्त्रीणां प्रियालोकफलो हि वेषः ॥२२॥

Seeing herself, appearing lovely in the mirror, with her long eyes steadfastly fixed, she became eager to meet Hara quickly; for a woman's dress receives its reward by being looked at by the loved one. (22).

अथाङ्गुलीभ्यां हरितालमार्द्रं माङ्गल्यमादाय मनःशिलां च ।
कर्णावसक्तामलदन्तपत्रं माता तदीयं मुखमुन्नमय्य ॥२३॥

Then her mother took in her fingers wet Haritāl and the auspicious Manaśilā adorned with ivory ornaments worked into a leaf, and raised her face. (23).

उमास्तनोद्भेदमनुप्रवृद्धो मनोरथो यः प्रथमं बभूव ।
तमेव मेना दुहितुः कथंचिद् विवाहदीक्षातिलकं चकार ॥२४॥

With the first desire of her heart, which grew with the budding of her breasts, Menā looked upon the auspicious tilak-mark she made as initiation of the marriage-rite as a token of her desire. (24).

बबन्ध चास्राकुलदृष्टिरस्याः स्थानान्तरे कल्पितसंनिवेशम् ।
धात्र्यङ्गुलिभिः प्रतिसार्यमाणम् ऊर्णामयं कौतुकहस्तसूत्रम् ॥२५॥

When her eyes were perplexed with tears welling up, a woollen amulet, put not in its proper place by the fingers of the wet-nurse, was tied to her wrist as an auspicious token of marriage-rite (by Menā). (25).

क्षीरोदवेलेव सफेनपुञ्जा पर्याप्तचन्द्रेव शरत् त्रियामा ।
नवं नवक्षौमनिवासिनी सा भूयो बभौ दर्पणमादधाना ॥२६॥

As she wore a fresh silken garment she mostly shone as the shore of the milky ocean with a welter of balls of foam; and, with a mirror in her hand, she shone like a night of autumn. (26).

तामर्चिताभ्यः कुलदेवताभ्यः कुलप्रतिष्ठां प्रणमय्य माता ।
अकारयत् कारयितव्यदक्षा क्रमेण पादग्रहणं सतीनाम् ॥२७॥

Then her mother, who was an adept in the knowledge of what was to be done, made her bow to the household deities who were duly worshipped and who were the very support of the family; and made her fall at the feet of chaste and saintly wives. (27).

अखण्डितं प्रेम लभस्व पत्युर् इत्युच्यते ताभिरुमा स्म नम्रा ।
तया तु तस्यार्धशरीरलाभात् पश्चात्कृता बन्धुजनाशिषोऽपि ॥२८॥

Then they said to Umā "Mayest thou win the undivided love of your husband;" but Umā, who was, modest, far exceeded their blessings by becoming a half of Hara's body. (28).

इच्छाविभूत्योरनुरूपमद्रिस् तस्याः कृती कृत्यमशेषयित्वा ।
सभ्यः सभायां सुहृदास्थितायां तस्थौ वृषाङ्कागमनप्रतीक्षः ॥२६॥

The mountain, having performed his duty by her suitably to his heart's desire and his high fortune;—he, this noble father, waited in the assembly of his relations, expecting to meet Hara. (29).

तावद्वरस्यापि कुबेरशैले तत्पूर्वपाणिग्रहणानुरूपम् ।
प्रसाधनं मातृभिरादृताभिर् न्यस्तं पुरस्तात् पुरशासनस्य ॥३०॥

Then the diligent (eight) mothers, placed before Hara (the chastiser of Pura), articles of decoration, preparatory to marriage, on mount Kailāsa. (30).

तद्गौरवान्मङ्गलमण्डनश्रीः सा पस्पृशे केवलमीश्वरेण ।
स एव वेषः परिणेतुरिष्टं भावान्तरं तस्य विभोः प्रपेदे ॥३१॥

Out of regard for them, the Lord merely touched at the wealth of ornaments; that very usual garb of his was transformed into the garb, usually worn by a bridegroom, (31).

बभूव भस्मैव सिताङ्गरागः कपालमेवामलशेखरश्रीः ।
उपान्तभागेषु च रोचनाङ्को गजाजिनस्यैव दुकूलभावः ॥३२॥

The ashes, applied to his body became the white unguent; his skull, the beautiful pure crest, and the elephant-hide became the silken garment, with marks of Gorocanā at the fringes. (32).

शङ्खान्तरद्योति विलोचनं यद् अन्तर्निविष्टामलपिङ्गतारम् ।
सांनिध्यपक्षे हरितालमय्यास् तदेव जातं तिलकक्रियायाः ॥३३॥

The eye, that was in the flat bone of his forehead, with the tawny pupils set in its centre, became the tilak mark in Haritāla. (33).

यथाप्रदेशं भुजगेश्वराणां करिष्यतामाभरणान्तरत्वम् ।
शरीरमात्रं विकृतिं प्रपेदे तथैव तस्थुः फणरत्नशोभाः ॥३४॥

The serpent—Lords, coiling round various parts of his person like the wrist etc. as ornaments, only had their bodies transformed; but the lustre of the gems on their hoods remained as it was before. (34).

दिवापि निष्ठ्यूतमरीचिभासा बाल्यादनाविष्कृतलाञ्छनेन ।
चन्द्रेण नित्यं प्रतिभिन्नमौलेश् चूडामणेः किं ग्रहणं हरस्य ॥३५॥

Why should Hara care for a crest-gem when the infant moon was his crest-ornament,—the moon, who emitted lustre even by day and whose spot was not visible owing to its small size ? (35).

इत्यद्भुतैकप्रभवः प्रभावात् प्रसिद्धनेपथ्यविधेर्विधाता ।
आत्मानमासन्नगणोपनीते खड्गे निषक्तप्रतिमं ददर्श ॥३६॥

Thus that god, the sole creator of marvels, who, through his power, fashioned the usual dress, saw his image reflected in the (polished) surface of a sword, brought by one of his Gaṇas, who was close by. (36).

स गोपतिं नन्दिभुजावलम्बी शार्दूलचर्मान्तरितोरुपृष्ठम् ।
तद्भक्तिसंक्षिप्तबृहत्प्रमाणम् आरुह्य कैलासमिव प्रतस्थे ॥३७॥

Supported by the arm of Nandi, he mounted a big bull whose hide back was covered by a tiger-skin, and who, out of devotion to the Lord, shrank in girth as if he was ascending mount Kailāsa. (37).

तं मातरो देवमनुव्रजन्त्यः स्ववाहनक्षोभचलावतंसाः ।
मुखैः प्रभामण्डलरेणुगौरैः पद्माकरं चक्रुरिवान्तरिक्षम् ॥३८॥

The seven Mothers, as they followed him,—their ear-ornaments swinging, as their mounts were swaying under them,—turned the sky into a lotus-lake, with their faces, red with the rays of the auriole, that surrounded their heads. (38),

तासां च पश्चात् कनकप्रभाणां काली कपालाभरणा चकाशे ।
बलाकिनी नीलपयोदराजिर् दूरं पुरःक्षिप्तशतह्रदेव ॥३९॥

Behind them, with their golden sheen, appeared dread Kālī, with her skull-ornaments, like a bank of clouds accompanied by flights of cranes, with lightning flickering ahead at a distance. (39).

ततो गणैः शूलभृतः पुरोगैर् उदीरितो मङ्गलतूर्यघोषः ।
विमानशृङ्गाण्यवगाहमानः शशंस सेवावसरं सुरेभ्यः ॥४०॥

Then the sound of auspicious musical instruments raised by the Gaṇas of Śiva, floating over the tops of their aerial cars, reminded them that it was time for them to wait upon the Lord (Śiva). (40).

उपाददे तस्य सहस्ररश्मिस् त्वष्ट्रा नवं निर्मितमातपत्रम् ।
स तद्दुकूलादविदूरमौलिर् बभौ वहन् गाङ्गमिव प्रवाहम् ॥४१॥

The sun held over an umbrella, newly fashioned by Tvaṣṭṛ; and his head, being near the silken cloth of the umbrella, he shone as when the Ganges fell upon his head. (41).

मूर्ते च गङ्गायमुने तदानीं सचामरे देवमसेविषाताम् ।
समुद्रगारूपविपर्ययेऽपि सहंसपाते इव लक्ष्यमाणे ॥४२॥

The Ganges and the Yamunā waited upon the Lord with chavries; and although their river-form was changed, they appeared to have flights of swan swooping down on them. (42).

समन्वगच्छत् प्रथमो विधाता श्रीवत्सलक्ष्मा पुरुषश्च साक्षात् ।
जयेति वाचा महिमानमस्य संवर्धयन्तौ हविषेव वह्निम् ॥४३॥

To him, first came the primeval Creator, and the first man Viṣṇu, both hailing him with the word 'Victory' and raising his glory. (43).

एकैव मूर्तिर्बिभिदे त्रिधा सा सामान्यमेषां प्रथमावरत्वम् ।
विष्णोर्हरस्तस्य हरिः कदाचिद् वेधास्तयोस्तावपि धातुराद्यौ ॥४४॥

Just one form was divided three-fold; equally great were they; sometimes Viṣṇu took precedence over Hara, sometimes Hara over Viṣṇu? sometimes Brahmā over both and sometimes both over Brahmā. (44).

तं लोकपालाः पुरुहूतमुख्याः श्रीलक्षणोत्सर्गविनीतवेषाः ।
दृष्टिप्रदाने कृतनन्दिसंज्ञास् तद्दर्शिताः प्राञ्जलयः प्रणेमुः ॥४५॥

The Guardians of the Quarters, Indra and others, assuming a modest attire, casting away their attributes of greatness, made signs to Nandi to take them to Hara; and led by him, bowed to him with folded hands. (45).

कम्पेन मूर्ध्नः शतपत्रयोनिं वाचा हरिं वृत्रहणं स्मितेन ।
आलोकमात्रेण सुरानशेषान् संभावयामास यथाप्रधानम् ॥४६॥

And Lord Śiva honoured Brahmā with a nod of his head, Hari with words, Indra with a smile, and the rest of the gods by mere looks according to their order. (46).

तस्मै जयाशीः ससृजे पुरस्तात् सप्तर्षिभिस्तान् स्मितपूर्वमाह ।
विवाहयज्ञे वितते ऽत्र यूयम् अध्वर्यवः पूर्ववृता मयेति ॥४७॥

The Saptarṣis gave him blessings for victory; he said to them smilingly, "You have been already chosen by me as chaplains for the sacrifice of the marriage-rite"; (47)

विश्वावसुप्राग्रहरैः प्रवीणैः संगीयमानत्रिपुरावदानः ।
अध्वानमध्वान्तविकारलङ्घ्यस् ततार ताराधिपखण्डधारी ॥४८॥

Then the moon-crested god, the laudations of whose marvellous deeds were sung by divine choristers to the accompaniment of the Lute, with Viśvāvasu at their lead, traversed the divine path, uncorrupted by temptation. (48).

खे खेलगामी तमुवाह वाहः सशब्दचामीकरकिंकिणीकः ।
तटाभिघातादिव लग्नपङ्के धुन्वन् मुहुः प्रोतघने विषाणे ॥४९॥

His mount, jogging along playfully, with small golden bells tinkling, shaking his horns to which bits of clouds had clung as if they were mud, sticking to them as when it was butting against the banks—carried him. (49).

स प्रापदप्राप्तपराभियोगं नगेन्द्रगुप्तं नगरं मुहूर्तात् ।
पुरोविलग्नैर्हरदृष्टिपातैः सुवर्णसूत्रैरिव कृष्यमाणम् ॥५०॥

That mountain, that never suffered an onslaught from foes, soon reached the city (of Oṣadhiprastha) guarded by the Lord of mountains, drawn by the glances of Hara as by golden chains.

तस्योपकण्ठे घननीलकण्ठः कुतूहलादुन्मुखपौरदृष्टः ।
स्वबाणचिह्नादवतीर्य मार्गादासन्नभूपृष्ठमियाय देवः ॥५१॥

In its suburbs God Nīlakaṇṭha, looked at with curiosity by the citizens, stepped down to the ground, descending (from his mount) at a path in the sky, marked by his arrow. (51).

तमृद्धिमद्बन्धुजनाधिरूढैर्वृन्दैर्गजानां गिरिचक्रवर्ती ।
प्रत्युज्जगामागमनप्रतीतः प्रफुल्लवृक्षैः कटकैरिव स्वैः ॥५२॥

The Lord of mountains went forth to meet him, accompanied by his relations mounting their elephants, as if they were his own spurs clad with trees in flowers. (52).

वर्गावुभौ देवमहीधराणां द्वारे पुरस्योद्घटितापिधाने ।
समीयतुर्दूरविसर्पिघोषौ भिन्नैकसेतू पयसामिवौघौ ॥५३॥

Groups of gods and mountains met at the city-gate, the portals of which were thrown open, as if they were streams of water whose loud sound rolled far in the distance, and which had burst its impounding walls. (53).

ह्रीमानभूद्भूमिधरो हरेण त्रैलोक्यवन्द्येन कृतप्रणामः ।
पूर्वं महिम्ना स हि तस्य दूरमावर्जितं नात्मशिरो विवेद ॥५४॥

The mountain was put to shame by Hara, who was an object of veneration to the three worlds by bowing down to him, he (the mountain) did not realise that his head was already bent before him (Hara), on account of his (Hara's) eminence. (54).

स प्रीतियोगाद् विकसन्मुखश्रीर् जामातुरग्रेसरतामुपेत्य ।
प्रावेशयन् मन्दिरमृद्धमेनम् आगुल्फकीर्णापणमार्गपुष्पम् ॥५५॥

The loveliness of his face was beaming on account of the contentment he felt; and he, going forward to meet his son-in-law, led him to the richly appointed house, along a road going along the market-place which was strewn with flowers upto the heel. (55).

तस्मिन् मुहूर्ते पुरसुन्दरीणाम् ईशानसंदर्शनलालसानाम् ।
प्रासादमालासु बभूवुरित्थं त्यक्तान्यकार्याणि विचेष्टितानि ॥५६॥

At that moment, the beautiful ladies of the city, eager to behold Hara from numerous places, were occupied with the (following) movements, to the exclusion of all other work. (56).

आलोकमार्गं सहसा व्रजन्त्या कयाचिदुद्वेष्टनवान्तमाल्यः ।
बद्धुं न संभावित एव तावत् करेण रुद्धोऽपि हि केशपाशः ॥५७॥

A certain damsel, going instantly to the window did not care to find her beautiful hair into a braid, although it was held by her in her hand from which (the braid) the flowers had dropped down getting loose from its coil. (57).

प्रसाधिकालम्बितमग्रपादम् आक्षिप्य काचिद् द्रवरागमेव ।
उत्सृष्टलीलागतिरागवाक्षाद् अलक्तकाङ्कां पदवीं ततान ॥५८॥

A certain damsel, withdrawing the toes of her feet from the hands of the female valet-de-chamber who had held them, traced, even while the paint was still wet on them and giving up her graceful gait, a line of foot-steps marked by the Alaktaka dye upto the window. (58).

विलोचनं दक्षिणमञ्जनेन संभाव्य तद्वञ्चितवामनेत्रा ।
तथैव वातायनसन्निकर्षं ययौ शलाकामपरा वहन्ती ॥५९॥

Still another damsel, adorning her right eye with collyrium, while the left was bereft of it, came near the window, still carrying the pencil of collyrium. (59).

जालान्तरप्रेषितदृष्टिरन्या प्रस्थानभिन्नां न बबन्ध नीवीम् ।
नाभिप्रविष्टाभरणप्रभेण हस्तेन तस्थाववलम्ब्य वासः ॥६०॥

Another woman, directing her eye through the window, did not tie the knot of her garment, which got loose by her (sudden) movement, but stood holding her garment by her hand, the sheen of its ornament, adorning her navel. (60).

अर्धाचिता सत्वरमुत्थितायाः पदे पदे दुर्निमिते गलन्ती ।
कस्याश्चिदासीद् रशना तदानीम् अङ्गुष्ठमूलार्पितसूत्रशेषा ॥६१॥

As another lady rose quickly, her girdle had at each step which was taken in confusion, the jewels dropping down; and it could be only half-strung, while what remained of it was only string looped round the root of the thumb. (61).

तासां मुखैरासवगन्धगर्भैर् व्याप्तान्तराः सान्द्रकुतूहलानाम् ।
विलोलनेत्रभ्रमरैर्गवाक्षाः सहस्रपत्राभरणा इवासन् ॥६२॥

The windows, which were filled with the faces wine-scented, of those ladies, whose curiosity was great, seemed to have been adorned with thousand-petalled lotuses, as their eyes flashed like swarms of bees. (62).

तावत् पताकाकुलमिन्दुमौलिर् उत्तोरणं राजपथं प्रपेदे ।
प्रासादशृङ्गाणि दिवापि कुर्वन् ज्योत्स्नाभिषेकद्विगुणच्छवीनि ॥६३॥

In the meanwhile, the moon-created god arrived into the royal road, beflagged densely with raised arches adorning it, making the tops of palaces shine with double refulgence, even day being bathed in moonlight. (63).

तमेकदृश्यं नयनैः पिबन्त्यो नार्यो न जग्मुर्विषयान्तराणि ।
तथा हि शेषेन्द्रियवृत्तिरासां सर्वात्मना चक्षुरिव प्रविष्टा ॥६४॥

Drinking him, the one cynosure of the eye, with their eyes, the ladies had no other object in mind; for, it seemed that the functions of all other senses were wholly concentrated in their eyes. (64).

स्थाने तपो दुश्चरमेतदर्थम् अपर्णया कोमलयापि तप्तम् ।
या दास्यमप्यस्य लभेत नारी सा स्यात् कृतार्था किमुताङ्कशय्याम् ।६५।

"It was proper that Pārvatī performed rigid penances, for obtaining him (for husband). Even she, who would become his slave, was blessed; how much more must be she, who would roll in his lap ?. (65).

परस्परेण स्पृहणीयशोभं न चेदिदं द्वन्द्वमयोजयिष्यत् ।
अस्मिन् द्वये रूपविधानयत्नः पत्युः प्रजानां विफलोऽभविष्यत् ॥६६॥

If the Creator had not designed this couple for each other,whose beauty was to be aspired by all, the Creator's endeavours to endue the two with beauty would have been vain. (66).

न नूनमारूढरुषा शरीरम् अनेन दग्धं कुसुमायुधस्य ।
व्रीडादमुं देवमुदीक्ष्य मन्ये संन्यस्तदेहः स्वयमेव कामः ॥६७॥

It was not through mounting wrath, that he consumed Kāma's body, but looking at this god, he (Kāma) felt crestfallen at his own humiliation by him, and himself shuffled off his body. (67).

अनेन संबन्धमवाप्य दिष्ट्या मनोरथप्रार्थितमीश्वरेण ।
मूर्धानमालि क्षितिधारणोच्चम् उच्चैस्तरं वक्ष्यति शैलराजः ॥६८॥

Having come into kinship with God Iśvara, which was sought by him in his heart's desire, he (Himālaya) would hold his head higher still, which was held already high by supporting the earth." (68).

इत्योषधिप्रस्थविलासिनीनां शृण्वन् कथाः श्रोत्रसुखास्त्रिनेत्रः ।
केयूरचूर्णीकृतलाजमुष्टि हिमालयस्यालयमाससाद ॥६९॥

Listening to this talk of the ladies of Oṣadhiprastha which was sweet to the ear, Hara came to the palace of

Himālaya, pounding to dust, the fried grains by the ends of his armlets. (69).

ततोऽवतीर्याच्युतदत्तहस्तः शरद्घनाद् दीधितिमानिवोक्ष्णः ।
क्रान्तानि पूर्वं कमलासनेन कक्षान्तराण्यद्रिपतेर्विवेश ॥७०॥

There, descending down from his bull like the moon from the clouds and supported by Viṣṇu, he entered the various chambers in the palace of Himālaya, already entered into by Brahman (the lotus-seated). (70).

तमन्वगिन्द्रप्रमुखाश्च देवाः सप्तर्षिपूर्वाः परमर्षयश्च ।
गणाश्च गिर्यालयमभ्यगच्छन् प्रशस्यमारम्भमिवोत्तमार्थाः ॥७१॥

Immediately after him, there came Indra and the other gods, preceded by the seven sages and other great sages; so also there came, to the palace of the mountain, the Gaṇas, like those who aim high to an auspicious undertaking. (71).

तत्रेश्वरो विष्टरभाग् यथावत् सरत्नमर्घ्यं मधुमच्च गव्यम् ।
नवे दुकूले च नगोपनीते प्रत्यग्रहीत् सर्वममन्त्रवर्जम् ॥७२॥

There, in that palace, Śiva received welcome offerings of gems and honeyed curds, and silken garments, as presented by the mountain, to the accompaniment of holy chants. (72).

दुकूलवासाः स वधूसमीपं निन्ये विनीतैरवरोधरक्षैः ।
वेलासकाशं स्फुटफेनराजिर् नवैरुदन्वानिव चन्द्रपादैः ॥७३॥

Vested in silken garments, he was led to the bride by the chamberlains that used to watch the harem attentively, as the ocean, flaked with foam, is led to the shore-line, by moon-beams. (73).

तया प्रवृद्धाननचन्द्रकान्त्या प्रफुल्लचक्षुःकुमुदः कुमार्या ।
प्रसन्नचेतःसलिलः शिवोऽभूत् संसृज्यमानः शरदेव लोकः ॥७४॥

By the loveliness of the waxing Moon of her face, the lake of the mind of Śiva, whose lotus-like eye was blooming, became lucid, like the world, when the autumn comes. (74).

तयोः समापत्तिषु कातराणि किञ्चिद्व्यवस्थापितसंहृतानि ।
ह्रीयन्त्रणामानशिरे मनोज्ञाम् अन्योन्यलोलानि विलोचनानि ॥७५॥

Their eyes, startled at chance meeting, slightly fixed and then withdrawn and thirsting for each other, were constrained through a sense of shame. (75).

तस्याः करं शैलगुरूपनीतं जग्राह ताम्राङ्गुलिमष्टमूर्तिः ।
उमातनौ गूढतनोः स्मरस्य तच्छङ्किनः पूर्वमिव प्ररोहम् ॥७६॥

The God who has eight forms, held her hand with its red fingers, as it was offered by Himavat, who was afraid of Śiva. This hand was, as it were, the sprout of love growing in the heart of Umā. (76).

रोमोद्गमः प्रादुरभूदुमायाः स्विन्नाङ्गुलिः पुंगवकेतुरासीत् ।
वृत्तिस्तयोः पाणिसमागमेन समं विभक्तेव मनोभवस्य ॥७७॥

There was horripilation on Umā's person, and the fingers of the Bull-emblemed God were wet with perspiration; through their being united in wedlock, love divided itself equally between them. (77).

प्रयुक्तपाणिग्रहणं यदन्यद् वधूवरं पुष्यति कान्तिमग्र्याम् ।
सांनिध्ययोगादनयोस्तदानीं किं कथ्यते श्रीरुभयस्य तस्य ॥७८॥

When, by the presence of these (Umā and Maheśa) other couples, on the eve of their marriage, attain a rare splendour, who could describe the glory of them both? (78)

प्रदक्षिणप्रक्रमणात् कृशानोर् उदर्चिषस्तन् मिथुनं चकाशे ।
मेरोरुपान्तेष्विव वर्तमानम् अन्योन्यसंसक्तमहस्त्रियामम् ॥७९॥

By going round the blazing fire, the couple shone like night and day, clinging to each other and revolving round the fringe of Mount Meru. (79).

तौ दंपती त्रिः परिणीय वह्निम् अन्योन्यसंस्पर्शनिमीलिताक्षौ ।
स कारयामास वधूं पुरोधास् तस्मिन् समिद्धार्चिषि लाजमोक्षम् ॥८०॥

The chaplain caused the couple who closed their eyes as they felt each other's touch, to go round the fire three times, and made the bride scatter fried grains into the blazing fire. (80).

सा लाजधूमाञ्जलिमिष्टगन्धं गुरूपदेशाद् वदनं निनाय ।
कपोलसंसर्पिशिखः स तस्या मुहूर्तकर्णोत्पलतां प्रपेदे ॥८१॥

That bride, instructed by the chaplain, breathed in the smoke of a handful of fried grains of agreeable smell; its crest, coming into ontact with her cheek, became for a moment, an ornament for her ear. (81).

तदीषदार्द्रारुणगण्डलेखम् उच्छ्वासिकालाञ्जनरागमक्ष्णोः ।
वधूमुखं क्लान्तयवावतंसम् आचारधूमग्रहणाद् बभूव ॥८२॥

The face of the bride, with the cheeks, moist and red

with perspiration, with the black collyrium in the eye slightly spreading out, with the yava sprout wilted, became so through the customary inhaling of smoke. (82).

वधूं द्विजः प्राह तवैष वत्से वह्निर्विवाहं प्रति पूर्वसाक्षी ।
शिवेन भर्त्रा सह धर्मचर्या कार्या त्वया मुक्तविचारयेति ॥८३॥

The chaplain said to the bride, "This fire is a witness unto thy marriage; thou shouldst perform religious duties with Śiva, your husband, unhesitatingly." (83).

आलोचनान्तं श्रवणे वितत्य पीतं गुरोस्तद् वचनं भवान्या ।
निदाघकालोल्बणभेवयेव माहेन्द्रमम्भः प्रथमं पृथिव्या ॥८४॥

Pārvatī drank in the words of her elders, stretching her ears to the corners of her eyes, as the earth, parched by the intense heat of summer, drinks the water of the first showers. (84).

ध्रुवेण भर्त्रा ध्रुवदर्शनाय प्रयुज्यमाना प्रियदर्शनेन ।
सा दृष्ट इत्याननमुन्नमय्य ह्रीसन्नकण्ठी कथमप्युवाच ॥८५॥

Her handsome husband, who was here for ever,urged her to look at Dhruva (the pole star), saw her, by raising her face; and she then spoke to him with difficulty in a voice, faint owing to shame. (85).

इत्थं विधिज्ञेन पुरोहितेन प्रयुक्तपाणिग्रहणोपचारौ ।
प्रणेमतुस्तौ पितरौ प्रजानां पद्मासनस्थाय पितामहाय ॥८६॥

Thus, when the chaplain, who was thoroughly versed in the procedure of the marriage rite, had performed their marriage, those parents of the world of men, then, paid their respects to Brahman, the lotus-seated. (86).

वधूं विधात्रा प्रतिनन्द्यते स्म कल्याणि वीरप्रसवा भवेति ।
वाचस्पतिः सन्नपि सोऽष्टमूर्तौ त्वाशास्यचिन्तास्तिमितो बभूव ॥८७॥

The Creator greeted the bride with the words, "Oh, auspicious one be the mother of a heroic son;" though he was the Lord of Speech, he was lost in thought as to the blessing he should give to Hara. (87).

क्लृप्तोपचारां चतुरस्रवेदीं तावेत्य पश्चात् कनकासनस्थौ ।
जायापती लौकिकमेषितव्यम् आर्द्राक्षतारोपणमन्वभूताम् ॥८८॥

They came to a square-altar, and there they were seated on golden seats; the couple experienced the sticking wet rice-grains which was usual and customary. (88).

पत्रान्तलग्नैर्जलबिन्दुवृन्दैर् आकृष्टमुक्ताफलजालशोभम् ।
तयोरुपर्यायतनालदण्डम् आधत्त लक्ष्मीः कमलातपत्रम् ॥८९॥

Goddess Lakṣmī, held over them a parasol of lotus, with a long stalk as the staff, at the fringe of whose petals, hung on assemblage of waterdrops, that gave it the beauty of tassels of pearls. (89).

द्विधा प्रयुक्तेन च वाङ्मयेन सरस्वती तन्मिथुनं नुनाव ।
संस्कारपूतेन वरं वरेण्यं वधूं सुखग्राह्यनिबन्धनेन ॥९०॥

Sarasvatī praised the couple in two ways : the most electable bridegroom in Sanskrit Speech which was adorned by grammatical purity; and the bride in Prākṛta Speech which was easy of comprehension (90).

तौ संधिषु व्यञ्जितवृत्तिभेदं रसान्तरेषु प्रतिभिन्नरागम् ।
अपश्यतामप्सरसां मुहूर्तं प्रयोगमाद्यं ललिताङ्गहारम् ॥९१॥

They witnessed for a while, the enactment of a drama by heavenly nymphs, in which there was graceful bodily acting; which displayed the four styles of speech at the various junctures and which had different melodies in the transition of emotions. (91).

देवास्तदन्ते हरमूढभार्यं किरीटबद्धाञ्जलयो निपत्य ।
शापावसानप्रतिपन्नमूर्तेर् ययाचिरे पञ्चशरस्य सेवाम् ॥९२॥

At its end, the gods, folding their hand on their crowned heads, begged him to accept the services of Kāma, whose life was restored to him. (92).

तस्यानुमेने भगवान् विमन्युर् व्यापारमात्मन्यपि सायकानाम् ।
काले प्रयुक्ता खलु कार्यविद्भिर् विज्ञापना भर्तृषु सिद्धिमेति ॥९३॥

The Lord, who was free from anger consented to the use of his (Kāma's) arrows against him; a request timely made to the master by those who know the proper occasion, bears fruit. (93).

अथ विबुधगणांस्तानिन्दुमौलिर्विसृज्य क्षितिधरपतिकन्यामाददानः करेण
कनककलशरक्षाभक्तिशोभासनाथं क्षितिविरचितशय्यं कौतुकागारमागात्

The moon-crested god, took his leave of the gods and taking the daughter of the mountain by the hand, entered the bed-chamber, where a golden pitcher was adorned with floral designs and where a bed was made on the floor. (94).

नवपरिणयलज्जाभूषणां तत्र गौरीं वदनमपहरन्तीं तत्कृतोत्क्षेपमीशः ।
अपि शयनसखीभ्यो दत्तवाचं कथंचित् प्रमथमुखविकारैर्हासयामास गूढम्

There the Lord drew towards himself Gaurī whose shyness, due to her recent-marriage was an adornment unto her, who averted her mouth, spoke with difficulty to her chamber-attendants; and Lord Śiva made her laugh by the grimaces of his Gaṇas. (95).

अष्टमः सर्गः

पाणिपीडनविधेरनन्तरं शैलराजदुहितुर्हरं प्रति ।
भावसाध्वसपरिग्रहादभूत् कामदोहदमनोहरं वपुः ॥१॥

Immediately after their marriage, the body of the daughter of the lord of mountains became lovely through intense desire of love, on account of her being intensely gripped with both love and fear. (1).

व्याहृता प्रतिवचो न संदधे गन्तुमैच्छदवलम्बितांशुका ।
सेवते स्म शयनं पराङ्मुखी सा तथापि रतये पिनाकिनः ॥२॥

She would not respond when spoken to, and desired to go when her garment was snatched, and averted her face by turning sideways in the bed and yet filled the heart of Pinākin with love. (2).

कैतवेन शयिते कुतूहलात् पार्वती प्रतिमुखं निपातितम् ।
चक्षुरुन्मिषति सस्मितं प्रिये विद्युदाहतमिव न्यमीलयत् ॥३॥

When Hara feigned sleep, Pārvatī looked at her husband's face with curiosity, and when he opened his eyes, she closed her eyes, as if she was struck by lightning. (3).

नाभिदेशनिहितः सकम्पया शंकरस्य रुरुधे तया करः ।
तन्नितम्बमथ चाभवत् स्वयं दूरमुच्छ्वसितनीविबन्धनम् ॥४॥

When Śaṅkara placed his hand in the region of her navel, she obstructed it; and her silken garment became of itself loose from its knot. (4).

एवमालि निगृहीतसाध्वसं शंकरो रहसि सेव्यतामिति ।
सा सखीभिरुपदिष्टमाकुला नास्मरत् प्रमुखवर्तिनि प्रिये ॥५॥

And when her companions advised her "Friend, curbing your fear, wait upon Śaṅkara thus in your privacy," she, however being confused, did not remember the advice of her friends. (5).

अप्यवस्तुनि कथाप्रवृत्तये प्रश्नतत्परमनङ्गशासनम् ।
वीक्षितेन परिगृह्य पार्वती मूर्धकम्पमयमुत्तरं ददौ ॥६॥

Pārvatī, finding that the chastiser of Ananga was inducing her to speak about unattainable objects, realising it by just glance, answered him by nodding her head. (6).

शूलिनः करतलद्वयेन सा संनिरुध्य नयने हृतांशुका ।
तस्य पश्यति ललाटलोचने मोघयत्नविधुरा रहस्यभूत् ॥७॥

Śūlin with his two hands covered her eyes but she obstructed it, when her garment was snatched away, but on seeing the eye in his forehead, she felt distressed, at the frustration of her efforts. (7).

चुम्बनेष्वधरदानवर्जितं सन्नहस्तमदयोपगूहने ।
क्लिष्टमन्मथमपि प्रियं प्रभोर् दुर्लभप्रतिकृतं वधूरतम् ॥८॥

In kissing, there was no biting of the lower lip, in their sexual congress; and the embrace was not close as the hands were wearied, in which love was not gratified;

that sexual congress knew no opposition from the bride. (8).

यन्मुखग्रहणमक्षताधरं दत्तमव्रणपदं नखं च यत् ।
यद्रतं च सदयं हरस्य तत् पार्वती विषहते स्म नेतरत् ॥९॥

The holding of her mouth without the biting of her lower lip, the scratching by the nails without leaving scratches, that mild love-play of the Lord, Pārvatī could well bear and not the hard one. (9).

रात्रिवृत्तमनुयोक्तुमुद्यतं सा विभातसमये सखीजनम् ।
नाकरोदपकुतूहलं ह्रिया शंसितुं तु हृदयेन तत्वरे ॥१०॥

Pārvatī did not satisfy the curiosity of her friends, when they asked for an account of what happened at night; but her heart quickened to narrate it. (10).

दर्पणे च परिभोगदर्शिनी पृष्ठतः प्रणयिनो निषेदुषः ।
प्रेक्ष्य बिम्बमनु बिम्बमात्मनः कानि कानि न चकार लज्जया ॥११॥

As her husband sat behind her, she watched the signs of her enjoyment in a mirror and seeing her face close to that of her husband, she acted in a variety of ways through a sense of shame. (11).

नीलकण्ठपरिभुक्तयौवनां तां विलोक्य जननी समाश्वसत् ।
भर्तृवल्लभतया हि मानसीं मातुरस्यति शुचं वधूजनः ॥१२॥

The mother cheered at seeing the enjoyment of her daughter's youthful body by her husband; for brides remove the mental pangs of their mothers through being loved by their husbands. (12).

वासराणि कतिचित् कथंचन स्थाणुना पदमकार्यत प्रिया ।
ज्ञातमन्मथरसा शनैः शनैः सा मुमोच रतिदुःखशीलताम् ॥१३॥

Śiva indulged in love-play with her, somehow, for a few days, knowing the flavour of love; Pārvatī gradually, forgot the pain of love-play. (13).

सस्वजे प्रियमुरोनिपीडिता प्रार्थितं मुखमनेन नाहरत् ।
मेखलाप्रणयलोलतां गतं हस्तमस्य शिथिलं रुरोध सा ॥१४॥

She embraced her lord, so that her breasts were pressed; she would not avert her mouth, when it was sought by him; she, but, gently obstructed his hand as it was extended, to snatch the girdle. (14).

भावसूचितमदृष्टविप्रियं चाटुमत् क्षणवियोगकातरम् ।
कैश्चिदेव दिवसैस्तयोस्तथा प्रेम रूढमितरेतराश्रयम् ॥१५॥

Their mutual love became a mystery to her friends, after a few days; it was indicated by emotions, it knew no conflict, it grew firm and it became apprehensive at even a momentary separation. (15).

तं यथात्मसदृशं वरं वधूर् अन्वरज्यत वरस्तथैव ताम् ।
सागरादनपगा हि जाह्नवी सोऽपि तन्मुखरसैकनिर्वृतिः ॥१६॥

As the bride was enamoured of her husband, so was the husband enamoured of his bride; for the Ganges does not recede from the ocean, so is the ocean given to tasting her mouth. (16).

शिष्यतां निधुवनोपदेशिनः शंकरस्य रहसि प्रपन्नया ।
शिक्षितं युवतिनैपुणं तया यत्तदेव गुरुदक्षिणीकृतम् ॥१७॥

Becoming the pupil of Hara in the act of sexual congress, in her privacy the skill, she acquired, among women, was offered by her as fee to her preceptor. (17).

दष्टमुक्तमधरोष्ठमम्बिका वेदनाविधुतपाणिपल्लवा ।
शीतलेन निरवापयत् क्षणं मौलिचन्द्रशकलेन शूलिनः ॥१८॥

Ambikā waved her hands to wipe out the pain she suffered from the biting of her lips, after it was released and she wiped the pain, by the coolness of the crescent of the moon in Śiva's crest. (18).

चुम्बनादलकचूर्णदूषितं शंकरोऽपि नयनं ललाटजम् ।
उच्छ्वसत्कमलगन्धये ददौ पार्वतीवदनगन्धवाहिने ॥१९॥

Śaṅkara too, put his third eye, smarting by the pain caused by the hair-powder, while he was kissing Pārvatī, in the way of the wind, breathed by the mouth of Pārvatī, which bore the fragrance of a blooming lotus. (19).

एवमिन्द्रियसुखस्य वर्त्मनः सेवनादनुगृहीतमन्मथः ।
शैलराजभवने सहोमया मासमात्रमवसद् वृषध्वजः ॥२०॥

Thus Vṛṣadhvaja, by his enjoyment of the path of sensual pleasure gratified Manmath (the god of love) and lived for a full month in the palace of the lord of mountain with Umā. (20).

सोऽनुमन्त्र्य हिमवन्तमात्मभूर् आत्मजाविरहदुःखपीडितम् ।
तत्र तत्र विजहार संपतन् अप्रमेयगतिना ककुद्मता ॥२१॥

There, taking leave of Himavat, who was pained at severance from his daughter, Śiva mounted on the back of Nandi, sported at various places, while Nandi jogged on with unimaginable gait. (21),

मेरुमेत्य मरुदाशुवाहनः पार्वतीस्तनपुरस्कृतः कृती ।
हेमपल्लवविभङ्गसंस्तरान् अन्वभूत् सुरतमर्दनक्षमान् ॥२२॥

Mounted on his bull, swift as the wind, he came to mount Meru, and there enjoyed rolling on beds of bits of leaves of gold, well capable of bearing the crush of sexual congress, and honoured by Pārvatī with her breasts. (22).

पद्मनाभवलयाङ्कितास्मसु प्राप्तवत्स्वमृतविप्रुषो नवाः ।
मन्दरस्य कटकेषु चावसत् पार्वतीवदनपद्मषट्पदः ॥२३॥

He, the bee snuggling in the lotus of Pārvatī's face, dwelt on the spurs of Mandara, stamped with the feet of Padmanābha (Viṣṇu) and splashed with drops of ambrosia. (23).

रावणध्वनितभीतया तया कण्ठसक्तघनबाहुबन्धनः ।
एकपिङ्गलगिरौ जगद्गुरुर् निर्विवेश विशदाः शशिप्रभाः ॥२४॥

The lord of the world, enjoyed on the Kailāsa mountain serene moonlight, where Pārvatī's hands were clasped round his neck, as she was frightened by (the blaring) voice of Rāvaṇa. (24).

तस्य जातु मलयस्थलीरतेर् धूतचन्दनवनः प्रियाक्लमम् ।
आचचाम सलवङ्गकेसरश् चाटुकार इव दक्षिणानिलः ॥२५॥

As, at times, he enjoyed sexual congress on the Malaya mountain, the Malaya breeze charged with the pollen of Lavaṅga (clove) which shook the sandal creeper; drank the drops of perspiration caused by love-play, and wheedled her like a sweet-tongued flatterer. (25).

हेमतामरसताडितप्रिया तत्कराम्बुविनिमीलितेक्षणा ।
सा व्यगाहत तरङ्गिणीमुमा मीनपङ्क्तिपुनरुक्तमेखला ॥२६॥

Umā indulged diving in the river, the fish rendering her girdle redundant, striking her husband, with golden lotuses, when her eyes were closed by his lotus-like hands. (26).

तां पुलोमतनयालकोचितैः पारिजातकुसुमैः प्रसाधयन् ।
नन्दने चिरमयुग्मलोचनः सस्पृहं सुरवधूभिरीक्षितः ॥२७॥

Adorning her with Pārijāta flowers fit for adorning the hair of Pulomā (the wife of Indra) god Śiva was seen with avidity by the wives of the gods. (27).

इत्यभौममनुभय शंकरः पार्थिवं च वनितासखः सुखम् ।
लोहितायति कदाचिदातपे गन्धमादनवनं व्यगाहत ॥२८॥

Thus enjoying earthly and heavenly pleasures with his beloved, he entered the gandhamādana forest at the westering of the sun (i.e. when the sun was reddening at his setting). (28).

तत्र काञ्चनशिलातलाश्रयो नेत्रगम्यमवलोक्य भास्करम् ।
दक्षिणेतरभुजव्यपाश्रयां व्याजहार सहधर्मचारिणीम् ॥२९॥

There seated on a golden slab and seeing the sun within the reach of his eye, Hara spoke to his beloved who was reclining on his left arm. (29).

पद्मकान्तिमरुणत्रिभागयोः संक्रमय्य तव नेत्रयोरिव ।
संक्षये जगदिव प्रजेश्वरः संहरत्यहरसावहर्पतिः ॥३०॥

"The sun, transferring the beauty of the lotus to her eyes, three parts of which were red, destroyed the day, as the Creator dissolves the world. (30).

शीकरव्यतिकरं मरीचिभिर् धूनयत्यवनते विवस्वति ।
इन्द्रचापपरिवेषशून्यतां निर्झरास्तव पितुर्व्रजन्त्यमी ॥३१॥

When the sun was hanging low on the western horizon, his rays not being in contact with particles of water, these rivulets flowing down the slopes of your father (mt. Himālaya) are no longer adorned by the halo of the rainbows. (31).

दष्टतामरसकेसरत्यजोः क्रन्दतोर्विपरिवृत्तकण्ठयोः ।
निघ्नयोः सरसि चक्रवाकयोरल्पमन्तरमनल्पतां गतम् ॥३२॥

The small distance between the Cakravāka pairs became very long (the Cakravāka-pairs) who were mutually dependent and who were crying, turning their necks away from one another; while they were biting the thread in the stalks of lotus. (32).

स्थानमाह्निकमपास्य दन्तिनः सल्लकीविटपभङ्गवासितम् ।
आविभातचरणाय गृह्णते वारि वारिरुहबद्धषट्पदम् ॥३३॥

The elephants, giving up their daily places, suck up in their trunks water which is infused with the scent of bits of Sallakī tendrils, and in which bees are clinging to lotus flowers, for the performance of their evening activities. (33).

पश्य पश्चिमदिगन्तलम्बिना निर्मितं मितकथे विवस्वता ।
दीर्घया प्रतिमया सरोऽम्भसां तापनीयमिव सेतुबन्धनम् ॥३४॥

O thou of few words, see, the sun, hanging on the skirts of the western horizon, seems by images in the waters of the lake to build a golden bridge. (34).

उत्तरन्ति विनिकीर्य पल्वलं गाढपङ्कमतिवाहितातपाः ।
दंष्ट्रिणो वनवराहयूथपा दष्टभङ्गुरबिसाङ्कुरा इव ॥३५॥

The leaders of wild boars, who had bitten the threads of lotus-stalks with huge tusks, having disturbed the mud in the lakes, passed the heat of the day therein. (35).

एष वृक्षशिखरे कृतास्पदो जातरूपरसवर्हमण्डलः ।
हीयमानमहरत्ययातपं पीवरोरु पिबतीव बर्हिणः ॥३६॥

Here is a peacock, O fair one, roosting at the top of the tree, with his plumage shining like liquid gold, and who seems to drink in the vanishing light of the sinking day. (36).

पूर्वभागतिमिरप्रवृत्तिभिर्व्यक्तपङ्कमिव जातमेकतः ।
खं हृतातपजलं विवस्वता भाति किञ्चिदिव शेषवत्सरः ॥३७॥

The sky in the east, being pervaded by darkness looked like a lake with but little water left in it and which seemed to expose mind in one part as the water in the form of his light was withdrawn by him. (37).

आविशद्भिरुटजाङ्गणं मृगैर्मूलसेकसरसैश्च वृक्षकैः ।
आश्रमाः प्रविशदग्निधेनवो बिभ्रति श्रियमुदीरिताग्नयः ॥३८॥

Hermitages, looking splendid with sacrificial fires blazing, marked by deer, entering their courts and by trees, that looked fresh as their roots were watered, were entered into by excellent cows.. (38).

बद्धकोशमपि तिष्ठति क्षणं सावशेषविवरं कुशेशयम् ।
षट्पदाय वसतिं ग्रहीष्यते प्रीतिपूर्वमिव दातुमन्तरम् ॥३९॥

The lotus, though it had furled itself into a bud, still stood awhile with an open aperture as if to give shelter to the bee that was seeking a home in love and affection. (39).

दूरमग्निपरिपेयरश्मिना वारुणी दिगरुणेन भानुना ।
भाति केसरवतेव मण्डिता बन्धुजीवतिलकेन कन्यका ॥४०॥

The western quarter, with the crimson sun, whose rays could be counted at a distance ahead, looked like a bride adorned by tilak mark of the Bandhujīva flower with filaments. (40).

सामभिः सहचराः सहस्रशः स्यन्दनाश्वहृदयंगमस्वरैः ।
भानुमग्निपरिकीर्णतेजसं संस्तुवन्ति किरणोष्मपायिनः ॥४१॥

Thousands of his companions (i.e. the Vālakhilyas and others), who drink the heat of his rays, laud the sun, who has transferred his rays to fire, with songs from the Sāmaveda, which appealed to the heart of horses of the chariot. (41).

सोऽयमानतशिरोधरैर्हयैः कर्णचामरविघट्टितेक्षणैः ।
अस्तमेति युगभुग्नकेसरैः संनिधाय दिवसं महोदधौ ॥४२॥

The sun, depositing the day in the great ocean, goes

to the setting mountain with his horses who have bent their heads, who have closed their eyes, as the hair in the Cāmara smart their eyes, and as the hair in the mane are ruffled by the yoke. (42).

खं प्रसुप्तमिव संस्थिते रवौ तेजसो महत ईदृशी गतिः ।
तत् प्रकाशयति यावदुद्गतं मीलनाय खलु तावतश्च्युतम् ॥४३॥

The sky seems to sleep when the sun sets; that is the way of great luminaries; it illumines all that it shines on, where it does not shine, that shrinks into nothingness. (43).

संध्ययाप्यनुगतं रवेर्वपुर्वन्द्यमस्तशिखरे समर्पितम् ।
येन पूर्वमुदये पुरस्कृता नानुयास्यति कथं तमापदि ॥४४॥

Twilight followed the sun's orb to the setting mountains; how can one who is first honoured by some one not follow him in his distress? (44).

रक्तपीतकपिशाः पयोमुचां कोटयः कुटिलकेशि भान्त्यमूः ।
द्रक्ष्यसि त्वमिति संध्यवेलया वर्तिकाभिरिव साधु मण्डिताः ॥४५॥

This twilight appears to have painted with a brush, the edges of clouds in red, yellow and brown colours and that you might see them, has well adorned them. (45).

सिंहकेसरसटासु भूभृतां पल्लवप्रसविषु द्रुमेषु च ।
पश्य धातुशिखरेषु भानुना संविभक्तमिव सांध्यमातपम् ॥४६॥

The sun seems to have distributed his evening light among the filament-like hair of the mane of the lions in the mountains, and the trees that burgeon forth with leaves and the peaks of mountains. (46).

पार्ष्णिमुक्तवसुधास्तपस्विनः पावनाम्बुरचिताञ्जलिक्रियाः ।
ब्रह्म गूढमभिसंध्यमादृताः शुद्धये विधिविदो गृणन्त्यमी ॥४७॥

Oh, daughter of the mountain, here are these hermits, who are such adepts in religious procedure, offering handfuls of water in their twilight orisons and eager to purify their souls, recite the Gāyatrī chant. (47)

तन्मुहूर्तमनुमन्तुमर्हसि प्रस्तुताय नियमाय मामपि ।
त्वां विनोदनिपुणः सखीजनो वल्गुवादिनि विनोदयिष्यति ॥४८॥

O sweet-tongued beloved deign to allow me to offer my evening prayer; you will be diverted by your friend, so skilled in humorous talk." (48).

निर्विभुज्य दशनच्छदं ततो वाचि भर्तुरवधीरणापरा ।
शैलराजतनया समीपगामाललाप विजयामहेतुकम् ॥४९॥

Thereupon, Pārvatī, showing by the pouting of her lips, as if she had not heard those words of her husband, began to talk casually to Vijayā (her friend), who was near her. (49).

ईश्वरोऽपि दिवसात्ययोचितं मन्त्रपूर्वमनुतस्थिवान् विधिम् ।
पार्वतीमवचनामसूयया प्रत्युपेत्य पुनराह सस्मितम् ॥५०॥

Iśvara, too, having offered his evening prayers, proper for day's decline, came back to Pārvatī, who seemed to be angry, and smilingly addressed her. (50).

मुञ्च कोपमनिमित्तकोपने संध्यया प्रणमितोऽस्मि नान्यया ।
किं न वेत्सि सहधर्मचारिणं चक्रवाकसमवृत्तिमात्मनः ॥५१॥

"O thou, that art angry without cause, I have been bowed down to by Sandhyā and by no other; don't you know me, your life's companion whose behaviour towards you is that of Cakravāka towards his mate. (51).

निर्मितेषु पितृषु स्वयंभुवा या तनुः सुतनु पूर्वमुज्झिता ।
सेयमस्तमुदयं च सेवते तेन मानिनि ममात्र गौरवम् ॥५२॥

When the self-born created the manes he abandoned the tiny Sandhyā; that is why she undergoes rise and fall; and so I honour her. (52).

तामिमां तिमिरवृत्तिपीडितां भूमिलग्नां स्वमिव संप्रति स्थिताम् ।
एकतस्तटतमालमालिनीं पश्य धातुरसनिम्नगामिव ॥५३॥

Oh daughter of the mountain, see this twilight troubled by increasing darkness, hanging to one side of the mountain's spur, like a river of liquid minerals, with Tamāla groves lining one bank. (53)

सांध्यमस्तमितशेषमातपं रक्तरेखमपरा बिभर्ति दिक् ।
संपरायवसुधा सशोणितं मण्डलाग्रमिव तिर्यगुज्झितम् ॥५४॥

The western quarter bears all the remaining gloam of the setting twilight as if it were a red streak, like a sanguinary battleground looking like the edge of a wheel, left in a slanting position. (54).

यामिनीदिवससंधिसंभवे तेजसि व्यवहिते सुमेरुणा ।
एतदन्धतमसं निरङ्कुशं दिक्षु दीर्घनयने विजृम्भते ॥५५॥

Oh, beloved with long eyes, Sumeru, having intercepted the light in the interval between night and day, this inspissated darkness, unobstructed, grows. (55).

नोर्ध्वमीक्षणगतिर्न चाप्यधो नाभितो न पुरतो न पृष्ठतः ।
लोक एष तिमिरौघवेष्टितो गर्भवास इव वर्तते निशि ॥५६॥

At night, this world is, as if, in a womb, surrounded by masses of darkness, so that it is unable to lift its eyes upwards, or bend them downwards, or cast around, or ahead or behind. (56).

शुद्धमाविलमवस्थितं चलं वक्रमार्जवगुणान्वितं च यत् ।
सर्वमेव तमसा समीकृतं धिङ् महत्त्वमसतां हृतान्तरम् ॥५७॥

Darkness has reduced to equality, all that is pure or impure, steady or moving or straight or crooked. Fie upon the greatness of the wicked, which makes no difference between good and evil. (57).

नूनमुन्नमति यज्वनां पतिः शार्वरस्य तमसो निषिद्धये ।
पुण्डरीकमुखि पूर्वदिङ्मुखं कैतकैरिव रजोभिराहतम् ॥५८॥

Here rises the moon, the lord of Brāhmins, to dispel the darkness of the night; Oh lotus-faced one, the eastern quarter seems to be struck by dust, white as Ketaka pollen. (58).

मन्दरान्तरितमूर्तिना निशा लक्ष्यते शशभृता सतारका ।
त्वं मया प्रियसखीभिरावृता श्रोष्यतेव वचनानि पृष्ठतः ॥५९॥

The night with stars, with moon, screened behind the

Mandāra mountain, appears like me, accompanied by my dear friend, with you behind us, listening to us. (59).

रुद्धनिर्गमनमादिनक्षयात् पूर्वदृष्टतनुचन्द्रिकास्मितम् ।
एतदुद्गिरति रात्रिनोदिता दिग् रहस्यमिव चन्द्रमण्डलम् ॥६०॥

Upto the end of the day, the moon was seen in the east; egged on by the night, seems to reveal the secret of the quarters, smiling with his own light. (60).

पश्य पक्वफलिनीफलत्विषा बिम्बलाञ्छितवियत्सरोऽम्भसा ।
विप्रकृष्टविवरं हिमांशुना चक्रवाकमिथुनं विडम्ब्यते ॥६१॥

The cool-rayed one imitates the Cakravāka pair, who are separated by a little distance; whose image, which shines like the ripe fruit of the Priyaṅgu, is reflected in the sky-lake, and in the waters. (61).

शक्यमोषधिपतेर्नवोदयाः कर्णपूररचनाकृते तव ।
अप्रगल्भयवसूचिकोमलाश् छेत्तुमग्रनखसंपुटैः कराः ॥६२॥

It is possible to divide the rays of the newly risen moon by the sharp nails, to fashion the ear-ornament, as if they are tender Yava sprouts. (62).

अङ्गुलीभिरिव केशसंचयं संनिगृह्य तिमिरं मरीचिभिः ।
कुड्मलीकृतसरोजलोचनं चुम्बतीव रजनीमुखं शशी ॥६३॥

The moon seems to kiss the mouth of the night who has closed into buds her lotus-eyes, collecting with his rays, as with his fingers, her hair in the form of darkness. (63).

पश्य पार्वति नवेन्दुरश्मिभिः सामिभिन्नतिमिरं नभस्तलम् ।
लक्ष्यते द्विरदभोगदूषितं संप्रसीदविव मानसं सरः ॥६४॥

See, Pārvatī, the sky that has its dense darkness dispersed by rays of the young moon, looks like the Mānasa lake, which is soiled by the elephants sporting in it, but soon recovering its serenity. (64).

रक्तभावमपहाय चन्द्रमा जात एष परिशुद्धमण्डलः ।
विक्रिया न खलु कालदोषजा निर्मलप्रकृतिषु स्थिरोदया ॥६५॥

The moon, giving up its redness, has now a bright orb; those that are pure in nature are not affected by change brought on by the fault of time. (65).

उन्नतेषु शशिनः प्रभा स्थिता निम्नसंश्रयपरं निशातमः ।
नूनमात्मसदृशी प्रकल्पिता वेधसेह गुणदोषयोर्गतिः ॥६६॥

The light of the moon stands in high places and the darkness of the night has fallen in low places; surely the creator has assigned to virtue and vice a position, proper to their nature. (66).

चन्द्रपादजनितप्रवृत्तयश् चन्द्रकान्तजलबिन्दवो गिरौ ।
मेखलातरुषु निद्रितानमून् बोधयन्त्यसमये शिखण्डिनः ॥६७॥

The mountain awakens the peacocks, sleeping beneath the trees on its spurs, at odd hours, by means of the spray of water, spurting from the moon-stones, as they are touched by the moon-beams. (67).

कल्पवृक्षशिखरेषु संप्रति प्रस्फुरद्भिरविकल्पसुन्दरि ।
हारयष्टिगणनामिवांशुभिः कर्तुमागतकुतूहलः शशी ॥६८॥

See, my beloved, the moon out of curiosity, now comes to arrange ropes of pearls, by his flashing rays on the tops of Kalpa trees. (68).

उन्नतावनतभागवत्तया चन्द्रिका सतिमिरा गिरेरियम् ।
भक्तिभिर्बहुविधाभिरर्पिता भाति भूतिरिव मत्तदन्तिनः ॥६९॥

The moon-light is mingled with darkness, owing to the high and low places in the mountain, and appears like the ornamental patches on the body of a wild elephant. (69).

एतदुच्छ्वसितपीतमैन्दवं वोढुमक्षममिव प्रभारसम् ।
मुक्तषट्पदविरावमञ्जसा भिद्यते कुमुदमा निबन्धनात् ॥७०॥

This night-lily, unable to hold the liquid light of the moon, bursts open, and, quickly letting forth the murmer of bees is opening from the stalk upwards. (70).

पश्य कल्पतरुलम्बि शुभ्रया ज्योत्स्नया जनितरूपसंशयम् ।
मारुते चलति चण्डि केवलं व्यज्यते विपरिवृत्तमंशुकम् ॥७१॥

Oh, irascible one, as the wind stirs, the moon-light as it hangs on the branch of the Kalpa-tree, imitates the form of a garment, that is shown as forcibly upturned. (71).

शक्यमङ्गुलिभिरुद्धृतैरधः शाखिनां पतितपुष्पपेशलैः ।
पत्रजर्जरशशिप्रभालवैरेभिरुत्कचयितुं तवालकान् ॥७२॥

It is possible to wreath into your hair bits of moon-light broken by leaves, which are gathered with fingers from underneath the trees and which are like delicate flowers. (72).

एष चारुमुखि योगतारया युज्यते तरलबिम्बया शशी ।
साध्वसादुपगतप्रकम्पया कन्ययेव नवदीक्षितो वरः ॥७३॥

O lovely one, here is the moon, united with the proper constellation—(the moon) whose orb is throbbing like a bride who is newly married to the bridegroom, who is quaking with fear. (73).

पाकभिन्नशरकाण्डगौरयोरुल्लसत्प्रतिकृतिप्रसन्नयोः ।
रोहतीव तव गण्डलेखयोश् चन्द्रबिम्बनिमिताक्षि चन्द्रिका ॥७४॥

The moon-light in thine eye seems to grow sprouts on your fair brow, which is naturally serene and which is white like ripe Śara grass. (74).

लोहितार्कमणिभाजनार्पितं कल्पवृक्षमधु बिभ्रती स्वयम् ।
त्वामियं स्थितिमतीमुपस्थिता गन्धमादनवनाधिदेवता ॥७५॥

Here is the presiding deity of gandhamādana, come to offer thee floral wine of Kalpa tree in goblets of jewels of the red beams of the sun. (75).

आर्द्रकेसरसुगन्धि ते मुखं मत्तरक्तनयनं स्वभावतः ।
अत्र लब्धवसतिर्गुणान्तरं किं विलासिनि मदः करिष्यति ॥७६॥

O, Pleasure-loving one! your face with its red and intoxicated eyes is naturally fragrant like wet saffron. What other feature of intoxication will there be when it begins to show itself on your face (after drinking wine)? (76).

मान्यभक्तिरथवा सखीजनः सेव्यतामिदमनङ्गदीपनम् ।
इत्युदारमभिधाय शंकरस् तामपाययत पानमम्बिकाम् ॥७७॥

Śaṅkara then made Ambikā drink wine, lauding it in words, "The amiable friend of love, whose devotion is approved." (77).

पार्वती तदुपभोगसंभवां विक्रियामपि सतीं मनोभवाम् ।
अप्रतर्क्यविधियोगनिर्मितामाम्रतेव सहकारतां ययौ ॥७८॥

Pārvatī underwent a delightful change as a result of drinking wine; the mango became the fragrant Sahakāra by an unimaginable process. (78).

तत्क्षणं विपरिवर्तितह्रियोः शिक्षतोः शयनमिद्धरागयोः ।
सा बभूव वशवर्तिनी द्वयोः शूलिनः सुवदना मदस्य च ॥७९॥

That lovely one became a slave unto two; Śaṅkara and the intoxication of wine as the two had lost all sense of shame, as their passions were inflamed, and as they carried themselves to the sleeping chamber. (79).

घूर्णमाननयनं स्खलत्कचं स्वेदबिन्दुमदकारणस्मितम् ।
आननेन न तु तावदीश्वरश् चक्षुषा चिरमुमामुखं पपौ ॥८०॥

Iśvara drank for long not only with his mouth, but also with his eyes the mouth of Pārvatī, (the mouth) the eyes in which were rolling, which was tripping in utterance, which was beaded with drops of perspiration and whose smiling was due to intoxication. (80).

तां विलम्बितपनीयमेखलामुद्वहन् जघनभारदुर्वहाम् ।
ध्यानसंभवविभूतिसंभृतं प्राविशन् मणिशिलागृहं हरः ॥८१॥

Iśvara, who had provided himself with the means of

enjoyment through his divine powers, carried her, who had worn the hanging golden girdle and who was difficult to be carried owing to her heavy thighs, to the house, constructed with crystal slabs. (81).

तत्र हंसधवलोत्तरच्छदं जाह्नवीपुलिनचारुदर्शनम् ।
अध्यशेत शयनं प्रियासखः शारदाभ्रमिव रोहिणीपतिः ॥८२॥

There he lay on a bed with Pārvatī, (the bed) which was covered with a counterpane, white like a swan, which thus looked lovely like the sandy bank of the Ganges; (she lay) as the lord of Rohiṇī sleeps on an autumnal cloud. (82).

क्लिष्टकेशमविलुप्तचन्दनं व्यत्ययार्पितनखं समत्सरम् ।
तस्य तच्छिदुरमेखलागुणं पार्वतीरतमभून्न तृप्तये ॥८३॥

The love-play with Pārvatī, in which the hair was disarranged, in which the sandal unguent was blurred, in which nail-marks were made in unlikely places, in which there were mock-quarrels and in which the girdle was about to snap, did not satisfy Lord Śiva. (83.)

केवलं प्रियतमादयालुना ज्योतिषामवनतासु पङ्क्तिषु ।
तेन तत्परिगृहीतवक्षसा नेत्रमीलनकुतूहलं कृतम् ॥८४॥

When the line of stars was declining on the horizon, Śiva, out of kindness for Pārvatī, simulated sleep while she clasped his bosom. (84).

स व्यबुध्यत बुधस्तवोचितः शातकुम्भकमलाकरैः समम् ।
मूर्छनापरिगृहीतकैशिकैः किंनरैरुषसि गीतमङ्गलः ॥८५॥

In the morning, Śiva was awakened along with the bed of golden lotus flowers, by auspicious hymns befitting wise people, sung by the Kinnars, who were thrumming on their vīṇā instrument musical notes in the ascending and descending order. (85).

तौ क्षणं शिथिलितोपगूहनौ दंपती रचितमानसोर्मयः ।
पद्मभेदपिशुनाः सिषेविरे गन्धमादनवनान्तमारुताः ॥८६॥

That couple, relaxing their embrace awhile, enjoyed the breezes from the interior of the gandhamādana forests, that raised ripples on the Mānasa lake and that indicated the bursting of one kind of lotus. (86).

ऊरुमूलनखमार्गराजिभिस् तत्क्षणं हृतविलोचनो हरः ।
वाससः प्रशिथिलस्य संयमं कुर्वतीं प्रियतमामवारयत् ॥८७॥

Hara, with his eyes attracted at that moment by the line of nail-marked on her thighs from their roots upwards, prevented Pārvatī from tightening her garment that had become loose. (87).

स प्रजागरकषायलोचनं गाढदन्तपदपीडिताधरम् ।
आकुलालकमरंस्त रागवान् प्रेक्ष्य भिन्नतिलकं प्रियामुखम् ॥८८॥

He, the passionate Hara, was delighted to see the beloved's face with its eyes reddening by keeping awake, with the lower lip bitten hard by teeth, with the hair dishevelled and Tilak-mark blurred. (88).

तेन भङ्गिविषमोत्तरच्छदं मध्यपिण्डितविसूत्रमेखलम् ।
निर्मलेऽपि शयनं निशात्यये नोज्झितं चरणरागलाञ्छितम् ॥८९॥

He did not leave the bed even when the night had worn to a clear dawn (the bed) with its counterpane crumpled, with the loose girdle lying all in a heap at its centre and soiled by the paint on her feet. (89).

स प्रियामुखरसं दिवानिशं हर्षवृद्धिजननं सिषेविषुः ।
दर्शनप्रणयिनामदृश्यतामाजगाम विजयानिवेदितः ॥९०॥

Desiring, night and day, to enjoy the kisses of his beloved, that heightened his joy, he became inaccessible to those that came to see him and who were announced by Vijayā. (90).

समदिवसनिशीथं सङ्गिनस्तत्र शम्भोः
शतमगमदृतूनां साग्रमेका निशेव ।
न तु सुरतसुखेभ्यश्छिन्नतृष्णो बभूव
ज्वलन इव समुद्रान्तर्गतस्तज्जलौघैः ॥९१॥

There, enjoying sexual pleasure on even days of the year right on upto midnight, Hara passed more than a hundred seasons as one night but he could not have his thirst quenched by sexual pleasure like the submarine fire with floods of water. (91).

———

नवमः सर्गः

तथाविधेऽनङ्गरसप्रसङ्गे मुखारविन्दे मधुरः प्रियायाः ।
संभोगवेश्म प्रविशन्तमन्तर्ददर्श पारावतमेकमीशः ॥१॥

At the time, when he was savouring the pleasure of love, he was like a bee in the lotus-like face of his beloved, and he saw a pigeon entering the house of pleasure. (1).

सुकान्तकान्तामणितानुकारं कूजन्तमाघूर्णितरक्तनेत्रम् ।
प्रस्फारितोन्नम्रविनम्रकण्ठं मुहुर्मुहुर्न्यञ्चितचारुपुच्छम् ॥२॥

Making a sound like the one, let out at the time of sexual pleasure, rolling his red eyes, stretching up his bent neck, and frequently contracting his tail. (2).

विशृङ्खलं पक्षतियुग्ममीषद् दधानमानन्दगतं मदेन ।
शुभ्रांशुवर्णं जटिलाग्रपादमितस्ततो मण्डलके चरन्तम् ॥३॥

Making his wings flutter, unstrained and in a manner so as to cause delight, full of exhilaration of the colour of the moon, with webbed feet, and moving round about in whirling movement. (3).

रतिद्वितीयेन मनोभवेन ह्रदात् सुधायाः प्रविगाह्यमानात् ।
तं वीक्ष्य फेनस्य चयं नवोत्थमवाप्यनन्दत् क्षणमिन्दुमौलिः ॥४॥

Śiva was delighted to see him for a while, white like a flake of foam rising on the lake of nectar as Madana, with Rati, dived into it for pleasure. (4).

तस्याकृतिं कामपि वीक्ष्य दिव्यामन्तर्भवच्छद्मविहंगमग्निम् ।
विचिन्तयन् संविविदे स देवो भ्रूभङ्गभीमश्च रुषा बभूव ॥५॥

Seeing his form, as divine in an ineffable manner, the god, as he reflected, recognised it as Agni disguised as a bird and became dreadful of aspect, as, in anger, he knitted his brow. (5).

स्वरूपमास्थाय ततो हुताशः श्वासस्खलत्कण्ठकृताञ्जलिः सन् ।
प्रवेपमानो नितरां स्मरारिमिदं वचो व्यक्तमथाभ्युवाच ॥६॥

The Fire, having assumed his own form, was much frightened and trembling violently, folded his hands in supplication and clearly addressed the enemy of Smara thus. (6).

असि त्वमेको जगतामधीशः स्वर्गौकसां त्वं विपदो निहंसि ।
अतः सुरेन्द्रप्रमुखाः प्रभो त्वामुपासते दैत्यवरैर्विधूताः ॥७॥

"You are the sole lord of the universe; you dispel the calamities of the gods; hence gods with Indra at their head, when worsted by the demons, seek thy help. (7).

त्वया प्रियाप्रेमवशंवदेन शतं व्यतीयेऽत्रभवन्नृतूनाम् ।
बहिः स्थितोऽपि त्वदवीक्षणार्तो दैन्यं परं प्राप सुरैः सुरेन्द्रः ॥८॥

When thou, who are fascinated by love of thy beloved, spent a hundred seasons in privacy for the sexual enjoyment, Indra, accompanied by the gods, experienced hard penury, being anxious for having not seen you. (8).

त्वदीयसेवावसरप्रतीक्षैरभ्यर्थितः शक्रमुखैः सुरैस्त्वाम् ।
उपागतोऽन्वेष्टुमहं विहंगरूपेण विद्वन्समयोचितेन ॥९॥

Besought by the gods, with Śakra at their head, waiting for an occasion to serve thee, I have come to seek thee, in the form of a bird which is proper to the occasion. (9).

इति प्रभो चेतसि संप्रधार्य तं नोऽपराधं भगवन् क्षमस्व ।
पराभिभूता वद किं क्षमन्ते कालातिपातं शरणार्थिनोऽमी ॥१०॥

Thinking, Oh Lord, thus in thy mind, pardon us, Holy Sire, our offence; being defeated, say, how can these, who are seeking refuge, brook delay? (10).

प्रभो प्रसीदाशु सृजात्मपुत्रं यं प्राप्य सेनान्यमसौ सुरेन्द्रः ।
स्वर्लोकलक्ष्मीप्रभुतामवाप्य जगत्त्रयं पाति तव प्रसादात् ॥११॥

Be pleased, Oh Lord; quickly send thy son, so that obtaining in him a commander, Indra, obtaining the mastery of the presiding deity of heaven, shall rule the three worlds, through thy favour." (11).

स शंकरस्तामिति जातवेदोविज्ञापनामर्थकरीं निशम्य ।
अभूत् प्रसन्नः परितोषयन्ति गीर्भिर्गिरीशा रुचिराभिरीशम् ॥१२॥

Lord Śaṅkara, having heard that meaningful prayer of Agni, was pleased; for those who are masters of speech, please their masters with agreeable and sweet words. (12).

प्रसन्नचेता मदनान्तकारी स तारकारेर्जयिनो भवाय ।
शक्रस्य सेनाधिपतेर्जयाय व्यचिन्तयच्चेतसि भावि किंचित् ॥१३॥

The destroyer of Madana, pleased in mind thought about the would-be birth of a commander of Indra's armies for victory over the demon Tāraka and thought a little about the future. (13).

युगान्तकालाग्निमिवाविषह्यं परिच्युतं मन्मथरङ्गभङ्गात् ।
रतान्तरेतः स हिरण्यरेतस्यथोर्ध्वरेतास्तदमोघमाधात् ॥१४॥

He who lived in celibacy, deposited into the Fire, his infallible semen, hot like the fire at the time of world-conflagration, being ejaculated after the interruption in his sexual enjoyment. (14).

अत्युष्णबाष्पानिलदूषितान्तर्विशुद्धमादर्शमिवात्मदेहम् ।
बभार भूम्ना सहसा पुरारिरेतःपरिक्षेपकुवर्णमग्निः ॥१५॥

Now Agni's pure body was soiled for the most part by the profuse semen of Lord Śiva; was like a mirror whose surface is blurred by hot breath. (15).

त्वं सर्वभक्षो भव भीमकर्मा कुष्ठाभिभूतोऽनलधूमगर्भः ।
इत्थं शशापाद्रिसुता हुताशं रुष्टा रतानन्दसुखस्य भङ्गात् ॥१६॥

Pārvatī, on account of the interruption she suffered in her sexual pleasure, was incensed and cursed Agni thus : "Be thou the consumer of everything; dreadful in your actions; suffering from leprosy and enveloped in smoke". (16).

दक्षस्य शापेन शशी क्षयीव प्लुष्टो हिमेनेव सरोजकोशः ।
वहन् विरूपं वपुरुग्ररेतश्चयेन वह्निः किल निर्जगाम ॥१७॥

Then Agni left the sleeping-chamber, bearing a body deformed by the quantity of Śiva's semen, like the moon a consumptive body, through the curse of Dakṣa; like a lotus bud, blasted by snow. (17).

स पावकालोकरुषा विलक्षां स्मरत्रपास्मेरविनम्रवक्त्राम् ।
विनोदयामास नगेन्द्रपुत्रीं शृङ्गारगर्भैर्मधुरैर्वचोभिः ॥१८॥

Śiva then diverted Pārvatī's mind with words sweet and full of love; she was embarrassed by anger at the sight of Agni; her face bent and smiling by the bashfulness when felt through love. (18).

हरो विकीर्णं घनघर्मतोयैर्नेत्राञ्जनाङ्कं सवयं प्रियायाः ।
द्वितीयकौपीनचलाञ्चलेनाहरन् मुखेन्दोरकलङ्किनोऽस्याः ॥१९॥

The collyrium, spread over the face of the beloved of Hara, by profuse perspiration in her eyes, was wiped out of Pārvatī's spotless moon of a face by Hara with the end of his upper garment. (19).

मन्देन स्विन्नाङ्गुलिना करेण कम्प्रेण तस्या वदनारविन्दात् ।
परामृशन् घर्मजलं जहार हरः सहेलं व्यजनानिलेन ॥२०॥

With his gently trembling hand, with its sweating fingers, Hara sportingly wiped out perspiration, removing it by fanning it. (20).

रतिश्लथं तत्कबरीकलापमंसावसक्तं विगलत्प्रसूनम् ।
स पारिजातोद्भवपुष्पमय्या स्रजा बबन्धामृतमूर्तिमौलिः ॥२१॥

That moon-crested god strung a Pārijāt wreath in her

braid, loosened in sexual enjoyment; (her braid) clinging on her shoulder from which flowers were dropping. (21).

कपोलपाल्यां मृगनाभिचित्रपत्रावलीमिन्दुमुखः सुमुख्याः ।
स्मरस्य सिद्धस्य जगद्विमोहमन्त्राक्षरश्रेणिमिवोल्लिलेख ॥२२॥

Hara painted on the cheeks of the beautiful lady Patrāvalī designs as if they were mantra-letters bewitching the world of the conquering god of love. (22).

रथस्य कर्णाविभि तन्मुखस्य ताटङ्कचक्रद्वितयं न्यधात् सः ।
जगज्जिगीषुर्विषमेषुरेष ध्रुवं यमारोहति पुष्पचापः ॥२३॥

Hara placed near her ears, wheels in the Tāṭaṅka ornaments for the chariot of her mouth which the world-conqueror god of uneven shafts will assuredly mount. (23).

तस्याः स कण्ठे पिहितस्तनाग्रां न्यधत्त मुक्ताफलहारवल्लीम् ।
या प्राप मेरुद्वितयस्य मूर्ध्नि स्थितस्य गङ्गौघयुगस्य लक्ष्मीम् ॥२४॥

He put in her neck a string of pearls which covered the tips of her breasts, and which attained the beauty of two streams of the Ganges falling on two Meru-peaks. (24).

नखव्रणश्रेणिधरे बबन्ध नितम्बबिम्बे रशनाकलापम् ।
बलस्वचेतोमृगबन्धनाय मनोभुवः पाशमिव स्मरारिः ॥२५॥

He tied a golden girdle round her plump buttocks lovely by a line of nail marks, a golden girdle for binding the deer of his mind, which was as it were a noose of the god of love. (25).

भालेक्षणाग्नौ स्वयमञ्जनं स भङ्क्त्वा दृशोः साधु निवेश्य तस्याः ।
नवोत्पलाक्ष्याः पुलकोपगूढे कण्ठे विनीलेऽङ्गुलिमुज्जघर्ष ॥२६॥

God Śiva, taking collyrium from the fire in the eye of his forehead, put it well in the eyes of his lotus-eyed beloved and he, then, wiped his finger on his blue and horripilated neck. (26).

अलक्तकं पादसरोरुहाग्रे सरोरुहाक्ष्याः किल संनिवेश्य ।
स्वमौलिगङ्गासलिलेन हस्तारुणत्वमक्षालयदिन्दुचूडः ॥२७॥

Having painted the lips of the lotus-feet of the lotus-eyed lady, the moon-crested god wiped the redness of his hand with water from the stream of the Ganges on his head. (27)

भस्मानुलिप्ते वपुषि स्वकीये सहेलमादर्शतलं विमृज्य ।
नेपथ्यलक्ष्मीपरिभावनार्थमदर्शयज्जीवितवल्लभां सः ॥२८॥

Having wiped the mirror gracefully with the ashes from his body, he held it before his beloved, that she may see the beauty of her attire in it. (28).

प्रियेण दत्ते मणिदर्पणे सा संभोगचिह्नं स्ववपुर्विभाव्य ।
त्रपावती तत्र घनानुरागं रोमाञ्चदम्भेन बहिर्बभार ॥२९॥

Seeing in the jewelled mirror, the signs of enjoyment by her beloved, filled with bashfulness, she manifested her deep love by the guise of horripilation. (29).

नेपथ्यलक्ष्मीं दयितोपक्लृप्तां सस्मेरमादर्शतले विलोक्य ।
अमंस्त सौभाग्यवतीषु धुर्यमात्मानमुद्धूतविलक्षभावा ॥३०॥

Smilingly looking in the mirror at the beauty of her attire arranged by her beloved giving up her crestfallen aspect, she considered herself as the foremost among chaste ladies. (30).

अन्तःप्रविश्यावसरेऽथ तत्र स्निग्धे वयस्ये विजया जया च ।
सुसंपदोपाचरतां कलानामङ्कस्थितां तां शशिखण्डमौलेः ॥३१॥

Then Jayā and Vijayā, two intimate friends of Pārvatī, entered at the proper occasion, and adorned with ornaments which all the wealth of arts devise Pārvatī who was seated in the lap of the moon-crested god. (31).

व्यधुर्बहिर्मङ्गलगानमुच्चैर्वैतालिकाश्चित्रचरित्रचारु ।
जगुश्च गन्धर्वगणाः सशङ्खस्वनं प्रमोदाय पिनाकपाणेः ॥३२॥

Outside, the bards loudly celebrated in song the splendid exploits of Hara, and the Gandharvas, too, sang, with conches blaring for the pleasure of Hara. (32).

ततः स्वसेवावसरे सुराणां गणांस्तदालोकनतत्पराणाम् ।
द्वारि प्रविश्य प्रणतोऽथ नन्दी निवेदयामास कृताञ्जलिः सन् ॥३३॥

Then, at the proper hour of their service, groups of gods, eager to see him, were announced by Nandī, who came to the door and bowed to him and folded his hands. (33).

महेश्वरो मानसराजहंसीं करे दधानस्तनयां हिमाद्रेः ।
संभोगलीलालयतः सहेलं हरो बहिस्तानभि निर्जगाम ॥३४॥

The great god, Hara, holding by the hand the daughter

of the mountain, the female swan of the Mānasa of his mind, gracefully came out of the pleasure-chamber to meet them. (34).

क्रमान् महेन्द्रप्रमुखाः प्रणेमुः शिरोभिरद्धाञ्जलयो महेशम् ।
प्रालेयशैलाधिपतेस्तनूजां देवीं च लोकत्रयमातरं ताम् ॥३५॥

The gods, Mahendra and others, folding their hands upon their crests, in due order bowed to him and to the daughter of the lord of mountains, the mother of the world. (35).

यथागतं तान् विबुधान् विसृज्य प्रसाद्य मानक्रियया प्रतस्थे ।
न नन्दिना दत्तभुजोऽधिरुह्य वृषं वृषाङ्कः सह शैलपुत्र्या ॥३६॥

Having taken their leave, in the order of their arrival, he pleased them by bestowing honours upon them, and mounted his bull, with Pārvatī; being given a lift by Nandī with his hand. (36).

मनोऽतिवेगेन ककुद्मता स प्रतिष्ठमानो गगनाध्वनोऽन्ते ।
वैमानिकैः साञ्जलिभिर्ववन्दे विहारहेलागतिभिर्गिरीशः ॥३७॥

Starting, mounted on a bull, which was swift as the mind, at the end of the path of the sky, he was bowed down to by the gods, who folded their hands, and who displayed sportive movements. (37).

स्वर्वाहिनीवारिविहारचारी रतान्तनारीश्रमशान्तिकारी ।
तौ पारिजातप्रसवप्रसङ्गो मरुत् सिषेवे गिरिजागिरीशौ ॥३८॥

Śiva and Pārvatī enjoyed the breezes, blowing and

sporting over the waters of the river of heaven, allaying the fatigue of a woman caused by sexual enjoyment; and fragrant by contact with the Pārijāta flowers. (38).

पिनाकिनापि स्फटिकाचलेन्द्रः कैलासनामा कलिताम्बराशः ।
धृतार्धसोमोऽद्भुतभोगिभोगो विभूतिधारी स्व इव प्रपेदे ॥३९॥

Śiva, too, came to the mount Kailāsa, as to his own soul,—Kailāsa that was made of crystal blocks, that covered a good part of the sky, that had the moon-crested Śiva, dwelling on it, that had wonderful python-bodies, sprawling about, and that was rich in costly minerals. (39).

विलोक्य यत्र स्फटिकस्य भित्तौ सिद्धाङ्गनाः स्वं प्रतिबिम्बमारात् ।
भ्रान्त्या परस्या विमुखीभवन्ति प्रियेषु मानग्रहिला नमत्सु ॥४०॥

The wives of the Siddhas seeing their reflections in the crystal walls from near from suspicion of rivals, turn averse from them, and take umbrage at their lovers, even when they bend before them (wives). (40).

सुबिम्बितस्य स्फटिकांशुगुप्तेश्चन्द्रस्य चिह्नप्रकरः करोति ।
गौर्यर्पितस्येव रसेन यत्र कस्तूरिकायाः शकलस्य लीलाम् ॥४१॥

The spot on the moon whose crystal rays are well preserved in that crystal mountain assumes the beauty of the Tilak-mark in musk, made by Pārvatī through pleasure. (41).

यदीयभित्तौ प्रतिबिम्बिताङ्गमात्मानमालोक्य रुषा करीन्द्राः ।
मत्तान्यकुम्भिभ्रमतोऽतिभीमदन्ताभिघातव्यसनं वहन्ति ॥४२॥

In whose crystal walls, majestic elephants, finding their reflections and fearing that they are rival elephants, wrathful, bear the severe pain of very hard blows of their tusks. (42).

निशासु यत्र प्रतिबिम्बितानि ताराकुलानि स्फटिकालयेषु ।
दृष्ट्वा रतान्तच्युततारहारमुक्ताभ्रमं बिभ्रति सिद्धवध्वः ॥४३॥

Where in the crystal palaces, the wives of the Siddhas, seeing the reflections of stars, think them to be big pearls, rolling from strings of pearls, dropped at the end of sexual congress. (43).

नभश्चरीमण्डनदर्पणश्रीः सुधानिधिर्मूर्धनि यस्य तिष्ठन् ।
अनर्घ्यचूडामणितामुपैति शैलाधिराजस्य शिवालयस्य ॥४४॥

The moon, resting on the Kailāsa peaks, assuming the beauty of a mirror for the nymphs of heaven, becomes the crest-ornament of Kailāsa, the abode of Śiva. (44).

समीयिवांसो रहसि स्मरार्ता रिरंसवो यत्र सुराः प्रियाभिः ।
एकाकिनोऽपि प्रतिबिम्बभाजो विभान्ति भूयोभिरिवाचिताः स्वैः ॥४५॥

Where gods, smitten by love, coming together in privacy to enjoy sexual pleasure with their loved ones, appear, though but to be many, owing to reflections. (45).

देवोऽपि गौर्या सह चन्द्रमौलिर्यदृच्छया स्फाटिकशैलशृङ्गे ।
शृङ्गारचेष्टाभिरनारताभिर्मनोहराभिर्व्यहरच्चिराय ॥४६॥

God Śiva, too, found pleasure in Gaurī's company on the peaks of the mount Kailāsa with love dalliance, beautiful and for long. (46).

वेवस्य तस्य स्मरसूदनस्य हस्तं समालम्ब्य सुविभ्रमश्रीः ।
सा नन्दिना वेत्रभृतोपविष्टमार्गा पुरोगेण कलं चचाल ॥४७॥

She moved gracefully, having possessed the glory of graces, holding the hand of the chastiser of Smara, and led by Nandī, who was carrying a cane in his hand, and who preceded her. (47).

चलच्छिखाग्रो विकटाङ्गभङ्गः सुवन्धुरः शुक्लसुतीक्ष्णतुण्डः ।
भ्रूवोपविष्टः स हि शंकरेण तस्या विनोदाय ननर्त भृङ्गी ॥४८॥

And being ordered by Lord Śaṅkara with the knitting of his brow, the tall Bhṛṅgī with the end of his crest-lock waving, and with violent twisting of his limbs, and with a fair and fiery face danced to divert her. (48).

कण्ठस्थलीलोलकपालमाला दंष्ट्राकरालाननमभ्यनृत्यत् ।
प्रीतेन तेन प्रभुणा प्रणुन्ना काली कलत्रस्य मुदे प्रियस्य ॥४९॥

And being ordered by Hara, in his pleasure, Kālī, with a string of human skulls dangling in her neck, and her face grim with her jaw-teeth, danced for the pleasure of his beloved spouse. (49).

भयंकरौ तौ विकटं नटन्तौ विलोक्य बाला भयविह्वलाङ्गी ।
सरङ्गमुत्सङ्गमनङ्गशत्रोर्गाढं प्रसह्य स्वमालिलिङ्ग ॥५०॥

Those fearsome Kālī and Bṛṅgi, danced so frantically, that the young bride, whose limbs were overpowered by fear at their sight, passionately clasped the lap of her husband. (50).

उत्तुङ्गपीनस्तनपीडपीडं ससंभ्रमं तत्परिरम्भमीशः।
प्रपद्य सद्यः पुलकोपगूढः स्मरेण रूढप्रमदो ममाद ॥५१॥

Iśa, with Pārvatī, climbing in his lap, being embraced through fear by her, bearing the hard pressure of her high and plump breasts, was thrilled with pleasure and exulted with passion. (51).

इति गिरितनुजाविलासलीलाविविधविभङ्गिभिरेषतोषितः सन् ।
अमृतकरशिरोमणिर्गिरीन्द्रे कृतवसतिर्वशिभिर्गणैर्ननन्द ॥५२॥

The moon-crested god, dwelling on Kailāsa pleased with various kinds of enjoyment with Pārvatī, rejoiced in the company of his submissive Gaṇas. (52).

दशमः सर्गः

आससाद शुनासीरं सदसि त्रिदशैः सह ।
एष त्र्यम्बकं तीव्रं वहन् वह्निर्महन्महः ॥१॥

And fire, bearing the strong semen of Śiva, came to Indra, who was in the assembly of gods. (1).

सहस्रेण दृशामीशो सुधवां सोऽतिसादरम् ।
दुर्दर्शनं ददर्शाग्निं धूम्रधूमिलमण्डलम् ॥२॥

Indra saw with his thousand eyes, Agni, with respect, with his (Agni's) vile body ugly to sight and enveloped in smoke. (2).

दृष्ट्वा तथाविधं वह्निमिन्द्रः क्षुब्धेन चेतसा ।
व्यचिन्तयच्चिरं किंचित् कंदर्पद्वेषिरोषजम् ॥३॥

Indra, seeing Agni, in that condition, thought with an agitated mind something, arising out of anger for the enemy of Kandarpa. (3).

स विलक्ष्यमुखैर्देवैर्वीक्ष्यमाणः क्षणं क्षणम् ।
उपाविशत् सुरेन्द्रेणाविष्टं सादरमासनम् ॥४॥

Seen every moment by the perplexed gods, he respectfully occupied the seat proferred by Indra. (4).

हव्यवाह त्वयासादि दुर्दशेयं दशा कुतः ।
इति पृष्टः सुरेन्द्रेण स निःश्वस्य वचोऽवदत् ॥५॥

And when asked by Indra, "Oh, Agni, how did you come to this sad plight?", he, sighing, said. (5).

अनतिक्रमणीयात्ते शासनात् सुरनायक ।
पारावतं वपुः प्राप्य वेपमानोऽतिसाध्वसात् ॥६॥

अभिगौरि रतासक्तं जगामाहं महेश्वरम् ।
कालस्येव स्मराराते: स्वं रूपमहमासदम् ॥७॥

"Oh, lord of gods, at the inviolable command, I assumed the body of a pigeon; I approached Hara, who was absorbed in the pleasure of love-dalliance with Pārvatī; as if, the enemy of Smara was the veritable god of death, I trembling through great fear, assumed my own form. (6), (7).

दृष्ट्वा छद्मविहंगं मां सुज्ञो विज्ञाय जम्भभित् ।
ज्वलज्ज्वालानले होतुं कोपनो माममन्यत ॥८॥

Oh, Indra, the slayer of Jambha, seeing me in the disguise of a bird, the wise one recognised me and thought of offering me as an oblation into blazing fire of his eye in his forehead. (8).

वचोभिर्मधुरैः सान्त्वैर्विनम्रेण मया स्तुतः ।
प्रीतिमानभवद्देवः स्तोत्रं कस्य न तुष्टये ॥९॥

The Lord, who was praised modestly by me, with sweet and significant speech, was pleased. Who is not gratified with eulogy ? (9).

शरण्यः सकलत्राता मामत्रायत शंकरः ।
क्रोधाग्नेर्ज्वलतो ग्रासत्रासतो दुर्निवारतः ॥१०॥

Hara, the refuge and protector of all, saved me from being a morsel into the irresistible fire of his wrath. (10).

परिहृत्य परीरम्भं रभसाद् दुहितुर्गिरेः ।
कामकेलिरसोत्सेकाद् व्रीडया विरराम सः ॥११॥

Giving up the pleasure of the embrace of Pārvatī he desisted, through shame, from the excessive pleasure of relishing flavour of love. (11).

रङ्गभङ्गच्च्युतं रेतस्तदमोघं सुदुर्वहम् ।
त्रिजगद्दाहकं सद्यो मद्विग्रहमधि न्यधात् ॥१२॥

He deposited in my body his world-consuming semen,

which was infallible and unbearable and which was ejaculated owing to interruption in his sexual pleasure. (12).

दुर्विषह्येण तेनाहं तेजसा वह्निनात्मना ।
निर्दग्धमात्मनो देहं दुर्वहं वोढुमक्षमः ॥१३॥

By that unbearable semen, which is of nature of fire, I am unable to sustain my heavy body, which is consumed. (13).

रौद्रेण दह्यमानस्य महसातिमहीयसा ।
मम प्राणपरित्राणप्रगुणो भव वासव ॥१४॥

Be thou known to fame, as the protector of my body, which is being consumed by a very terrific lustre (semen)". (14).

इति श्रुत्वा वचो वह्नेः परितापोपशान्तये ।
हेतुं विचिन्तयामास मनसा विबुधेश्वरः ॥१५॥

Having heard the words of Agni, the lord of the gods thought in his mind of a means to allay that malady. (15).

तेजोदग्धानि गात्राणि पाणिनास्य परामृशन् ।
किंचित् कृपीटयोनिं तं दिवस्पतिरभाषत ॥१६॥

Caressing his body which was burnt by the lustre (semen) of Hara, the lord of heaven spoke to Agni thus : (16).

प्रीतः स्वाहास्वधाहन्तकारैः प्रीणयसे स्वयम् ।
देवान्पितॄन्मनुष्यांस्त्वमेकस्तेषां मुखं यतः ॥१७॥

"Oh, Agni, pleased with offerings made with the words "Svāhā," "Svadhā" and "Hanta", thou dost thyself please gods, manes and men. (17).

त्वयि जुह्वति होतारो हवींषि ध्वस्तकल्मषाः ।
भुञ्जन्ति स्वर्गमेकस्त्वं स्वर्गप्राप्तौ हि कारणम् ॥१८॥

The sacrificers offer to thee oblations and are purged of sins; thou alone, art the cause of attaining heaven. (18).

हवींषि मन्त्रपूतानि हुताश त्वयि जुह्वतः ।
तपस्विनस्तपःसिद्धिं यान्ति त्वं तपसां प्रभुः ॥१९॥

Anchorites, by pouring oblations consecrated by sacred spells in thee, accomplish the end of their penances; for thou art the master of penances. (19).

निधत्से हुतमर्काय स पर्जन्योऽभिवर्षति ।
ततोऽन्नानि प्रजास्तेभ्यस्तेनासि जगतः पिता ॥२०॥

Thou givest to the Sun, what oblations are poured in thee; thereby he sends showers of rain; from that is produced food; from food subjects spring; for that reason thou art the father of the world. (20).

अन्तश्चरोऽसि भूतानां तानि त्वत्तो भवन्ति च ।
ततो जीवितभूतस्त्वं जगतः प्राणदोऽसि च ॥२१॥

Thou dwellest in the hearts of beings; they spring

from thee; thou art their life-breath, and thou givest life to the world. (21).

जगतः सकलस्यास्य त्वमेकोऽस्युपकारकृत् ।
कार्योपपादने तत्र त्वत्तोऽन्यः कः प्रगल्भते ॥२२॥

Thou art the sole benefactor of the whole world; who else has the power to enable us to accomplish our object? (22).

अमीषां सुरसंघानां त्वमेकोऽर्थसमर्थने ।
विपत्तिरपि संश्लाघ्योपकारव्रतिनोऽनल ॥२३॥

Thou alone art able to help the gods to achieve their ends; Oh Fire, even the misfortune of those whose vow is to oblige, is praiseworthy. (23).

देवी भागीरथी पूर्वं भक्त्यास्माभिः प्रतोषिता ।
निमज्जतस्तवोदीर्णं तापं निर्वापयिष्यति ॥२४॥

We have already thoroughly gratified Goddess Bhāgīrathī, so that when you immerse in her waters, she would forthwith allay your very violent fever. (24).

गङ्गां तद्गच्छ मा कार्षीर्विलम्बं हव्यवाहन ।
अर्थेष्ववश्यकार्येषु सिद्धये क्षिप्रकारिता ॥२५॥

Oh, Fire, don't tarry; immediately go to the Ganges; in matter of duties necessarily to be performed absence of delay leads to accomplishment. (25).

शंभोरम्भोमयी मूर्तिः सैव देवी सुरापगा ।
त्वत्तः स्मरद्विषो बीजं दुर्धरं धारयिष्यति ॥२६॥

That Ganges, the watery form of God Śiva, that River

of the gods will take over the unbearable seed of Lord Śiva, and shall bear it." (26).

इत्युदीर्य शुनासीरो विरराम स चानलः ।
तद्विसृष्टस्तमामन्त्र्य प्रतस्थे स्वधुनीमभि ॥ २७॥

Indra, having spoken thus, stopped ; and Fire, disengaged by him, took leave of him, and started towards the river of heaven. (27).

हिरण्यरेतसा तेन देवी स्वर्गतरङ्गिणी ।
तीर्णाध्वना प्रपेदे सा निःशेषाघविनाशिनी ॥२८॥

That Fire, going along the way, reached the river of heaven, that destroys all afflictions; (28).

स्वर्गारोहणनिःश्रेणिर्मोक्षमार्गाधिदेवता ।
उदारदुरितोद्गारहारिणी दुर्गतारिणी ॥२९॥

A ladder for ascending to heaven, the presiding deity of the way to redemption, averting numerous severe calamities, and helping to cross the difficult path of worldly existence; (29).

महेश्वरजटाजूटवासिनी पापनाशिनी ।
सगरान्वयनिर्वाणकारिणी धर्मचारिणी ॥३०॥

Living in the matted locks of Śiva, destroying sin, giving redemption to the family of Sagara, and the supporter of Dharma; (30).

विष्णुपादोदकोद्भूता ब्रह्मलोकादुपागता ।
त्रिभिः स्रोतोभिरश्रान्तं पुनाना भुवनत्रयम् ॥३१॥

Sprung from the water from Viṣṇu's foot, and coming from the world of Brahman, and with her triple streams; purifying, unwearied, the three worlds; (31).

जातवेदसमायान्तमूर्मिहस्तैः समुच्छ्रितैः ।
आजुहावार्थसंसिद्ध्यै सुप्रसादधरेव सा ॥३२॥

She, who was most serene in her aspect, invited Fire, who was coming, (invited) with her hands of her rising waves, for the accomplishment of her purpose. (32).

संमिलद्भिर्मरालैः सा कलं कूजद्भिरुन्मदैः ।
ददे श्रेयांसि दुःखानि निहन्मीति तमभ्यधात् ॥३३॥

Through the voice of throhging swans, that were crying sweetly and that were intoxicated, she told him that she would give him happiness and destroy sorrows. (33).

कल्लोलैरुद्गतैरर्वाचीनं तटमभिव्रजैः ।
प्रीतेव तमभीयाय स्वधुनी जातवेदसम् ॥३४॥

The river of heaven came to meet Agni, as if she was pleased, with her rising and rippling waves swirling towards the lower bank. (34).

अथाभ्युपेतस्तापार्तो निममज्जानलः किल ।
विपदा परिभूताः किं व्यवस्यन्ति विलम्बितुम् ॥३५॥

Now came Fire, afflicted by fever and plunged (into her waters); can those, overpowered by calamities, brook delay? (35).

गङ्गावारिणि कल्याणकारिणि श्रमहारिणि ।
स मग्नो निर्वृतिं प्राप पुण्यकारिणि तारिणि ॥३६॥

Immersed into her waters, he obtained relief; into those waters, which bring happiness, remove fatigue, enable men to accumulate merit, and help them to cross (the waters of worldly existence). (36).

तत्र माहेश्वरं धाम संचक्राम हविर्भुजः ।
गङ्गायामिद्धभङ्गायामन्तस्तापविपद्धृति ॥३७॥

The seed (semen) of Hara, passed from the Fire to the Ganges, whose waves were swirling up and who was suffering the distress of internal fever. (37).

कृशानुरेतसो रेतस्याहृते सरिता तया ।
निश्चक्राम ततः सौख्यं हव्यवाहो वहन्बहु ॥३८॥

When the semen of Hara was received from Fire by the Ganges, Agni emerged from her waters, feeling immensely happy. (38).

सुधासारैरिवाम्भोभिः परिषिक्तो हुताशनः ।
यथागतं जगामाथ परां निर्वृतिमावहत् ॥३९॥

And Fire, bathing in those waters, as if they were of the essence of ambrosia, feeling immensely happy, went his way. (39).

सा सुदुर्विषहं कामं धाम कामजितो महत् ।
प्रादधाना परीतापमवाप व्योमवाहिनी ॥४०॥

The Ganges, the river of the sky, bearing the weighty seed of Hara, was greatly troubled by intense fever. (40).

वह्निरार्ता युगान्ताग्नेस्तप्तानीव शिखाशतैः ।
हित्वोष्माणि जलान्यस्या निर्जग्मुर्जलजन्तवः ॥४१॥

The creatures in water, scorched by hundreds of flames of the fire that consumes at the end of an aeon, leaving her hot waters, issued out of them. (41).

तेजसा तेन रौद्रेण तप्तानि सलिलान्यपि ।
समुदञ्चन्ति चण्डानि दुर्भराणि बभार सा ॥४२॥

And the Ganges bore those waters, which were heated by the fire (the semen) of Hara, which (waters) were furiously swirling up and were hard to hold. (42).

जगच्चक्षुषि चण्डांशौ किंचिदभ्युदयोन्मुखे ।
जग्मुः षट्कृत्तिका माघे मासि स्नातुं सुरापगाम् ॥४३॥

When the sun, the eye of the world, was about to rise, the six Kṛttikās went to the river of the gods for bathing in the month of Māgha. (43).

शुभ्रै रभ्रंकषैरूर्मिशतैः स्वर्गमनं सताम् ।
कथयन्तीमिवालोकावगाहाचमनादिना ॥४४॥

She seemed to describe her sorrows with hundreds of her waves that were white and that scoured the sky, to the gods that were seeing her, bathing in her, and sipping her water. (44).

सुस्नातानां मुनीन्द्राणां बलिकर्मोचितैरलम् ।
बहिः पुष्पोत्करैः कीर्णतीरां दूर्वाक्षतान्वितैः ॥४५॥

Her bank outside was bespattered with clusters of flowers with Dūrvā and rice-seeds, enough for the offerings, of great sages that had bathed well. (45).

ब्रह्मध्यानपरैर्योगिवरैर्ब्रह्मासनस्थितैः ।
योगनिद्रागतैर्योगपट्टबन्धैरुपाश्रिताम् ॥४६॥

She was occupied by sages who were meditating on Brahma, practising Yoga, and had assumed the Brahma-posture, and who were experiencing Yaugic sleep, and who had wound the Yogapaṭṭa round their knees; (46).

पादाङ्गुष्ठाग्रभूमिष्ठैः सूर्यसंविष्टदृष्टिभिः ।
ब्रह्मर्षिभिः परं ब्रह्म गृणद्भिरुपसेविताम् ॥४७॥

(Sages), resorted to by the seven sages, standing on the tips of their big toes, who had fixed their gaze on the sun and invoking Brahma. (47).

अथ दिव्यां नदीं देवीमभ्यनन्दन् विलोक्य ताः ।
कं नाभिनन्दयत्येषा दृष्टा पीयूषवाहिनी ॥४८॥

The Kṛttikās, on seeing the divine river, were over-joyed; whose heart, she, this river of ambrosia, does not rejoice ! (48).

चन्द्रचूडामणिर्देवो यामुद्वहति मूर्धनि ।
यस्या विलोकनं पुण्यं श्रद्दधुस्तां मुदा हृदि ॥४९॥

In their hearts, they had faith in her, who is borne on his head by the moon-crested head and whose sight produces merit. (49).

दिव्यां विष्णुपदीं देवीं निर्वाणपदवेशिनीम् ।
निर्धूतकल्मषां मूर्ध्ना सुप्रह्वास्तां ववन्दिरे ॥५०॥

The Kṛttikās bent low in devotion to the divine river, the giver of redemption, who purges the world of sin, who issues from the foot of Viṣṇu— (50).

सौभाग्यैः खलु सुप्रापां मोक्षप्रतिभुवं सतीम् ।
भक्त्या प्रतुष्टुवुस्तां ताः श्रद्दधाना दिवोधुनीम् ॥५१॥

She who was easily to be won by one's good fortune, who was a pledge of heaven. They through their devotion, pleased her, and had faith in the river of heaven. (51).

मुक्तिस्त्रीसङ्गदौत्यज्ञैस्तत्र ता विमलैर्जलैः ।
प्रक्षालितमलाः सस्नुः सुस्नातास्तपसान्विताः ॥५२॥

There they washed themselves clean with her pure waters that were redemption's messenger of love, and bathed themselves thoroughly in the company of ascetics. (52).

स्नात्वा तत्र सुलभ्यायां भाग्यैः परिपचेलिमैः ।
चरितार्थं स्वमात्मानं बहु ता मेनिरे मुदा ॥५३॥

Having bathed in that river, who was to be gained through ripening good fortune, they considered, in joy, to have achieved the purpose of their life. (53).

कृशानुरेतसो रेतस्तासामभिकलेवरम् ।
अमोघं संचचाराथ सद्यो गङ्गावगाहनात् ॥५४॥

As they bathed in the waters of the Ganges, the infallible semen of Hara was immediately transferred to their bodies. (54).

रौद्रं सुदुर्धरं धाम दधाना दहनात्मकम् ।
परितापमवापुस्ता मग्ना इव चिन्ताम्बुधौ ॥५५॥

Bearing the unbearable semen of Rudra, which was of the nature of fire, they were extremely troubled and seemed to be immersed in the sea of poison. (55).

अक्षमा दुर्वहं वोढुमम्बुनो बहिरातुराः ।
अग्निं ज्वलन्तमन्तस्ता दधाना इव निर्ययुः ॥५६॥

Unable to bear the unbearable seed, they issued out of the waters being troubled as if they were holding, internally the blazing fire. (56).

अमोघं शांभवं बीजं सद्यो नद्योज्झितं महत् ।
तासामभ्युदरं दीप्तं स्थितं गर्भत्वमागमत् ॥५७॥

The great, lustrous and fructified seed of Śambhu, abandoned by the Ganges and deposited in their womb, was transformed into foetus. (57).

सुज्ञा विज्ञाय ता गर्भीभूतं तद्वोढुमक्षमाः ।
विषादमवापुः सद्यो गाढं भर्तृभिया ह्रिया ॥५८॥

The wise Kṛttikās, knowing that they were not able to bear it, were dejected for fear of their husbands and were filld with shame. (58).

ततः शरवणे सार्धं भयेन व्रीडया सह ।
तद्गर्भजातमुत्सृज्य ता गृहानभितो ययुः ॥५९॥

Then in the forest of reeds, with shame and fear, they left what was born from their womb and went home (59).

ताभिस्तत्रामृतकरकलाकोमलं भासमानं
तन्निक्षिप्तं क्षणमभिनभो गर्भमम्युज्जिहानैः ।
स्वैस्तेजोभिर्बिनपतिशतस्पर्धमानैरमानैर्
वक्त्रैः षड्भिः स्मरहरगुरुस्पर्धया चाजनीव ॥६०॥

They delivered from their womb, the foetus, shining softly as the digit of the moon into the middle of the sky, which was born with various immeasurable splendour, with six mouths, as if out of rivalry with the preceptor of Hara (i. e. Brahman). (60).

एकादशः सर्गः

अभ्यर्थ्यमाना विबुधैः समग्रैः प्रह्वैः सुरेन्द्रप्रमुखैरुपेत्य ।
तं पाययामास सुधातिपूर्णं सुरापगा स्वं स्तनमाशु मूर्ता ॥१॥

The Ganges, whom all the humble gods headed by Surendra supplicated, having come to her, (the Gange) immediately became visible and fed him with her own breast full of nectar-like milk. (1).

पिबन् स तस्याः स्तनयोः सुधौघं क्षणं क्षणं साधु समेधमानः ।
प्रापाकृतिं कामपि षड्भिरेत्य निषेव्यमाणः खलु कृत्तिकाभिः ।२॥

Drinking her breasts full of nectar-like milk and growing in good proportion, he, being attended upon by six Kṛttikās, became possessed by an indescribable form. (2).

भागीरथीपावककृत्तिकानामानन्दवाष्पाकुललोचनानाम् ।
तं नन्दनं दिव्यमुपात्तुमासीत् परस्परं प्रौढतरो विवादः ।३॥

There was a great dispute between the Gange the

fire and the Kṛittikās, whose eyes were troubled with tears of joy to take the divine child. (3).

अत्रान्तरे पर्वतराजपुत्र्या समं शिवः स्वैरविहारहेतोः ।
नभो विमानेन विगाहमानो मनोऽतिवेगेन जगाम तत्र ॥४॥

In the meanwhile, Śiva with Pārvatī, climbed into an aerial car with a speed which was speedier than that of the mind and flew to the sky, according to their free will, and came there. (4).

निसर्गवात्सल्यवशाद् विवृद्धचेतःप्रमोदौ गलदश्रुनेत्रौ ।
अपश्यतां तं गिरिजागिरीशौ षडाननं तद्दिनजातमात्रम् ॥५॥

Girijā, and Girīśa, with the joy of their mind increased by their natural filial love (with tears welling up out of their eyes) saw Sadānana, who was born only six days ago. (5).

अथाह देवी शशिखण्डमौलिं कोऽयं शिशुर्दिव्यवपुः पुरस्तात् ।
कस्याथवा धन्यतमस्य पुंसो मातास्य का भाग्यवतीषु धुर्या ॥६॥

Then Pārvatī asked the moon-crested God, "who is the child before us; who is the mother, the foremost amongst the fortunate ladies, of him, who is the most blessed amongst men? (6).

स्वर्णापगापावकलोऽयमेताः षट्कृत्तिकाः किं कलहायमानाः ।
पुत्रो ममायं न तवायमित्थं मिथोऽतिवैलक्ष्यमुदाहरन्ति ॥७॥

This river of heaven, this fire and these Kṛittikās, mutually disputing "this is my child", "this is your child", futilely quarrel between themselves. (7).

एतेषु कस्येदमपत्यमीशाखिलत्रिलोकीतिलकायमानम् ।
अन्यस्य कस्याप्यथ देवदैत्यगन्धर्वसिद्धोरगराक्षसेषु ॥८॥

Oh, Īśa, whose child among these, is this, the Tilaka ornament of the three worlds or whose, from among the Gods, the Siddhas, the demons, the Gandharvas, the serpents, the Rākṣasas ?" (8).

श्रुत्वेति वाचं हृदयप्रियायाः कौतूहलिन्या विमलस्मितश्रीः ।
सान्द्रप्रमोदोदयसौख्यहेतुभूतं वचोऽवोचत चन्द्रचूडः ॥९॥

Having heard these words of the beloved of his heart, who was full of curiosity, Candracūḍa, with the glory of a serene smile on his face, spoke words that were full of the happiness of a rising and intense joy. (9).

जगत्त्रयीनन्दन एष वीरः प्रवीरमातुस्तव नन्दनोऽस्ति ।
कल्याणि कल्याणकरः सुराणां त्वत्तोऽपरस्याः कथमेष सर्गः ॥१०

"This hero, giving delight to the three worlds, blessed one, is your son; he is the giver of delight to gods; who else could give birth to this child ? (10).

देवि त्वमेवास्य निदानमास्से सर्गे जगन्मङ्गलगानहेतोः ।
सत्यं त्वमेवेति विचारयस्व रत्नाकरे युज्यत एव रत्नम् ॥११॥

Oh Goddess, thou art the cause of the birth of this child, the theme of the auspicious songs of the world. Think for thyself truly; a gem deserves to be in the ocean. (11).

अतः शृणुष्वावहितेन वृत्तं बीजं यदग्नौ निहितं मया तत् ।
संक्रान्तमन्तस्त्रिदशापगायां ततोऽवगाहे सति कृत्तिकासु ॥१२॥

गर्भत्वमाप्तं तदमोघमेतत्ताभिः शरस्तम्बमपि न्यधायि ।
बभूव तत्रायमभूतपूर्वो महोत्सवोऽशेषचराचरस्य ॥१३॥

Listen, therefore, O beloved, with an attentive mind, the seed that I cast in fire, was transferred from him to the river of the gods, and from her to the Kṛittikās, when they plunged into her; that infallible seed developed into a foetus, which they deposited into a clump of reeds; there he was born, an extraordinary great festivity of movable and immovable beings. (12 & 13).

अशेषविश्वप्रियदर्शनेन धुर्या त्वमेतेन सुपुत्रिणीनाम् ।
अलं विलम्ब्याचलराजपुत्रि स्वपुत्रमुत्सङ्गतलं विधेहि ॥१४॥

The most lovely to the eyes of the whole world thou art; by reason of this child, the foremost of good mothers. Oh, daughter of the lord of mountains ! Don't tarry; put this thy child into thy lap." (14).

अथेतिवादिन्यमृतांशुमौलौ शैलेन्द्रपुत्री रभसेन सद्यः ।
सान्द्रप्रमोदेन सुपीनगात्री धात्री समग्रस्य चराचरस्य ॥१५॥

किरीटबद्धाञ्जलिभिर्नभःस्थैर्नमस्कृता सत्वरनाकिलोकैः ।
विमानतोऽवातरदात्मजं तं ग्रहीतुमुत्कण्ठितमानसाभूत् ॥१६॥

When Candramaulī had spoken thus, Pārvatī, the mother of all creatures of well-developed limbs, hastily climbed down from the aerial car, she was immediately bowed down to by the gods, who had folded their hands on their coronets, and was very eager in her mind to take the child. (15-16).

स्वर्गापगापावककृत्तिकादीन्कृताञ्जलीनानमतोऽपि भूयः ।
हित्वोत्सुका तं सुतमाससाद पुत्रोत्सवे माद्यति को न हर्षात् ॥१७॥

Pārvatī, eager to celebrate the festivity of her son's birth, disregarding the Kṛittikās, the fire-god, the heavenly river, and other gods, got hold of her son; who is not maddened with joy, at the festival of a son's birth? (17).

प्रमोदबाष्पाकुललोचना सा न तं ददर्श क्षणमग्रतोऽपि ।
परिस्पृशन्ती करकुड्मलाभ्यां सुखान्तरं प्राप किमप्यपूर्वम् ॥१८॥

Her eyes filled with tears of joy; she could not see him, though he lay before her; only caressing him with her bud-like finger, she attained joy ineffable. (18).

सुविस्मयानन्दविकस्वरायाः शिशुर्गलद्बाष्पतरङ्गितायाः ।
विवृद्धवात्सल्यरसोत्तराया देव्या दृशोर्गोचरतां जगाम ॥१९॥

When the child came within sight of the Goddess; her eyes dialated in wonder and joy, rippling with welling tears, full of growing motherly love. (19).

तमीक्षमाणा क्षणमीक्षणानां सहस्रमाप्तुं विनिमेषमैच्छत् ।
सानन्दनालोकनमङ्गलेषु क्षणं क्षणं तृप्यति कस्य चेतः ॥२०॥

Looking at the child for a while, she wished to have a thousand of unwinking eyes; whose mind is satisfied at any moment with looking at the auspicious sight of a son? (20).

विनम्रदेवासुरपृष्ठगाभ्यामादाय तं पाणिसरोरुहाभ्याम् ।
नवोदयत्पार्वणचन्द्रचारुं गौरी स्वमुत्सङ्गतलं निनाय ॥२१॥

Pārvatī took the child, sweet like the newly risen full moon, into her lap, with her lotus-like hands, going behind the backs of gods and demons. (21).

स्वमङ्कमारोप्य सुधानिधानमिवात्मनो नन्दनमिन्दुवक्त्रा ।
तमेकदेवं जगदेकदेवी बभूव पूज्या धुरि पुत्रिणीनाम् ॥२२॥

Putting that child, the one hero in the world, a store of nectar, into her lap, the moon-faced Pārvatī, became the foremost and adorable among mothers. (22).

निसर्गवात्सल्यरसौघसिक्ता सान्द्रप्रमोदामृतपूरपूर्णा ।
तमेकपुत्रं जगदेकमाताभ्युत्सङ्गगं प्रस्नविणी बभूव ॥२३॥

Drenched with natural motherly love and filled with the nectar of intense joy, this one mother of the world, putting that unique child in her lap, had her breasts dripping with milk. (23).

अशेषलोकत्रयमातुरस्याः षाण्मातुरः स्तन्यसुधामधासीत् ।
सुरस्रवन्त्यानलकृत्तिकाभिर्मुहुर्मुहुः सस्पृहमीक्ष्यमाणः ॥२४॥

Kārttikeya sucked the nectar-like milk from the breasts of this mother of all the three worlds and she was avidly and frequently looked at by the Ganges and the Kṛittikās. (24).

सुखाश्रुपूर्णेन मृगाङ्कमौलेः कलत्रमेकेन मुखाम्बुजेन ।
तस्यैकनालोद्गतपञ्चपद्मलक्ष्मीं क्रमात्षड्वदनीं चुचुम्ब ॥२५॥

Pārvatī, Śiva's spouse, with the lotus of her mouth, suffused with tears of joy, kissed in due order his six mouths, which had the glory of a cluster of lotuses, standing on the self-same stalk. (25).

हैमं फलं हेमगिरेर्लतेव विकस्वरं नाकनदीव पद्मम् ।
पूर्वेव दिङ्नूतनमिन्दुमाभात्तं पार्वती नन्दनमादधाना ॥२६॥

Pārvatī, holding that child, shone like a creeper on the snow-mountain, bearing a golden fruit or like the river of heaven, bearing a blooming lotus, or like the East, bearing the new moon. (26).

प्रीतात्मना सा प्रयतेन दत्तहस्तावलम्बा शशिशेखरेण ।
कुमारमुत्सङ्गतले दधाना विमानमभ्रंलिहमारुरोह ॥२७॥

She was supported by the hands of the self-controlled Śiva and putting her son in her lap, climbed into a sky-scraping aerial car. (27).

महेश्वरोऽपि प्रमदप्ररूढरोमोद्गमो भूधरनन्दनायाः ।
अङ्कादुपादत्तदङ्कतः सा तस्यास्तु सोऽप्यात्मजवत्सलत्वात् ॥२८॥

Śaṅkara, too, thrilled with the pleasure of great joy, took the child into his own lap, from that of Pārvatī, and she from his, and again he from hers, out of love for their son. (28).

दधानया नेत्रसुधैकसत्रं पुत्रं पवित्रं सुतया तयाऽद्रेः ।
संश्लिष्यमाणः शशिखण्डधारी विमानवेगेन गृहान् जगाम ॥२९॥

The moon-crested god, who was closely embraced by that daughter of the mountain, holding her son, who was pure and who was a perennial source of nectar to the eye, went to his palace, with the swiftness of his aerial car. (29).

अधिष्ठितः स्फाटिकशैलशृङ्गे तुङ्गे निजं धाम निकामरम्यम् ।
महोत्सवाय प्रमथप्रमुख्यान्पृथून् गणान् शंभुरथादिदेश ॥३०॥

Residing in his own very beautiful palace on the peak of the crystal mountain, Śambhu commanded his big gaṇa hosts, of which the Pramatha host was the chief, for the celebration of a great festival. (30).

पृथुप्रमोदः प्रगुणो गणानां गणः समग्रो वृषवाहनस्य ।
गिरीन्द्रपुत्र्यास्तनयस्य जन्मन्यथोत्सवं संववृते विधातुम् ॥३१॥

The entire host of Śiva, whose joy was intense, and who was efficient, started to celebrate the festival at the birth of Pārvatī's son. (31).

स्फुरन्मरीचिच्छुरिताम्बराणि संतानशाखिप्रसवाञ्चितानि ।
उच्चिक्षिपुः काञ्चनतोरणानि गणा वराणि स्फटिकालयेषु ॥३२॥

In the crystal palaces, the hosts of Śiva hung big garlands of Santānaka flowers strung with gold-thread, that covered the sky, with their flashing rays, (32).

दिक्षु प्रसर्पंस्तदधीश्वराणामथामराणामिव मध्यलोके ।
महोत्सवं शंसितुमाहतोऽन्यैर्दध्वान घोरः पटहः पटीयान् ॥३३॥

Solemn and deep sounded the drums, as they were beaten by the servants of the gods, guardians of the quarters, and it rolled through the quarters to announce to the earth the great festival. (33).

महोत्सवे तत्र समागतानां गन्धर्वविद्याधरसुन्दरीणाम् ।
संभावितानां गिरिराजपुत्र्या गृहेऽभवन्मङ्गलगीतकानि ॥३४॥

At that festival there assembled at the palace, Gandharva and Vidyādhara ladies, who were honoured by Pārvatī, and they sang auspicious songs. (34),

सुमङ्गलोपायनपात्रहस्तास्तं मातरो मातृवदभ्युपेताः ।
विधाय दूर्वाक्षतकानि मूर्ध्नि निन्युः स्वमङ्कं गिरिजातनूजम् ॥३५॥

The divine mothers, bearing vessels, containing auspicious presents, came to him like his mother, and putting Dūrvas and Rice-seeds upon his head, put the child in their lap. (35).

ध्वनत्सु तूर्येषु सुमन्द्रमङ्क्यालिङ्ग्योर्ध्वकेष्वप्सरसो रसेन ।
सुसंधिबन्धं ननृतुः सुवृत्तगीतानुगं भावरसानुविद्धम् ॥३६॥

As the musical instruments āṅkya, āliṅgya, and ūrdhvaka sounded, the Apsaras danced according to the lilt of wellmeasured songs, with relish, to the accompaniment of songs, dripping with emotions and sentiments in which words coalesed well. (36).

वाता ववुः सौख्यकराः प्रसेदुराशा विधूमो हुतभुग्दिदीपे ।
जलान्यभूवन्विमलानि तत्रोत्सवेऽन्तरिक्षं प्रससाद सद्यः ॥३७॥

At that festival, pleasant breezes blew, the quarters brightened and fire blazed smokeless, the waters grew limpid and clear and the sky became immediately serene. (37).

गम्भीरशङ्खध्वनिमिश्रमुच्चैर्मृदु होङ्कृता दुन्दुभयः प्रणेदुः ।
दिवौकसां व्योम्नि विमानसंघा विमुच्य पुष्पप्रचयान्प्रसस्रुः ॥३८॥

The musical drums (at Śiva's palace) sounded softly, blended with the deep blare of the conches, and groups of aerial cars of gods in heaven scattered showers of flowers and sped away. (38).

इत्थं महेशाद्रिसुतासुतस्य जन्मोत्सवे संमदयांचकार ।
चराचरं विश्वमशेषमेतत्परं चकम्पे किल तारकश्रीः ॥३९॥

Thus the festival at the birth of the son of Siva aud Pārvatī gladdened the world, together with all movable and immovable beings, but the royal glory of Tāraka was shaken. (39).

ततः कुमारः स मुदां निदानैः स बाललीलाचरितैर्विचित्रैः ।
गिरीशगौर्योर्हृदयं जहार मुदे न हृद्या किमु बालकेलिः ॥४०॥

Then Kumāra carried away the hearts of Girīśa by his childish play which excited great joy; whose heart is not moved through joy, by a child's play that captivates the heart? (40).

महेश्वरः शैलसुता च हर्षात्सतर्षमेकेन मुखेन गाढम् ।
अजातदन्तानि मुखानि सूनोर्मनोहराणि क्रमतश्चुचुम्ब ॥४१॥

Both Maheśwara and Pārvatī avidly kissed one after the other the toothless and lovely mouths of their son. (41).

क्वचित्स्खलद्भिः क्वचिदस्खलद्भिः क्वचित्प्रकम्पैः क्वचिदप्रकम्पैः ।
बालः स लीलाचलनप्रयोगैस्तयोर्मुदं वर्धयति स्म पित्रोः ॥४२॥

The child heightened the joy of his parents by his attempts at walking gracefully in which he slipped at places, and trembled at others and was steady at still others. (42).

अहेतुहासच्छुरिताननेन्दुर्गृहाङ्गणक्रीडनधूलिधूम्रः ।
मुहुर्ववन्किचिदलक्षितार्थं मुदं तयोरङ्कगतस्ततान ॥४३॥

And sitting in the lap of his parents, the child gladdened their hearts by lisping meaningless words, his moon-like face flashing with a causeless smile; and grey with the dust in the court-yard of the house, where he played. (43).

गृह्णन्विषाणे हरवाहनस्य स्पृशन्नुमाकेसरिणं सलीलम् ।
स भृङ्गिणः सूक्ष्मतरं शिखाग्रं कर्षन्बभूव प्रमादाय पित्रोः ॥४४॥

He was the joy of his parents, as he touched the horns of Śiva's bull and sportingly touched Uma's Lion, or pulled a fine hair from the crest-lock of Bhṛṅgin. (44).

एको नव द्वौ दश पञ्च सप्तेत्यजीगणन्नात्ममुखं प्रसार्य ।
महेशकण्ठोरगदन्तपंक्ति तदङ्कगः शैशवमौग्ध्यमेशिः ॥४५॥

The child of Īśa seated in his lap, in his childish prank, counted the lines of fangs in the mouths of serpents in the neck of his father to the number of ten. (45).

कपर्दिकण्ठान्तकपालदाम्नोऽङ्गुलि प्रवेश्याननकोटरेषु ।
दन्तानुपात्तुं रभसो बभूव मुक्ताफलभ्रान्तिकरः कुमारः ॥४६॥

शंभोः शिरोऽन्तः सरितस्तरंगान्विगाह्य गाढं शिशिरान्रसेन ।
स जातजाड्यं निजपाणिपद्ममतापयद्भालविलोचनाग्नौ ॥४७॥

Kumāra became impetuous to count the teeth in the cavernlike mouths of the skulls, in the string of skulls in the neck of Śiva, thinking them to be pearls. He plunged his lotus-like hand in the waves of the Ganges on the head of Śambhu, with relish because of its coolness, and when it was benumbed with cold, warmed it in the fire of his eye in his forehead. (46-47).

किंचित्कलं भङ्गुरकंधरस्य मनज्जटाजूटधरस्य शम्भोः ।
प्रलम्बमानं किल कौतुकेन चिरं चुचुम्बे मुकुटेन्दुखण्डम् ॥४८॥

The child, whose neck was wobbling, touched for long the lovely crescent of the moon in Śiva's crest with curiosity, hanging from his loose matted locks. (48).

इत्थं शिशोः शैशवकेलिवृत्तै र्मनोऽभिरामैर्गिरिजागिरीशौ ।
मनोविनोदैकरसप्रसक्तौ दिवानिशं नाविदतां कदाचित् ॥४९॥

Girijā and Girīśa, as they were absorbed in the charming childish pranks of their child, which were a source of diversion to the mind, did not know night from day. (49).

इति बहुविधं बालक्रीडाविचित्रविचेष्टितं
ललितललितं सान्द्रानन्दं मनोहरमाचरन् ।
अलभत परां बुद्धिं षष्ठे दिने नवयौवनं
स किल सकलं शास्त्रं शस्त्रं विवेद विभुर्यथा ॥५०॥

Thus indulging in various most graceful childish games, which gave intense delight, he attained on the sixth day, fresh youth and great talents, and he became a master of the art of weapons and all the lores. (50).

द्वादशः सर्गः

अथ प्रपेदे त्रिदशैरशेषैः क्रूरासुरोपप्लवदुःखितात्मा ।
पुलोमपुत्रीदयितोऽन्धकारिं पत्रीव तृष्णातुरितः पयोदम् ॥१॥

Now came Indra with all the gods to God Śiva, troubled as they were by the harassment of a powerful demon as does the Cātaka parched by thirst, to a cloud. (1).

दृप्तारिसंत्रासखिलीकृतात्म कथञ्चिदम्भोदविहारमार्गात् ।
अवाततारादिगिरिं गिरीशगौरीपदन्यासविशुद्धमिन्द्रः ॥२॥

Embarrassed by fear of the proud demon, Indra descended to the mountain from the path, where clouds disport themselves, hallowed by the tread of the feet of Śiva and Gaurī. (2).

संक्रन्दनः स्यन्दनतोऽवतीर्य मेघात्मनो मातलिदत्तहस्तः ।
पिनाकिनोऽथालयमुच्चचाल शुचौ पिपासाकुलितो यथाम्भः ॥३॥

Indra, then, having climbed down from his cloud-chariot, supported by Mātali, moved to Śiva's abode, as in summer a person, parched by thirst, moves towards water. (3).

इतस्ततोऽथ प्रतिबिम्बभाजं विलोकमानः स्फटिकाद्रिभूमौ ।
आत्मानमप्येकमनेकधा स व्रजन्विभोरास्पदमाससाद ॥४॥

He, then, reached the abode of Lord Śiva, multiplied into many, though one, through his reflections in the crystal mountain, as he walked about there. (4).

विचित्रकाञ्चनमणिभङ्गिसङ्गं सौवर्णदण्डं दधताऽतिचण्डम् ।
स नन्दिनाऽधिष्ठितमभ्यतिष्ठत्सौधाङ्गणद्वारमनङ्गशत्रोः ॥५॥

He, then, reached the port of the courtyard to Śiva's palace, which was adorned by multicoloured gems, where Nandī, with a gold-encased and fearsome cane in his hand, kept guard. (5).

ततः स कक्षाहितहेमदण्डो नन्दी सुरेन्द्रं प्रतिपद्य सद्यः ।
प्रतोषयामास सुगौरवेण गत्वा शशंस स्वयमीश्वरस्य ॥६॥

Then putting his gold-encased cane in an adjoining room, Nandī immediately approached Indra, pleased him by the great respect, and himself announced to him (Īśa's coming). (6).

भ्रूसंज्ञयाऽनेन कृताभ्यनुज्ञः सुरेश्वरं तं जगदीश्वरेण ।
प्रवेशयामास सुरैः पुरोगः समं स नन्दी सदनं सदस्यः ॥७॥

Commanded by a sign of his eye-brow, by the Lord of the World, Nandī, preceded by the Gods, ushered Indra into that excellent palace. (7).

स चण्डिभृङ्गिप्रमुखैर्गरिष्ठैर्गणैरनेकैर्विविधस्वरूपैः ।
अधिष्ठितं संसदि रत्नमय्यां सहस्रनेत्रः शिवमालुलोके ॥८॥

Indra saw in the jewel-bedecked assembly-hall Śiva, which was occupied by such weighty Gaṇas, as Bhṛṅgi and others of various forms. (8).

कपर्दमुद्बद्धमहीनमूर्धरत्नांशुभिर्भासुरमुल्लसद्भिः ।
दधानमुच्चैस्तरमिद्धधातोः सुमेरुशृङ्गस्य समत्वमाप्तम् ॥९॥

His matted locks were tied by Lords of serpents whose hoods were flashing with the lustre of their crest-gems, thus attaining the semblance of the peak of Sumeru, rich in minerals. (9).

बिभ्राणमुत्तुङ्गतरङ्गमालां गङ्गां जटाजूटतटं भजन्तीम् ।
गौरीं तदुत्सङ्गजुषं हसन्तीमिव स्वफेनैः शरदभ्रशुभ्रैः ॥१०॥

The Ganges, swirling with high rippling waves, on the edge of his matted locks, laughing to scorn Gaurī, seated in Hara's lap, with masses of foam white like autumnal clouds. (10).

गङ्गातरङ्गप्रतिबिम्बितैः स्वैर्बहूभवन्तं शिरसा सुधांशुम् ।
चलन्मरीचिप्रचयैस्तुषारगौरैर्हिमद्योतितमुद्वहन्तम् ॥११॥

Bearing the moon on his head, that became many owing to his reflections in the waves of the Ganges, the moon, who shone white, illumined white by snow and by moving masses of rays, white like frost. (11).

भालस्थले लोचनमेधमानधामाधरीभूतरवीन्दुनेत्रम् ।
युगान्तकालोचितहव्यवाहं मीनध्वजप्लोषणमादधानम् ॥१२॥

Possessing an eye in the region of the forehead, whose brilliance was growing and which obscured the brilliance of the eyes, in the form of the sun and the moon and which was like the fire at the end of an aeon, fit to consume the fish-bannered God. (13).

महार्हरत्नाञ्चितयोरुदारं स्फुरत्प्रभामण्डलयोः समन्तात् ।
कर्णस्थिताभ्यां शशिभास्कराभ्यामुपासितं कुण्डलयोश्छलेन ॥१३॥

Wearing ear-rings studded with costly gems, which spread their circle of light all round and which seemed to be the sun, and the moon, under their guise; (13).

स्वबद्धया कण्ठिकयेव नीलमाणिक्यमय्या कुतुकेन गौर्याः ।
नीलस्य कण्ठस्य परिस्फुरन्त्या कान्त्या महत्या सुविराजमानम् ॥१४॥

Shining with great splendour, by the flashing lustre of his blue neck, as if by the necklace of sapphire, put round her neck by Gaurī out of liking for it, (14).

कालार्पितानां त्रिदशासुराणां चितारजोभिः परिपाण्डुराङ्गम् ।
महन्महेभाजिनमुद्गताभ्रप्रालेयशैलश्रियमुद्वहन्तम् ॥१५॥

Bearing the beauty of the snowy mountain, where a great cloud seemed to appear, on account of the huge elephanthide (which he wore) his body smeared with the ashes from the funeral pyre of Gods and demons, taken toll of by the dread god of death. (15).

पाणिस्थितब्रह्मकपालपात्रं वैकुण्ठभाजाऽपि निषेव्यमाणम् ।
नरास्थिखण्डाभरणं रणान्तमूलं त्रिशूलं कलयन्तमुच्चैः ॥१६॥

Attended to by Viṣṇu; who abides in Vaikuṭṇha, bearing in his hand a Brahmin's skull, adorned by shreds of human bones, and holding aloft a trident, the instrument of death to his enemies. (16).

पुरातनीं ब्रह्मकपालमालां कण्ठे वहन्तं पुनराश्वसन्तीम् ।
उद्गीतवेदां मुकुटेन्दुवर्षत्सुधाभरौघाप्लवलब्धसंज्ञाम् ॥१७॥

Wearing in his neck a string of ancient skulls of

Brāhmaṇas, coming to life through the streams of ambrosia flowing from the moon in his crown, reciting Vedic chants. (17).

सलीनमङ्कस्थितया गिरीन्द्रपुत्र्या नवाष्टापदवल्लिभासा ।
विराजमानं शरदभ्रखण्डं परिस्फुरन्त्याऽचिररोचिषेव ॥१८॥

Shining like an autumnal cloud, by the flashes of the quickly quivering lightning, and shining by Gaurī, gracefully sitting in his lap, flashing like a creeper of new gold. (18).

दृप्तान्धकप्राणहरं पिनाकं महासुरस्त्रीविधवत्वहेतुम् ।
करेण गृह्णन्तमगृह्यमन्यैः पुरा स्मरप्लोषणकेलिकारम् ॥१९॥

Wielding in his hand the Pinãka bow, which is impossible to be lifted by others, taking the life of Andhaka and giving widowhood to the wives of the great demons, which (Pināka) formerly indulged in the sport of consuming Smara. (19).

भद्रासनं काञ्चनपादपीठं महार्हमाणिक्यविभङ्गिचित्रम् ।
अधिष्ठितं चन्द्रमरीचिगौरैरुद्वीज्यमानं चमरैर्गणाभ्याम् ॥२०॥

शस्त्रास्त्रविद्याभ्यसनैकसक्ते सविस्मयैरेत्य गणैः सुदृष्टे ।
नीराज्यमाने स्फटिकाचलेन सानन्दनिर्दिष्टदृशं कुमारे ॥२१॥

Seated on an auspicious seat, variegated with arrangements of costly rubies, on a golden throne, and fanned by chowries, white like moon-beams, by the Gaṇas; and looking gleefully at Kumāra, engaged in the practice of weapons and missiles, and the Gaṇas, coming, looked admiringly at him, who was waved by the crystal mountain in person. (20-21).

तथाविधं शैलसुताधिनाथं पुलोमपुत्रीदयितो निरीक्ष्य ।
आसीत्क्षणं क्षोभपरो नु कस्य मनो न हि क्षुभ्यति धामधाम्नि ॥२२॥

Indra, the spouse of Paulomi, saw Śiva, the husband of Umā, in that condition and was full of agitation for a while; whose mind is not agitated at the sight of great splendour? (22).

विकस्वराम्भोजवनश्रिया तं दृशां सहस्रेण निरीक्षमाणः ।
रोमालिभिः स्वर्गपतिर्बभासे पुष्पोत्कराकीर्ण इवाम्रशाखी ॥२३॥

Looking him with a thousand eyes, that resembled a multitude of blooming lotuses, the lord of heaven with lines of horripilation of his person, looked like a mango-tree, covered with clusters of blossoms. (23).

दृष्ट्वा सहस्रेण दृशां महेशमभूत्कृतार्थोऽतितरां महेन्द्रः ।
सर्वाङ्गजातं तदथो विरूपमिव प्रियाकोपकरं विवेद ॥२४॥

Mahendra felt very blest on seeing Maheśa; then he realised that gawkiness of his whole body, the cause of anger in his spouse. (24).

ततः कुमारं कनकाद्रिसारं पुरंदरः प्रेक्ष्य धृतास्त्रशस्त्रम् ।
महेश्वरोपान्तिकवर्तमानं शत्रोर्जयाशां मनसा बबन्ध ॥२५॥

Then Mahendra, seeing Kumāra, by his father's side,

practising his missiles and weapons, felt a profound hope in his heart about victory. (25).

श्रीनीलकण्ठद्युपतिः पुरोऽस्ति त्वयि प्रणामावसरं प्रतीच्छन् ।
सहस्रनेत्रेऽत्र भव त्रिनेत्र दृष्ट्या प्रसादप्रगुणो महेश ॥२६॥

इति प्रबद्धाञ्जलिरेत्य नन्दी निधाय कक्षामभि हेमवेत्रम् ।
प्रसादपात्रं पुरतो भविष्णु रथ स्मरारातिमुवाच वाचम् ॥२७॥

Then Nandī, who had folded his hands in supplication, placing his gold-encased cane at the door, said to the destroyer of the (three) cities, "Nīlakaṇṭha, the Lord of heaven stands before thee, awaiting to be favoured by thee, O Trinetra, be thou pleased to favour with thy glance this thousand-eyed Indra, who stands before thee, to be the receptacle of thy favours." (26-27).

पुरा सुरेन्द्रं सुरसङ्घसेव्यं त्रिलोकसेव्यस्त्रिपुरासुरारिः ।
प्रीत्या सुधासारनिधारिणेव ततोऽनुजग्राह विलोकनेन ॥२८॥

And then, the enemy of the demon Tripura, who was waited upon by the three worlds, honoured Indra, waited upon by all the gods, with a glance, dripping with the very essence of Nectar. (28).

किरीटकोटिच्युतपारिजातपुष्पोत्करेणानमितेन मूर्ध्ना ।
स्वर्गैकवन्द्यो ज॰॰देकवन्द्यं तं देवदेवं प्रणनाम देवः ॥२९॥

Then, Indra, the one God, honoured in heaven bowed to the god, the only one, to be honoured by the whole world, with his bent head, from the edge of whose coronet were slipping clusters of Pārijāta. (29).

अनेकलोकैकनमस्क्रियार्हं महेश्वरं तं त्रिदशेश्वरः सः ।
भक्त्या नमस्कृत्य कृतार्थतायाः पात्रं पवित्रं परमं बभूव ॥३०॥

Groups of gods, and groups of Gaṇas, who were full of devotion bowed down to Śiva, with heads humbled low and felt blest becomingly. (30).

सुभक्तिभाजामधि पादपीठं प्रान्तक्षितिं नम्रतरैः शिरोभिः ।
ततः प्रणेमुः पुरतो गणानां गणाः सुराणां क्रमतः पुरारिम् ॥३१॥

Groups of gods and Gaṇas with heads bowed in humility, stood at the edge of the foot-stool in proper order, and then bowed to Purāri. (31).

गणोपनीते प्रभुणोपदिष्टः शुभासने हेममये पुरस्तात् ।
प्रापोपविश्य प्रमुदं सुरेन्द्रः प्रभुप्रसादो हि मुदे न कस्य ॥३२॥

Indra, then occupied the fine golden seat, placed by a Gaṇa, at the command of Lord (Śiva); and was filled with joy; who is not filled with joy at the favour of his master? (32).

क्रमेण चान्येऽपि विलोकनेन संभाविताः सस्मितमीश्वरेण ।
उपाविशंस्तोषविशेषमाप्ता दृग्गोचरे तस्य सुराः समग्राः ॥३३॥

And in due order, all the other gods were smilingly honoured by the lord eyeing them, and sat within sight of him, and were full of great satisfaction. (33).

अथाह देवो बलवैरिमुख्यान्गीर्वाणवर्गान्करुणार्द्रचेताः ।
कृताञ्जलीकानसुराभिभूतान्ध्वस्तश्रियः श्रान्तमुखानवेक्ष्य ॥३४॥

Then to the gods, headed by Indra, who had lost their splendour and who were overpowered by the demon, who had folded their hands, and had wearied faces, the lord touched with tenderness and addressed them thus:—(34).

अहो बतानन्तपराक्रमाणां दिवौकसो वीरवरायुधानाम् ।
हिमोदबिन्दुग्लपितस्य किं यः पद्मस्य दैन्यं दधते मुखानि ॥३५॥

"Oh ye gods, who possess weapons, worthy of great warriors, and capable of achieving innumeral feats, why do your faces appear wilted like lotuses, smitten by frost ? (35).

स्वर्गौकसः स्वर्गपरिच्युताः किं स्वपुण्यराशौ सुमहत्तमेऽपि ।
चिह्नं चिरोढं न तु यूयमेते निजाधिपत्यस्य परित्यजध्वम् ॥३६॥

Oh ye gods, how have you lost heaven, even when your merit stood pretty high. Do not cast away the insignia of royalty, long borne by you. (37).

दिवौकसो देवगृहं विहाय मनुष्यसाधारणतामवाप्ताः ।
यूयं कुतः कारणतश्चरध्वं महीतले मानभृतो महान्तः ॥३७॥

Oh Ye gods, why have you left heaven, and attaining community with man, whence do you, of lofty pride, wander the earth ? (37).

अनन्यसाधारणसिद्धमुच्चैस्तद्दैवतं धाम निकामरम्यम् ।
कस्मादकस्माद्भिरगाद्भवद्भिरराजितं पुण्यमिवापचारात् ॥३८॥

How did you come to lose your extraordinarily lovely

abode, like a heap of merit, slipping away through some henious sin? (38).

विवौकसो वो हृदयस्य कस्मात्तथाविधं धैर्यमहार्यमार्याः ।
अगादगाधस्य जलाशयस्य ग्रीष्मातितापाद्विवशादिवाम्भः ॥३९॥

Oh ye Gods, whence did you lose that ineffable courage like the water of an unfathomable lake through the tremendous heat of summer? (39).

सुराः सुराधीशपुरःसराणां समीयुषां वः सममातुराणाम् ।
तद्ब्रूत लोकत्रयजित्वरात्कि महासुरात्तारकतो विरुद्धम् ॥४०॥

Oh ye Gods, say whence your opposition of Tāraka, the great demon, the conqueror of the three worlds—you, who, all led by Indra, have come together in distress. (40).

पराभवं तस्य महासुरस्य निषेद्धुमेकोऽहमलंभविष्णुः ।
दावानलप्लोषविपत्तिमन्यो महाम्बुदात्कि हरते वनानाम् ॥४१॥

I alone am able to condemn his reprisal of you; who else than a cloud is able to extinguish the blaze of the conflagration-fire which consumes entire forests? (41).

इतीरिते मन्मथमर्दनेन सुराः सुरेन्द्रप्रमुखा मुखेषु ।
सान्द्रप्रमोदाश्रुतरङ्गितेषु वपुः श्रियं सत्वरमाश्वसन्तः ॥४२॥

When thus addressed by Śiva, the gods headed by Mahendra, taking quick comfort, immediately wore a mien bearing glory, and which was rippling with waves of intense joy. (42).

ततो गिरीशस्य गिरां विरामे जगाद लब्धेऽवसरे सुरेन्द्रः ।
भवन्ति वाचोऽवसरे प्रयुक्ता ध्रुवं फलाविष्टमहोदयाय ॥४३॥

When Giriśa ended his speech, Surendra, finding the occasion, spake,—speech, properly timed, leads to great prosperity, blest with fruit. . (43).

ज्ञानप्रदीपेन तमोपहेनाविनश्वरेणास्खलितप्रभेण ।
भूतं भवद्भावि च यच्च किंचित्सर्वज्ञ सर्वं तव गोचरं तत् ॥४४॥

Oh Lord, the omniscient, with the imperishable light of knowledge, of unfailing lustre; all, the past, the present, and the future is accessible to thee. (44).

दुर्वारदोरुद्यमदुःसहेन यस्तारकेणामरघस्मरेण ।
तदीशतामाप्तवता निरस्ता वयं दिवोऽमी वद किं न वेत्सि ॥४५॥

Oh, Lord, dost thou not know, that Tāraka, the destroyer of gods, with his puissant and irresistible arms, has obtained the sovereignty of heaven, and has expelled us, therefrom ? (45).

विधेरमोघं स हरप्रसादमासाद्य सद्यस्त्रिजगज्जिगीषुः ।
सुरानशेषानहकप्रमुख्यान्दोर्दण्डचण्डो मनुते तृणाय ॥४६॥

Having obtained an infallible boon from the Creator, that conqueror of the three worlds, he, who was haughty through (the might of) his puissant arms, regarded as trifling as grass, the gods, each considering himself as the chief. (46).

स्तुत्या पुराऽस्माभिरुपासितेन पितामहेनेति निरूपितं नः ।
सेनापतिः संयति दैत्यमेतं पुरः स्मरारातिसुतो निहन्ति ॥४७॥

Oh holy sire ! formerly, Brahman, the grand sire, pleased by our supplications, told us, that some day, in the future, a son of the enemy of the cities (Siva) will slay this demon. (47).

अहो ततोऽनन्तरमक्षयावत्सुदुःसहां तस्य पराभवार्तिम् ।
विषेहिरे हन्त हृदन्तशल्यमाज्ञानिवेशं त्रिदिवौकसोऽमी ॥४८॥

Oh holy sire ! Since that day up-to-date, the gods have endured the humiliation of defeat at his hands and also his commands, as unbearable barbs rankling in their hearts, gods, though they are. (48).

निदाघधामक्लमविक्लवानां नवीनमम्भोदमिवौषधीनाम् ।
सुनन्दनं नन्दनमात्मनो नः सेनान्यमेतं स्वयमादिश त्वम् ॥४९॥

Oh holy Sire, do you order this thy good son, to be commander-in-chief, like a new cloud to the medicinal herbs, parched by the intense heat of summer?' (49).

त्रैलोक्यलक्ष्मीहृदयैकशल्यं समूलमुत्खाय महासुरं तम् ।
अस्माकमेषां पुरतो भवन्सन्दुःखापहारं युधि यो विधत्ते ॥५०॥

He who would remove our grief in battle by bearing the brunt in our fight, by uprooting that great demon, a barb in the heart of the rough glory of three worlds. (50).

महाहवे नाथ तवास्य सूनोः शस्त्रैः शितैः कृत्तशिरोधराणाम् ।
महासुराणां रमणीविलापैर्दिशो दशैता मुखरीभवन्तु ॥५१॥

Let the ten quarters resound with the cries of laments of the wives of the great demons, whose heads are lopped off with sharp weapons in the severe battle. (51).

महारणक्षोणिपशूपहारीकृतेऽसुरे तत्र तवात्मजेन ।
बन्दिस्थितानां सुदृशां करोतु वेणीप्रमोक्षं सुरलोक एषः ॥५२॥

There, offered, as victim-beasts, on the great battle-field, by thy son, let the gods unloosen the braid of hair of the imprisoned lovely damsels. (52).

इत्थं सुरेन्द्रे वदति स्मरारिः सुरारिदुश्चेष्टितजातरोषः ।
कृतानुकम्पस्त्रिदशेषु तेषु भूयोऽपि भूताधिपतिर्बभाषे ॥५३॥

When Indra had spoken thus, the lord of beings infuriated by the foul deeds of the demon, took pity on the gods, and once more addressed them thus: (53).

अहो अहो देवगणाः सुरेन्द्रमुख्याः शृणुध्वं वचनं ममैते ।
विचेष्टते शंकर एष देवः कार्याय सज्जो भवतां सुताद्यैः ॥५४॥

Oh ye gods, Indra and others, listen to my words, here, I, Śaṅkara, am ready to help your cause, myself, my sons and others. (54).

पुरा मयाऽकारि गिरीन्द्रपुत्र्याः प्रतिग्रहोऽयं नियतात्मनाऽपि ।
तत्रैष हेतुः खलु तद्भवेन वीरेण यद्वध्यत एव शत्रुः ॥५५॥

Formerly, I, though, a Yogin, married the daughter of the lord of mountains, my object in doing so was that the son born to me, through marriage, might slay the foe. (55).

अत्रोपपन्नं तदमी नियुज्य कुमारमेनं पृतनापतित्वे ।
निघ्नन्तु शत्रुं सुरलोकमेष भुनक्तु भूतोऽपि सुरैः सहेन्द्रः ॥५६॥

Therefore, your task is proper: Appoint this Kumāra to the command of the army, and kill your enemy and let Mahendra once again rule heaven with the gods. (55).

इत्युदीर्य भगवांस्तमात्मजं घोरसंगरमहोत्सवोत्सुकम् ।
नन्दनं हि जहि देवविद्विषं संयतीति निजगाद शंकरः ॥५७॥

So saying, the holy sire, Śaṅkara, said to his son, avidly thirsting for the gruelling fight, "Kill the enemy of the gods in battle." (57).

शासनं पशुपतेः स कुमारः स्वीचकार शिरसाऽवनतेन ।
सर्वथैव पितृभक्तिरतानामेष एव परमः खलु धर्मः ॥५८॥

Kumāra accepted the command of his father, with his bent head; this is indeed, the nature of those devoted to their fathers. (58).

असुरयुद्धविधौ विबुधेश्वरे पशुपतौ वदतीति तमात्मजम् ।
गिरिजया मुमुदे सुतविक्रमे सति न नन्दति का खलु वीरसूः ॥५९॥

When the lord of the gods had spoken thus to his son about the battle, Girijā was delighted, what mother of heroes does not exult in the exploits of her son? (59).

सुरपरिवृढः प्रौढं वीरं कुमारमुमापते-
र्बलवदमरारातिस्त्रीणां दृगञ्जनभञ्जनम् ।
जगदभयदं सद्यः प्राप्य प्रमोदपरोऽभव-
द्ध्रुवमभिमते पूर्णे को वा मुदा न हि माद्यति ॥६०॥

The Lord of the gods, having secured him, this brave son of god Śiva, immediately, who wholly wiped away the collyrium from the eyes of the wives of the demons, and who was the giver of freedom from fear to the world, was delighted very much; who is not maddend with joy, when the desire of his heart is fulfilled ? (60).

त्रयोदशः सर्गः

प्रस्थानकालोचितचारुवेषः स स्वर्गिवर्गैरनुगम्यमानः ।
ततः कुमारः शिरसा नतेन त्रैलोक्यभर्तुः प्रणनाम पादौ ॥१॥

Then Kumāra, dressed in a splendid attire, proper for marching forth, and followed by the gods, bowed at the feet of (his father), the lord of the three worlds. (1).

जहीन्द्रशत्रुं समरेऽमरेशपदं स्थिरत्वं नय वीर वत्स ।
इत्याशिषा तं प्रणमन्तमीशो मूर्धन्युपाघ्राय मुदाऽभ्यनन्दत् ॥२॥

"Kill the enemy of Indra, and secure fixity to his position, as the lord of the gods." Thus Īśa blessed him with joy and smelt his head, as he bowed down at his feet. (2).

प्रह्वीभवन्नम्रतरेण मूर्ध्ना नमश्चकाराङ्घ्रियुगं स्वमातुः ।
तस्याः प्रमोदाश्रुपयःप्रवृत्तिस्तस्याभवद्वीरवराभिषेकः ॥३॥

Becoming humble, with his head bent very low, he bowed at the pair of toes of his mother; her showers of tears of joy became the water, for consecrating as king, a great hero. (3).

समङ्कमारोप्य सुता हिमाद्रेराश्लिष्य गाढं सुतवत्सला सा ।
शिरस्युपाघ्राय जगाद शत्रुं जित्वा कृतार्थीकुरु वीरसूं माम् ॥४॥

Putting him in her lap, that affectionate mother smelt him on his head and said to him, "Conquer the enemy and make me, the mother of a hero, happy." (4).

उद्दामदैत्येशविपत्तिहेतुः श्रद्धालुचेताः समरोत्सवस्य ।
आपृच्छ्य भक्त्या गिरिजागिरीशौ ततः प्रतस्थेऽभि दिवं कुमारः ॥५॥

Kumāra, the cause of the death of the overweening demon, and having faith in the festivity of battle, devotedly took leave of Girijā and Girīśa, and started towards heaven. (5).

देवं महेशं गिरिजां च देवीं ततः प्रणम्य त्रिदिवौकसोऽपि ।
प्रदक्षिणीकृत्य च नाकनाथपूर्वाः समस्तास्तमथानुजग्मुः ॥६॥

All the gods, headed by Indra, bowed to Śiva and Pārvatī, and going round them, followed him. (6).

अथ व्रजद्भिस्त्रिदशैरशेषैः स्फुरत्प्रभाभासुरमण्डलैस्तैः ।
नभो बभासे परितो विकीर्णं दिवापि नक्षत्रगणैरिवोग्रैः ॥७॥

As all the gods went along, flashing with shining aurioles, the sky appeared to be pervaded all round with brilliantly shining stars. (7).

रराज तेषां व्रजतां सुराणां मध्ये कुमारोऽधिककान्तिकान्तः ।
नक्षत्रताराग्रहमण्डलानामिव त्रियामारमणो नभोन्ते ॥८॥

Among the gods marching along, was Kumāra shining

with greater brilliance, as in the sky shines the moon in circle of constellations, stars and planets. (8).

गिरीशगौरीतनयेन सार्धं पुलोमपुत्रीदयितादयस्ते ।
उत्तीर्य नक्षत्रपथं मुहूर्तात्प्रपेदिरे लोकमथात्मनीनम् ॥९॥

Those gods, with Indra, at their head, along with son of Girīśa and Gaurī, traversed the path of the stars, and reached the place (heaven) beneficial to them. (9).

ते स्वर्गलोकं चिरकालदृष्टं महासुरत्रासवशंवदत्वात् ।
सद्यः प्रवेष्टुं न विषेहिरे तत्क्षणं व्यलम्बन्त सुराः समग्राः ॥१०॥

They could not bear to enter the world of heaven seen after a long time, under the yoke of fear of the great demon, but all the gods lingered awhile. (10).

पुरो भव त्वं न पुरो भवामि नाहं पुरोगोऽस्मि पुरःसरस्त्वम् ।
इत्थं सुरास्तत्क्षणमेव भीताः स्वर्गं प्रवेष्टुं कलहं वितेनुः ॥११॥

All the gods, who were afraid of (Tāraka) quarelled among themselves thus, when entering the heaven: "Enter thou first, I am unable to enter", "No, you enter first." (11).

सुरालयालोकनकौतुकेन मुदा शुचिस्मेरविलोचनास्ते ।
दधुः कुमारस्य मुखारविन्दे दृष्टिं द्विषत्साध्वसकातरां ताम् ॥१२॥

They (gods) with their eyes lit up through a brilliant smile through joy, caused by looking at heaven, fixed their glances, filled with fright through fear of the enemy, on the lotus-like face of Kumāra. (12).

सहेलहासच्छुरिताननेन्दुस्ततः कुमारः पुरतो भविष्णुः ।
स तारकापातमपेक्षमाणो रणप्रवीरो हि सुरानवोचत् ॥१३॥

Then Kumāra, desiring to go ahead, his face brightened by a playful smile, spoiling for a fight with the demon; this hero in battle spoke to the gods. (13).

भीत्यालमद्य त्रिदिवौकसोऽमी स्वर्गं भवन्तः प्रविशन्तु सद्यः ।
अत्रैव मे दृक्पथमेतु शत्रुर्महासुरो यः खलु दृष्टपूर्वः ॥१४॥

"Have no fear all ye gods; may, you immediately enter heaven; let the great demon, that you have already seen, (come within my sight here). (14).

स्वर्लोकलक्ष्मीकचकर्षणाय दोर्मण्डलं वल्गति यस्य चण्डम् ।
इहैव तच्छोणितपानकेलिमह्नाय कुर्वन्तु शरा ममैते ॥१५॥

He, whose puissant arms are moving to drag the presiding deity of heaven by the hair, let these shafts of mine, immediately drink just here the blood of that demon. (15).

शक्तिर्ममासावहतप्रचारा प्रभावसारा सुमहःप्रसारा ।
स्वर्लोकलक्ष्म्या विपदापहारैः शिरो हरन्तो विदधातु मुदं वः ॥१६॥

Let my Śakti, whose power is irresistible, which is strong in its power, and which is all-sweeping in its might, give you joy by relieving the suffering of heaven's presiding deity and by lopping off the head of the demon Tāraka, the enemy." (16).

इत्यन्धकारातिसुतस्य दैत्यवधाय युद्धोत्सुकमानसस्य ।
सर्वं शुचिस्मेरमुखारविन्दं गीर्वाणवृन्दं वचसा ननन्द ॥१७॥

Having heard these words of the son of Śiva, the enemy of Andhaka, whose mind was eager to kill the demon, all the gods, with their lotus-like faces, irradiated by a smile, were filled with delight. (17).

सान्द्रप्रमोदात्पुलकोपगूढः सर्वाङ्गसंफुल्लसहस्रनेत्रः ।
तस्योत्तरीयेण निजाम्बरेण निरुञ्छनं चारु चकार शक्रः ॥१८॥

Indra embraced with horripilation due to intense joy and with his thousand eyes dialated all over his body, exchanged with him, (Kumāra) his fine upper garment. (18).

घनप्रमोदाश्रु तरंगिताक्षैर्मुखैश्चतुर्भिः प्रचुरप्रसादैः ।
पपौ प्रभुर्ब्रह्मचिराविवृद्धः षडाननं षट्सु शिरःसु चित्रम् ॥१९॥

The primeval old Brahman, his eyes welling up with tears of joy, with his four very serene mouths, touched the six heads of Kumāra. (19).

तं साधु साध्वित्यभितः प्रशस्य मुग्धा कुमारं त्रिपुरासुरारेः ।
प्रानन्दयन्वीर जयेति वाचा गन्धर्वविद्याधरसिद्धसंघाः ॥२०॥

Gandharvas, Vidyādharas and groups of Siddhas praised him loudly with the words "Bravo, Bravo", this son of Śiva and gladdened his heart. (20).

दिव्यर्षयः शत्रुविजेष्यमाणं तमभ्यनन्दन्किल नारदाद्याः ।
निरुञ्छनं चक्रुरथोत्तरीयैश्चामीकरीयैर्निजवल्कलैश्च ॥२१॥

Divine sages like Nārada and others congratulated him

upon his success over his enemy, and exchanged their barks with his gold-woven upper garment. (21).

ततः सुराः शक्तिधरस्य तस्यावष्टम्भतः साध्वसमुत्सृजन्तः ।
उत्सेहिरे स्वर्गमनन्तशक्तेर्गन्तुं वनं यूथपतेरिवेभाः ॥२२॥

Then the gods, giving up their fear with the support of the mighty hero, the wielder of Śakti, were emboldened to enter the heaven, as the elephants, through the support of mighty hero, (are emboldened) to enter the forest. (22).

अथाभिपृष्ठं गिरिजासुतस्य पुरंदरारातिवधं चिकीर्षोः ।
सुरा निरीयुस्त्रिपुरं दिधक्षोरिव स्मरारेः प्रमथाः समन्तात् ॥२३॥

Then the gods stood behind the back of the son of Girijā, desirous to kill the enemy of Indra, like the Pramathas, of Lord Śiva, desirous of burning Tripura. (23).

सुराङ्गनानां जलकेलिभाजां प्रक्षालितैः संततमङ्गरागैः ।
प्रपेदिरे पिञ्जरवारिपूरां स्वर्गौकसः स्वर्गधुनीं पुरस्तात् ॥२४॥

By the unguents from the bodies of the wives of the gods, who were indulging in a plunge in the waters of the river of the gods, the river ahead was filled with yellow colour. (24).

दिग्दन्तिनां वारिविहारभाजां कराहतैर्भीमतरैस्तरंगैः ।
आप्लावयन्तीं मुहुरालवालश्रेणीं तरूणां निजतीरजानाम् ॥२५॥

(The river) who was flooding a series of basins of the

trees on her banks, with the mighty waves lashed up by the trunks of the quarter-elephants at play in her waters. (25).

लीलारसाभिः सुरकन्यकाभिर्हिरण्मयीभिः सिकताभिरुच्चैः ।
माणिक्यगर्भाभिरुपाहिताभिः प्रकीर्णतीरां वरवेदिकाभिः ॥२६॥

(The river) whose banks had high platforms of golden sand, studded with rubies, constructed by the daughters of the gods in their ardour for sport. (26).

सौरभ्यलुब्धभ्रमरोपगीतैर्हिरण्यहंसावलिकेलिलोलैः ।
चामीकरीयैः कमलैर्विनिद्रैश्च्युतैः परागैः परिपिङ्गतोयाम् ॥२७॥

(The river) whose waters were yellowish, with the pollen of the blooming golden lotuses, garrulous with the murmur of bees which coveted their fragrance and shaken by flights of golden swans, in their play. (27),

कुतूहलाद्द्रष्टुमुपागताभिस्तीरस्थिताभिः सुरसुन्दरीभिः ।
अम्भूर्मिराजि प्रतिबिम्बिताभिर्मुदं दिशन्तीं व्रजतां जनानाम् ॥२८॥

(The river was) giving joy to the people, passing about, by the reflections in her serried waves, of nymphs, standing on her banks, drawn there by curiosity. (28).

ननन्द सद्यश्चिरकालदृष्टां विलोक्य शक्रः सुरदीर्घिकां ताम् ।
अवर्णयत्सावरमद्रिपुत्रीमहेशपुत्राय ततः पुरोगः ॥२९॥

Indra was delighted instantly on seeing the divine river, seen after a long time; then going ahead, showed her respectfully to the son of the daughter of the mountain. (29).

स कार्त्तिकेयः पुरतः परीतः सुरैः समस्तैः सुरनिम्नगां ताम् ।
अपूर्वदृष्टामवलोकमानः सविस्मयः स्मेरविलोचनोऽभूत् ॥३०॥

Kārttikeya, surrounded by all the gods, on seeing the divine river, not seen before, was filled with wonder, and his face was lit up with a smile. (30).

उपेत्य तां तत्र किरीटकोटिन्यस्ताञ्जलिर्भक्तिपरः कुमारः ।
गीर्वाणवृन्दैः प्रणुतां प्रणुत्य नम्रेण मूर्ध्ना मुदितो ववन्दे ॥३१॥

Going near her, Kumāra, who was full of devotion, putting his folded hands upon the edge of his coronet, praised the river, praised by the gods, and bowed to her with a bent head and was filled with joy. (31).

प्रनर्तितस्मेरसरोजराजिः पुरः परीरम्भमिलन्महोर्मिः ।
कपोलपालिश्रमवारिहारि भेजे गुहं तं सरितः समीरः ॥३२॥

Kārttikeya, then enjoyed the breeze from the river, making the series of lotuses wearing the bloom of a smile and swirling together great waves ahead of it, and removing the fatigue from the edges of the cheeks. (32).

ततो व्रजन्नन्दननामधेयं लीलावनं जम्भजितः पुरस्तात् ।
विभिन्नभग्नोद्धृतशालसंघं प्रेक्षांचकार स्मरशत्रुसूनुः ॥३३॥

Then the son of the enemy of Smara, going to Nandana, the pleasure-garden of Indra, saw it with the Sāla groves, riddled with holes by shafts and uprooted. (33).

सुरद्विषोपप्लुतमेवमेतद्वनं बलस्य द्विषतो गतश्रि ।
इत्थं विचिन्त्यारुणलोचनोऽभूद्भ्रूभङ्गदुष्प्रेक्ष्यमुखः स कोपात् ॥३४॥

Reflecting that the garden of Indra was devastated by the demons, the enemies of the gods, and had lost its glory, his eyes flared up scarlet, and a frown being formed on his brows, his face was terrible to look at. (34).

निर्लूनलीलोपवनामपश्यद्दुःसंचरीभूतविमानमार्गाम् ।
विध्वस्तसौधप्रचयां कुमारो विश्वेकसाराममरावतीं सः ॥३५॥

Then he saw the city of Āmarāvatī, the jewel of the worlds where the paths of the aerial cars were difficult to traverse, where the line of palaces was razed to the ground. (35).

गतश्रियं वैरिवराभिभूतां वशां सुदीनामभितो वधानाम् ।
नारीमवीरामिव तामवेक्ष्य स बाढमन्तः करुणापरोऽभूत् ॥३६॥

At the sight of the city of Amarāvatī, overwhelmed by the formidable enemy, and wearing a gloomy aspect like a woman whose husband is impotent, his heart was, indeed, touched with a deep tenderness. (36.).

कुध्रे स्थिते देवरिपौ सरोषस्तस्याविषण्णः समराय चोत्कः ।
तथाविधां तां स विवेश पश्यन्सुरैः सुराधीश्वरराजधानीम् ॥३७॥

Then Kumāra, wrathful on account of the misdeeds of the demon and ready and eager for the fight with the demon, accompanied by the gods, entered the capital of Indra which was in that sad plight. (37).

दैतेयदन्तावलदन्तघातैः क्षुण्णान्तराः स्फाटिकहर्म्यपंक्तीः ।
महाहिनिर्मोकपिनद्धजालाः स वीक्ष्य तस्यां विषसाद सद्यः ॥३८॥

He was instantly saddeded at sight of the crystal palaces, with their interior shattered by the butting of the tusks of the elephants of the demons, and whose lattices were bound by the sloughs of huge pythons. (38).

उत्कीर्णचामीकरपङ्कजानां दिग्दन्तिदानद्रवदूषितानाम् ।
हिरण्यहंसव्रजवर्जितानां विदीर्णवैदूर्यमहाशिलानाम् ॥३९॥

प्राविर्भवद्बालतृणाञ्चितानां तदीयलीलागृहदीर्घिकाणाम् ।
स दुर्दशां वीक्ष्य विरोधिजातां विषादवैलक्ष्यभरं बभार ॥४०॥

He bore the burden of misery at sight of Indra's pleasure-ponds, in his pleasure-houses, devastated by the enemies, whose (ponds) margins were strewn with sprouting fresh grass, whose golden lotuses were uprooted, and were soiled by the rut of the quarter-elephants, and which were abandoned by the golden swans, whose huge sapphire-slabs were smashed to smithereens. (39-40).

तद्दन्तिदन्तक्षतहेमभित्ति सुतन्तुजालाकुलरत्नजालाम् ।
निन्ये सुरेन्द्रेण पुरोगतेन स वैजयन्ताभिधमात्मसौधम् ॥४१॥

Kumāra was led by Indra to Vaijayant, his palace, whose gold-plastered walls were smashed by the tusks of the enemies' elephants, whose strings of gems were enveloped in cob-webs. (41).

निर्विघ्नवर्त्मा विबुधेश्वरेण सुरैः समग्रैरनुगम्यमानः ।
स प्राविशत्तं विविधाश्मरश्मिच्छिन्नेन सोपानपथेन सौधम् ॥४२॥

He (Kumāra) was led by him (Indra) into that palace by way of the stairway, whose many-coloured gems were prized out by the enemies, and he (Kumāra) was followed by all the gods. (42).

निसर्गकल्पद्रुमतोरणं तं स पारिजातप्रसवस्रगाढ्यम् ।
विप्रैः कृतस्वस्त्ययनं मुनीन्द्रैरन्तःप्रविष्टप्रमदं प्रपेदे ॥४३॥

Kumāra, then, reached the palace, where wish-yielding trees naturally formed the archway; which (palace) was festooned with leaves and flowers of the Pārijāta tree; which was blessed with auspicious reading by the great divine sages; and wherein (celestial) ladies had already entered. (43).

पादौ महर्षेः किल कश्यपस्य कुलाविवृद्धस्य सुरासुराणाम् ।
प्रदक्षिणीकृत्य कृताञ्जलिः सन्षड्भिः शिरोभिः स नतैर्ववन्दे ॥४४॥

He perambulated round the feet of Kāśyapa, the progenitor of the races of gods and the demons, and folding his hands in worship, bowed to him low with all his six heads bent. (44).

स देवमातुर्जगदेकवन्द्यौ पादौ तथैव प्रणनाम कामम् ।
मुनेः कलत्रस्य च तस्य भक्त्या प्रह्वीभवञ्शैलसुतातनूजः ॥४५॥

He bowed to the feet of the gods' mother, the spouse of the Muni, the object of worship of the world, bending in devotion before them. (45).

स कश्यपः सा जननी सुराणां तमेवयामासतुराशिषा द्वौ ।
तया यया नैकजगज्जिगीषु र्जेता मृधे तारकमुग्रवीर्यम् ॥४६॥

Kāśyapa and the mother of the gods, blessed him with good fortune; and through their blessings, he would be enabled to vanquish Tāraka the conqueror of the three worlds. (46).

स्वदर्शनार्थं समुपेयुषीणां सुदेवतानामदितिश्रितानाम् ।
पादौ ववन्दे पतिदेवतास्तमाशीर्वचोभिः पुनरभ्यनन्दन् ॥४७॥

He bowed to the feet of the goddesses, who resorted to the feet of Aditi; and who had come to see him; and the devoted wives wished him well by blessing him. (47).

पुलोमपुत्रीं विबुधाधिभर्तुस्ततः शची नाम कलत्रमेषः ।
नमश्चकार स्मरशत्रुसूनुस्तमाशिषा सा समुपाचरच्च ॥४८॥

Kumāra, the son of Smara's enemy bowed to Śaci, the the daughter of Puloma, and the wife of Indra, and she greeted him with her blessings. (48).

अथादितीन्द्रप्रमदाः समेतास्ता मातरः सप्त घनप्रमोदाः ।
उपेत्य भक्त्या नमते महेशपुत्राय तस्मै ददुराशिषः प्राक् ॥४९॥

Now, Aditi, and other ladies together with the seven mothers, full of intense joy, approached the son of Maheśa, and greeted him with blessings as he bowed to them. (49).

समेत्य सर्वेऽपि मुदं दधाना महेन्द्रमुख्यास्त्रिदिवौकसोऽथ ।
आनन्दकल्लोलितमानसं तं समभ्यषिञ्चन्पृतनाधिपत्ये ॥५०॥

All the gods, headed by Indra, met together and were full of joy; and their minds were rippling with joy, like the Mānasa lake undulating with waves, they invested him with the office of the commander-in-chief. (50).

All the gods, whose grief was wholly wiped out, entertained hopes of victory over the enemy and found an opportunity for battle, as the son of Hara, of unlimited prowess, attained the full glory of the godly hosts. (51).

सकलविबुधलोकः स्रस्तनिःशेषशोकः
कृतरिपुविजयाशः प्राप्तयुद्धावकाशः ।
अजनि हरसुतेनानन्तवीर्येण तेना-
खिलविबुधचमूनां प्राप्य लक्ष्मीमनूनाम् ॥५१॥

चतुर्दशः सर्गः

रणोत्सुकेनान्धकशत्रुसूनुना समं प्रयुक्तैस्त्रिदशैर्जिगीषुणा ।
महासुरं तारकसंज्ञकं द्विषं प्रसह्य हन्तुं समनह्यत द्रुतम् ॥१॥

Egged on by the conquering son of the enemy of Andhaka, all together quickly girded up their loins, to kill forcibly their enemy, the great demon Tāraka. (1).

स दुर्निवारं मनसोऽतिवेगिनं जयश्रियः संनयनं सुदुःसहम् ।
विजित्वरं नाम तदा महारथं धनुर्धरः शक्तिधरोऽध्यरोहयत् ॥२॥

He, arming himself with a bow and Śakti, climbed into his chariot Vijitvara by name, which was irresistible and swifter than the mind, and unbearable in its onset, and bringing the glory of battle. (2).

सुरालयश्रीविपदां निवारणं सुरारिसंपत्परितापकारणम् ।
केनापि वध्रेऽस्य विरोधिवारणं सुचारु चामीकरघर्मवारणम् ॥३॥

There was held on his head by some one, a beautiful

golden umbrella, which warded off the distress of the glory of heaven, which was the cause of the sorrow of the fortune of the enemy of the gods and which tore the opponents to pieces. (3).

शरज्ज्वरज्ज्वन्द्रमरीचिपाण्डुरैः स वीज्यमानो वरचारुचामरैः ।
पुरःसरैः किंनरसिद्धचारणैः रणेच्छुरस्तूयत वाग्भिरुल्बणैः ॥४॥

By the Kinnaras, the Siddhās, and the Cāraṇas, who drew themselves before him were waved the chowries, white like moon-beams, over him, who was extolled by them with high-sounding phrases and who was eager for battle. (4).

प्रयाणकालोचितचारुवेषभृद्वज्रं वहन्पर्वतपक्षदारणम् ।
ऐरावतं स्फाटिकशैलसोदरं ततोऽधिरुह्य द्युपतिस्तमन्वगात् ॥५॥

He was followed by Indra, dressed suitably for moving out, wielding his thunderbolt that lopped the wings of mountains, mounting on his Airāvata who was like a crystal mountain. (5).

तमन्वगच्छद्गिरिशृङ्गसोदरं मदोद्धतं मेषमधिष्ठितः शिखी ।
विरोधिविद्वेषरुषाधिकं ज्वलन्महोमहीयस्तरमायुधं दधत् ॥६॥

He was followed by Agni, mounting a goat, huge as a mountain-peak, and overbearing with conceit, and who was wielding a weapon flaming. (6).

अथेन्द्रनीलाचलचण्डविग्रहं विषाणविध्वस्तमहापयोधरम् ।
अधिष्ठितः कासरमुद्धतं मुदा वैवस्वतो दण्डधरस्तमन्वगात् ॥७॥

Yama, the chastiser, gladly mounted his fearsome

buffalo, whose body was huge and fearsome as a mountain of sapphire that had split the big clouds with his horns. (7).

मदोद्धतं प्रेतमथाधिरूढवांस्तमन्वकर्द्धे षितनूजमन्वगात् ।
महासुरद्वेषविशेषभीषणः सुरोषणश्चण्डरणाय नैर्ऋतः ॥८॥

Then a very Nairṛta (Rākṣasa), mounting a Piśāca, over-bearing with conceit, very fearsome owing to his hatred of the great demon Tāraka, followed Kumāra, for a fierce struggle. (8).

नवोद्यदम्भोधरघोरदर्शने युद्धाय रूढो मकरे महत्तरे ।
दुर्वारपाशो वरुणो रणोल्बणस्तमन्वियाय त्रिपुरान्तकात्मजम् ॥९॥

Then Varuṇa, with his infallible noose, formidable in battle, mounted a huge alligator who looked formidable like a rising cloud and followed that son of the enemy of Tripura. (9).

विगम्बराधिक्रमणोल्बणं क्षणान्मृगं महीयांसमरुद्धविक्रमम् ।
अधिष्ठितः सगरकेलिलालसो मरुन्महेशात्मजमन्वगाद्द्रुतम् ॥१०॥

Fierce in his onset, like God Śiva, the god of wind mounted a deer, fleet of foot, unsurpassable in traversing, spoiling for a fight, and quickly followed the son of Maheśa. (10).

विरोधिनां शोणितपारणैषिणीं गदामनूनां नरवाहनो वहन् ।
महाहवाम्भोधिविगाहनोद्धतं यियासुमन्वागमदीशनन्दनम् ॥११॥

Kubera, carrying a huge club, desiring its glut of the enemies' blood, followed the son of Īśa, eager to plunge into the great cream of battle. (11).

महाहिनिबद्धजटाकलापिनो ज्वलत्त्रिशूलप्रबलायुधा युधे ।
रुद्रास्तुषाराद्रिसखं महावृषं ततोऽधिरूढास्तमयुः पिनाकिनः ॥१२॥

The Rudras, mounted on bulls resembling the snow-mountain, and their matted locks bound by coils of large serpents, and armed with Pināka bows, and wielding flaming tridents in their hands, followed him in the great battle. (12).

अन्येऽपि संनह्य महारणोत्सवश्रद्धालवः स्वर्गिगणास्तमन्वयुः ।
स्ववाहनानि प्रबलान्यधिष्ठिताः प्रमोदविस्मेरमुखाम्बुजश्रियः ॥१३॥

Other gods, too, girding up their loins, having great faith in battle, riding their strong mounts, with the beauty of their lotus-like faces, irradiated by smiles of delight, followed him. (13).

उद्दण्डहेमध्वजदण्डसंकुलाश्चञ्चद्विचित्रातपवारणोज्ज्वलाः ।
चलद्रूघनस्यन्दनघोषभीषणाः करीन्द्रघण्टारवचण्डचीत्कृताः ॥१४॥

स्फुरद्विचित्रायुधकान्तिमण्डलं रद्द्योतिताशावलयाम्बरान्तराः ।
दिवौकसां सोऽनुवहन्महाचमूः पिनाकपाणेस्तनयस्ततो ययौ ॥१५॥

Then the son of the Pināka-wielder, leading the godly hosts, full of golden flags, with tall staves, bright with umbrellas, shining and of a variety of colours, frightening with the loud sound of chariots, as of the rumble of mountains, and full of the tinkling of bells of great elephants, and of their fearsome trumpetings, filling the spaces of the sky, between the circles of quarters, by the circle of the flashing light of the different weapons, was followed by them. (14-15).

कोलाहलेनोच्चलतां दिवौकसां महाचमूनां गुरुभिर्ध्वजव्रजैः ।
घनैर्निरुच्छ्वासमभूदनन्तरं दिङ्मण्डलं व्योमतलं महीतलम् ॥१६॥

As the numerous godly hosts moved on with great noise, the circle of the quarters, the earth and the heavens lost all difference and became breathless owing to the great multitude of flags. (16).

सुरारिलक्ष्मीपरिकम्पहेतवो दिक्चक्रवालप्रतिनादमेदुराः ।
नभोन्तकुक्षिंभरयो घनाः स्वनां निहन्यमानैः पटहैर्वितेनिरे ॥१७॥

The drums, when beaten, produced a sound that filled the hollows of the sky augmented by the reverberations in the circle of quarters, that made the glory of the demons quake through fright. (17).

प्रमथ्यमानाम्बुधिगर्जितर्जनैः सुरारिनारीगणगर्भपातनैः ।
नभश्चमूधूलिकुलैरिवाकुलं ररास गाढं पटहप्रतिस्वनैः ॥१८॥

By the echoes of the loud sound of the drums, that brought about miscarriages of the wives of the demons, surpassing the rumble of the ocean as it was being churned, the sky was filled with clouds of dust, and seemed to wail loudly. (18).

क्षुण्णं रथैर्वाजिभिराहतं खुरैः करीन्द्रकर्णैः परितः प्रसारितम् ।
धूतं ध्वजैः काञ्चनशैलजं रजो वातैर्हृतं व्योम समारुहत्क्रमात् ॥१९॥

The dust of the mountain of gold, trodden by the wheels of the chariots, kicked up by the hooves of the horses, gradually rose into the sky. (19).

खातं खुरै रथ्यतुरंगपुंगवै रुपत्यकाहाटकमेदिनीरजः ।
गतं दिगन्तान्मुखरैः समीरणैः सुविभ्रमं भूरि बभार भूयसा ॥२०॥

The dust of the golden foot-hills, beaten up by hooves of chariot-horses, was carried to the ends of the quarters by the howling winds, where it bore a peculiar charm. (20).

अधस्तयोर्ध्वं पुरतोऽथ पृष्ठतोऽभितोऽपि चामीकररेणु रुच्चकैः ।
चमूषु सर्पन्मरुदाहतोऽहरन्नवीनसूर्यस्य च कान्ति संभवम् ॥२१॥

The golden dust, dispersed by the wind, below and above, before and ahead of the army, surpassed the abundance of the splendour of the morning sun. (21).

बलोद्धतं काञ्चनभूमिजं रजो बभौ दिगन्तेषु नभःस्थले स्थितम् ।
अकालसंध्याघनरागपिङ्गलं घनं घनानामिव वृन्दमुद्यतम् ॥२२॥

The dust raised by the army from the golden ground in the ends of the quarters, as it was hanging in the sky, like a bank of clouds risen in the sky, was tawny owing to the profuse glow of untimely twilight. (22).

हेमावनीषु प्रतिबिम्बमात्मनो मुहुर्विलोक्याभिमुखं महागजाः ।
रसातलोत्तीर्णगजभ्रमात्क्रुधा दन्तप्रकाण्डप्रहृतानि तेनिरे ॥२३॥

Big elephants seeing their reflections in the golden floor, thinking that they were (rival) elephants sprung from the nether regions, angrily struck them with their staff-like tusks. (23).

सुजातसिन्दूरपरागपिञ्जरैः कलं चलद्भिः सुरसैन्यसिन्धुरैः ।
शुद्धासु चामीकरशैलभूमिषु नादृश्यत स्वं प्रतिबिम्बमग्रतः ॥२४॥

The elephants in the armies of the gods, as they moved gracefully, were tawny with the particles of the excellent vermilion dye and were not able to notice reflections in the clean floor of gold before them. (24).

इति क्रमेणामरराजवाहिनी महाहवाम्भोधिविलासलालसा ।
अयातरत्काञ्चनशैलतो द्रुतं कोलाहलाक्रान्तविधूतकन्दरा ॥२५॥

Thus gradually Indra's army desirous of sporting in the ocean of a great battle, shaking the caves with their loud rullabaloo quickly descended from the golden mountain (Meru). (25).

महाचमूस्यन्दनचण्डचीत्कृतैर्विलोलघण्टेभपतेश्च बृंहितैः ।
सुरेन्द्रशैलेन्द्रमहागुहाशयाः सिंहा महत्स्वप्नसुखं न तत्यजुः ॥२६॥

The lions in the caves of mount Meru gave up their dreams of enjoying sound sleep, being disturbed by the loud sound of the rumbling of the chariots in the great army, and by the trumpetings of the elephants which had bells dangling from their bodies. (26).

गम्भीरभेरिध्वनितैर्भयंकरैर्महागुहान्तप्रतिनादमेदुरैः ।
महारथानां गुरुनेमिनिःस्वनैरनाकुलैस्तैर्मृगराजताऽजनि ॥२७॥

The lions were rightly lords of beasts, since they were unperturbed by the deep reverberations, augmented inside the deep caverns, of the profound rumblings of the drums, and by the sound of the wheels of the great chariots. (27).

समुत्थितेन त्रिदिवौकसां महाचमूरवेणाद्रितटान्तदारिणा ।
प्रपेदिरे केसरिणोऽधिकं मदं स्ववीर्यलक्ष्मीमृगराजतावशात् ॥२८॥

By the noise of the numerous godly hosts, that tore up the mountain-spoors, the lions became more conceited by their lordship of beasts, which was endowed with glory of their own heroism. (28).

भिया सुरानीकविमर्दजन्मना विदुद्रुवुर्दूरतरं द्रुतं मृगाः ।
गुहागृहान्ताद्बहिरेत्य हेलया तस्थुर्विशङ्कं नितरां मृगाधिपाः ॥२९॥

The deer were frightened by the tumultuous noise of the godly hosts and ran to a great distance, and the lions, all of a sudden, left the interior of the caves and boldly stood out. (29).

विलोकिताः कौतुकिनाऽमरावतीजनेन जुष्टप्रमदेन दूरतः ।
सुराचलप्रान्तभुवः प्रपेदिरे सुविस्तृतायाः प्रसरं सुसैनिकाः ॥३०॥

The inhabitants of Indra's capital together with their wives, saw the soldiers descended to the extensive regions of the foot-hills of the mountain of the gods. (30).

पीतासितारक्तसितैः सुराचलप्रान्तस्थितैर्धातुरजोभिरम्बरम् ।
अयत्नगन्धर्वपुरोदयभ्रमं बभार भूम्नोत्पतितैरितस्ततः ॥३१॥

The sky easily bore the illusion of the city of the

Gandharvas with the dust of minerals of the Sumeru,—black, yellow, red and white,—that was blown about all round. (31).

महास्वनः सैन्यविमर्दसंभवः कर्णान्तकूलंकषतामुपेयिवान् ।
पयोनिधेः क्षुब्धतरस्य वर्धनो बभूव भूम्ना भुवनोदरंभरिः ॥३२॥

The great noise engendered by the crush of the loud army, split the hollows of the ears, and filling the hollows of the world, made the waters of the ocean swirl up to a great height. (32).

महागजानां गुरुबृंहितैस्ततैः सुहेषितैर्घोरतरैश्च वाजिनाम् ।
घनै रथानां गुरुचण्डचीत्कृतैस्तिरोहितोऽभूत्पटहस्य निःस्वनः ॥३३॥

The sound of the drums was muffled by the trumpetings of the great elephants, and by the very loud neighings of the horses, and by the loud rumbling noise of the chariots. (33).

महासुराणामवरोधयोषितां कचाक्षिपक्ष्मस्तनमण्डलेषु च ।
ध्वजेषु नागेषु रथेषु वाजिषु क्षणेन तस्थौ सुरसैन्यजं रजः ॥३४॥

The dust, kicked up by the godly hosts, settled for a while on the hair, the eyelashes and the nipples of the orbed breasts of the wives of great Asuras and on the flags, the elephants, the chariots, and the horses. (34).

घनैर्विलोक्य स्थगितार्कमण्डलं भ्रमूरजोभिर्निचितं नभःस्थलम् ।
प्रयायि हंसैरभिमानसं घनभ्रमेण सानन्दमनर्ति केकिभिः ॥३५॥

The swans seeing the sky pervaded by the dust, kicked

up by the army, covering the sky, and obscuring the sun's orb, started to go to the Mānasa lake, and the peacocks danced with delight, under the illusion that it was a cloud. (35).

सान्द्रैः सुरानीकरजोभिरम्बरे नवाम्बुदानीकनिभैरभिश्रिते ।
चकाशिरे स्वर्णमया महाध्वजाः परिस्फुरन्तस्तडितां गणा इव ।।३६।।

When the thick clouds of dust, raised by the godly hosts, pervaded the sky, like banks of clouds, the great golden flags flashed all round, like multitudinous lightning. (36).

विलोक्य धूलीपटलैर्भृशं भृतं द्यावापृथिव्योरलमन्तरं महत् ।
किमूर्ध्वतोऽधः किमधस्त ऊर्ध्वतो रजोऽभ्युपैतीति जनैरतर्क्यत ।।३७।।

Seeing the great interspace between the earth and the sky, fully pervaded by clouds of dust, the people wondered whether the dust rose from the earth to the sky or fell from the sky to the earth. (37).

नोर्ध्वं न चाधो न पुरो न पृष्ठतो न पार्श्वतोऽभूत्खलु चक्षुषोर्गतिः ।
सूच्यग्रभेद्यैः पृतनारजश्चयैराच्छादिता प्राणिगणस्य सर्वतः ।।३८।।

The cloud of dust, raised by the army, was so thick that it could be penetrated by the point of a needle, so that the sight of all living beings could reach neither above, nor behind, nor ahead, nor to the back, nor to the sides. (38).

दिगन्तदन्तावलदाननहारिभिर्विमानरन्ध्रप्रतिनादमेदुरैः ।
अनेकधावाद्यध्वनितैरनारतैर्जगर्ज गाढं गुरुभिर्नभस्तलम् ।।३९।।

By the uninterrupted sound of musical instruments, that dried up the ichor of many an elephant in the numerous directions, and augmented by echoes in the hollows of aerial cars, the sky sounded deeply. (39).

भुवं विगाह्य प्रययो महाचमूः क्वचिन्न मान्ती महतीं दिवं खलु ।
सुसंकुलायामपि तत्र निर्भरात्किंकर्तव्यतामवाप नाकुला ॥४०॥

The great army covered the earth, and not contained therein, went to the heavens, and there, through its weight, it became confused and did not know what to do. (40).

उद्दामदानद्विपवृन्दबृंहितैर्नितान्तमुत्तुङ्गतुरंगहेषितैः ।
चलद्घनस्यन्दननेमिनिःस्वनैरभून्निरुच्छ्वासमिवाकुलं जगत् ॥४१॥

The world seemed to have lost its breath, owing to the trumpetings of the elephants dripping with profuse ichor, and by the loud neighings of the very tall stallions, and by the rumbling sound of the chariots on the move as of the clouds scudding before the wind. (41).

महागजानां गुरुभिस्तु गर्जितैर्विलोलघण्टारणितै रणोल्बणैः ।
वीरप्रणादैः प्रमदप्रमेदुरैर्वाचालतामादधिरे तरां दिशः ॥४२॥

The quarters were extremely garrulous by the loud trumpetings of the great elephants, and by the janglings of the dangling bells, and by the loud war-cries of the warriors, full of joy and delight. (42).

दन्तीन्द्रदानद्रववारिवीचिभिः सद्योऽपि नद्यो बहुधा पुपूरिरे ।
धारा रजोभिस्तुरगैः क्षतैर्भुवं ता याः पङ्कतामेत्य रथैः स्थलीकृताः ॥४३॥

By the rippling waves of the water of the ichor of huge tuskers, the rivers were flooded; and the rivers that were filled with the dust, pounded by the hooves of the horses, became full of clammy mud, which was turned into solid ground by the wheels of the chariots. (43).

निम्नाः प्रदेशाः स्थलतामुपानमन्निम्नत्वमुच्चैरपि सर्वतश्च ते ।
तुरंगमाणां व्रजतां खुरैः क्षता रथैर्गजेन्द्रैः परितः समीकृताः ॥४४॥

Low lands became level, and high lands became low all round being trodden by hooves of moving horses, and made level by the movements of the horses and the chariots. (44).

नभोदिगन्तप्रतिघोषभीषणैर्महामहीभृत्तटदारणोल्बणैः ।
पयोधिनिर्घूननकेलिभिर्जगद्बभूव भेरीध्वनितैः समाकुलम् ॥४५॥

The world was full of turmoil by the sound of instruments, that delighted in the sport of stirring the ocean, frightening by the echoes in the ends of the quarters of the sky, and strong in rending the spoors of great mountains. (45).

इतस्ततो वातविधूतचञ्चलैर्निरन्ध्रिताशागमनैर्ध्वजांशुकैः ।
लक्षैः क्वणत्काञ्चनकिङ्किणीकुलैरमज्जि धूलीजलधौ नभोगते ॥४६॥

A lac of flags, which were flitting about, as they were shaken by the wind, making it impossible to move in the quarters with strings of tinkling golden bells attached to them, plunged in the ocean of dust. (46).

घण्टारवं रौद्रतरैर्निरन्तरं विसृत्वरैर्गर्जरवैः सुभैरवैः ।
मत्तद्विपानां प्रथयांबभूविरे न वाहिनीनां पटहस्य निःस्वनाः ॥४७॥

By the constant dreadful clangour of the bells, and by the spreading and very frightful trumpetings of wild elephants, the sound of the drums in the army was drowned. (47).

करालवाचालमुखाभ्रमूस्वनैर्ध्वस्ताम्बरा वीक्ष्य दिशो रजस्वलाः ।
तिरोबभूवे गहनैर्विनेश्वरो रजोन्धकारैः परितः कुतोऽप्यसौ ॥४८॥

The sun disappeared somewhere in the mass of dust, seeing the quarters soiled by dust whose openings were dreadfully sounding and where the sky was lost in the tumult of the army. (48).

आक्रान्तपूर्वा रभसेन सैनिकैर्दिगङ्गना व्योम रजोभिदूषिता ।
भेरीरवाणां प्रतिशब्दितैर्गजैर्जगर्ज गाढं घनमत्सरादिव ॥४९॥

The sky sounded deeply and the ladies of the quarters were forcibly molested by the soldiers; and by the echoes of the sounding drums, it sounded deeply as through deep envy. (49).

गुरुसमीरसमीरितभूधरा इव गजा गगनं विजगाहिरे ।
गुरुतरा इव वारिधरा रथा भुवमितोह विवर्त इवाभवत् ॥५०॥

The elephants, like mountains, swirled up by stormy winds, dived into the skies, and the chariots, like huge clouds, rushed on the earth, and there was an alteration in condition of state. (50).

बलमवसुरलोकानल्पकल्पान्तकाले
निरवधय इवाम्भोराशयो घोरघोषाः ।

गुरुतरपरिमज्जद्भूभृतो देवसेना
ववृधुरपि सुपूर्णा व्योमभूम्यन्तराले ॥५१॥

The big mountains, and the numerous godly hosts diving deeply into the interspaces of the sky and the earth, although full, yet grew, like boundless oceans, in the short time of the end of an aeon, of the powerful world of gods. (51).

पञ्चदशः सर्गः

सेनापतिं नन्दनमन्धकद्विषो युधे पुरस्कृत्य बलस्य शात्रवः ।
सैन्यैरुपैतीति सुरद्विषां पुरोऽभूत्किंवदन्ती हृदयप्रकम्पिनी ॥१॥

That Indra, the enemy of the demon Bala, putting at the van of battle, the son of the enemy of Andhaka, is coming with his armies; this news, that made the hearts tremble, was heard by the Asuras. (1).

चमूप्रभुं मन्मथमर्दनात्मजं विजित्वरीभिर्विजयश्रियाश्रितम् ।
श्रुत्वा सुराणां पृतनाभिरागतं चित्ते चिरं चुक्षुभिरे महासुराः ॥२॥

The great demons were for a long time agitated in their minds, as they heard that the son of the killer of Manmatha, as the commander, was leading the conquering godly hosts attended by the goddess of victory, against them. (2).

समेत्य दैत्याधिपतेः पुरे स्थिताः किरीटबद्धाञ्जलयः प्रणम्य ते ।
न्यवेदयन्मन्मथशत्रुसूनुना युयुत्सुना जम्भजितं सहागतम् ॥३॥

The great demons coming together in the city of Tāraka folded their hands upon their coronets, and bowing, reported that Kumāra, desiring fight had come with Indra. (3).

दासीकृताशेषजगत्त्रयं न मां जिगाय युद्धे कतिशः शचीपतिः ।
गिरीशपुत्रस्य बलेन सांप्रतं ध्रुवं विजेतेति स काकुतोऽहसत् ।।४।।

How many times has Indra conquered me—the conqueror of the three worlds and he is sure to conquer me with the army of the son of Girīśa, so he laughed ironically. (4).

ततः क्रुधा विस्फुरिताधरः सन् स तारको दर्पितदोर्बलोद्धतान् ।
युधे त्रिलोकीजयकेलिलालसः सेनापतीन्संनहनार्थमाविशत् ।।५।।

Then in rage, his lower lip throbbing, the demon Tāraka, desirous of the sport of conquering the three worlds, ordered his commanders, inflated with pride of the strength of their puissant arms, to gird up their loins for battle. (5).

महाचमूनामधिपाः समन्ततः संनह्य सद्यः सुतरामुदायुधाः ।
तस्थुर्विनम्रक्षितिपालसंकुले तदङ्गणद्वारवरप्रकोष्ठके ।।६।।

The commanders of the great armies immediately lifting up their weapons and girding up their loins stood in the middle of the court-yard of his palace, where waited vassal kings in humble postures. (6).

स द्वारपालेन पुरः प्रदर्शितान्कृतानतीन्बाहुधरानधिष्ठितान् ।
महाहवाम्भोधिविधूननोद्धतान्ददर्श राजा पृतनाधिपान्बहून् ।।७।।

That king Tāraka saw many commanders of armies, who were announced by the porter as they stood before him in humble postures with puissant arms, ready to shake up boldly the ocean of the great battle. (7).

बली बलारातिबलातिशातनं दिग्दन्तिनादप्रघनाशनस्वनम् ।
महीधराम्भोधिमवारितक्रमं ययौ रथं घोरमथाधिरुह्य सः ॥८॥

The powerful warrior went forth climbing into a formidable chariot, whose movement could not be arrested by either mountain or ocean, which drowned the trumpetings of the quarters-elephants, and which brought about the attrition of the forces of Indra. (8).

युगक्षयक्षुब्धपयोधिनिःस्वनाश्चलत्पताकाकुलवारितातपाः ।
धरारजोग्रस्तदिगन्तभास्कराः पतिं प्रयान्तं पृतनास्तमन्वयुः ॥९॥

And the armies, kicking up a row, like the rumblings of the sea, agitated, at the end of an aeon, that warded off the heat by the waving flags, that obscured the ends of quarters and the sun by the dust of the earth, followed him, as he marched forth. (9).

चमूरजः प्राप दिगन्तदन्तिनां महासुरस्याभिसुरं प्रसर्पिणः ।
दन्तप्रकाण्डेषु सितेषु शुभ्रतां कुम्भेषु दानाम्बुघनेषु पङ्कताम् ॥१०॥

The dust raised by the army of the great Asura Tāraka that was marching against the gods, looked white on the long tusks of the quarter-elephants, and became clammy mud, on their temples thickly covered with ichor. (10).

महीभृतां कन्दरदारणोल्बणैस्तद्वाहिनीनां पटहस्वनैर्घनैः ।
उद्वेलिताश्चुक्षुभिरे महार्णवा नभःस्रवन्ती सहसाऽभ्यवर्धत ॥११॥

By the deep sound of his army-drums, that were loud enough to split the caves of mountains, swollen into floods, the great oceans were agitated and the river of the sky was in high flood. (11).

सुरारिनाथस्य महाचमूस्वनैर्विगाह्यमाना तुमुलैः सुरापगा ।
प्रत्युच्छ्रितैरूर्मिशतैश्च वारिभिरक्षालयन्नाकनिकेतनावलीम् ॥१२॥

The river of the gods, in which the great tumultuous armies of the great asura plunged, whose waters were swirled up by hundreds of waves, laved the rows of gods' palaces. (12).

अथ प्रयाणाभिमुखस्य नाकिनां द्विषः पुरस्तादशुभोपदेशिनी ।
अगाधदुःखाम्बुधिमध्यमज्जनं बभूव चोत्पातपरम्परा तदा ॥१३॥

And in front of the enemy of the gods, there occurred a series of evil portents that augured that he would be plunged into the ocean of misery. (13).

प्रागामिदैत्याशनकेलिकांक्षिणी कुपक्षिणां घोरतरा परम्परा ।
बधौ पदं व्योम्नि सुरारिवाहिनीरुपर्युपर्येत्य निवारितातपा: ॥१४॥

And flights of dreadful and evil birds, expecting a feast of the corpses of the demons rose high into the sky, without warding off the sun's heat. (14).

मुहुर्विभग्नातपवारणध्वजश्चलद्धराधूलिकलाकुलेक्षणः ।
धुताश्वमातङ्गमहारथाकरानवेक्षणोऽभूत्प्रसभं प्रभञ्जनः ॥१५॥

A stormy wind arose, which broke the banners that warded off the heat, that made it impossible for the eyes to see on account of the dust from the earth, making it impossible for men to see the numerous horses, the elephants and the great chariots, that were shaken by it. (15).

सद्यो विभिन्नाञ्जनपुञ्जतेजसो मुखैर्विषाग्नि विकिरन्त उच्चकैः ।
पुरः पथोऽतीत्य महाभुजंगमा भयंकराकारभृतो भृशं ययुः ॥१६॥

Great pythons of terrific forms, who were as lustrous as pounded antimony, hurling forth poisonous flames from their mouths, crossed the path ahead and frequently went along. (16).

मिलन्महाभीमभुजंगभीषणं प्रभुर्दिनानां परिवेषमादधौ ।
महासुरस्य द्विषतोऽतिमत्सरादिवान्तमासूचयितुं भयंकरः ॥१७॥

The lord of day (the sun) assumed a halo, dreadful as several huge serpents, meeting together as if to suggest the death of the enemy, the great Asura, and so was very frightening. (17).

त्विषामधीशस्य पुरोऽधिमण्डलं शिवाः समेताः परुषं ववाशिरे ।
सुरारिराजस्य रणान्तशोणितं प्रसह्य पातुं द्रुतमुत्सुका इव ॥१८॥

In the orb of the sun, female jackals, coming together ahead of it, cried rancorously, as if to drink forcibly, and quickly the blood of the Asura, as he fell on the battle-field. (18).

दिवापि तारास्तरलास्तरस्विनीः परापतन्तीः परितोऽथ वाहिनीः ।
विलोक्य लोको मनसा व्यचिन्तयत्प्राणव्ययान्तं व्यसनं सुरद्विषः ॥१९॥

And round the armies, even by day the people saw

the quivering stars falling with force, and thought that the end of the enemy of the gods was near. (19).

ज्वलद्भिरुच्चैरभितः प्रभाभरैरुद्भासिताशेषदिगन्तराम्बरम् ।
रवेण रौद्रेण हृदन्तदारणं पपात वज्रं नभसो निरम्बुदात् ॥२०॥

And there fell from a cloudless sky, a thunderbolt, illumining the sky around in all the quarters by highly flaming lustres, and rending the hearts, with its frightning noise. (20).

ज्वलद्भिरङ्गारचयैर्नभस्तलं ववर्ष गाढं सह शोणितास्थिभिः ।
धूमं ज्वलन्तो व्यसृजन्मुखै रजो दधुर्दिशो रासभकण्ठधूसरम् ॥२१॥

The sky rained down masses of burning cinders thickly together with bones and blood, and the quarters hurled flaming and smoke-like dust from the openings, of the colour of an asse's neck. (21).

निर्घातघोषो गिरिशृङ्गशातनो घनोऽम्बराशाकुहरोदरंभरिः ।
बभूव भूम्ना श्रुतिभित्तिभेदनः प्रकोपिकालार्जितगर्जितर्जनः ॥२२॥

The roar of lightning, threatening like the roar of the irate Yama, rending the peaks of mountains, and filling the inside of the hollows of the sky and quarters, greatly rent the walls of the ears. (22).

स्खलन्महीभं प्रपतत्तुरङ्गमं परस्पराश्लिष्टजनं समन्ततः ।
प्रक्षुभ्यदम्भोधिविभिन्नभूधराकुलं द्विषोऽभूदवनिप्रकम्पात् ॥२३॥

And through the quaking of the earth and the splitting of mountains by the agitating ocean, the army of the enemy had its horses falling and its soldiers rushing into each other, all round. (23).

ऊर्ध्वीकृतास्या रविबद्धदृष्टयः समेत्य सर्वे सुरविद्विषः पुरः ।
श्वानः स्वरेण श्रवणान्तशातिना मिथो रुदन्तः करुणेन निर्ययुः ॥२४॥

All dogs coming together and raising their heads towards the sun, bayed aloud with a loud sound so as to split the inside of the ear, and wept together and piteously slunk away before the enemy of the gods. (24).

अपीति पश्यन्परिणामदारुणां महत्तमां गाढमरिष्टसंततिम् ।
दुर्दैवदष्टो न खलु न्यवर्तत क्रुधा प्रयाणव्यवसायतोऽसुरः ॥२५॥

On seeing the very great series of ill-boding omens, bitten by ill-luck, the Asura did not in anger retreat from his endeavour of marching (against the enemy). (25).

अरिष्टमाशङ्क्य विपाकदारुणं निवार्यमाणोऽपि बुधैर्महासुरः ।
पुरः प्रतस्थे महतां वृथा भवेदसद्ग्रहान्धस्य हितोपदेशनम् ॥२६॥

Although fearing disaster, terrible in its effect and although dissuaded by the gods, he marched forth; the counsel of the great is lost upon those who are blinded by a thoughtless resolve. (26).

क्षितौ निरस्तं प्रतिकूलवायुना तदीयचामीकरधर्मवारणम् ।
रराज मृत्योरिव पारणाविधौ प्रकल्पितं हाटकभाजनं महत् ॥२७॥

And his golden umbrella, which shaded him from the sun, was flung on to the earth, by an adverse wind, and there shone as a big golden vessel to satisfy the hunger of the god of death. (27).

विजानता भाविशिरोनिकृंतनं प्रसभेन शोकादिव तस्य मौलिना ।
मुहुर्गलद्भिस्तरलैरलंतरामरोदि मुक्ताफलबाष्पबिन्दुभिः ॥२८॥

And his wise coronet, anticipating the imminent lopping of Tāraka's head, wept bitterly as through sorrow, with tears in the form of quick-dropping pearls. (28).

निवार्यमाणैरभितोऽनुयायिभिर्गृहीतुकामैरिव तं मुहुर्मुहुः ।
अपाति गृध्रैरभि मौलिमाकुलैर्भविष्यदेतन्मरणोपदेशिभिः ॥२९॥

The vultures swooped upon his head, going round him, desirous of often grasping him, prognasticating that his time of death was nigh. (29).

सद्यो निकृत्ताञ्जनसोदरद्युति फणामणिप्रज्वलदंशुमंडलम् ।
निर्यद्विषोल्कानलगर्भफूत्कृतं ध्वजे जनस्तस्य महाहिमैक्षत ॥३०॥

And above his banner people saw a great serpent, of the colour of antimony freshly pounded, with the circle of the light of the gem on his hood flaming, his hissings full of the fire of poison issuing as if from firebrands of poison. (30).

रथाश्वकेशावलिकर्णचामरं ददाह बाणासनबाणबाणधीन् ।
अकाण्डतश्चण्डतरो हुताशनस्तस्यातनुस्यन्दनधुर्यगोचरः ॥३१॥

A great fire blazing up, all of a sudden, burnt up the hair and the Cāmaras of the horses of his chariot and the quivers of the arrows of his bow, appearing at the opening of his chariot. (31).

इत्याद्यरिष्टैरशुभोपदेशिभिर्विहन्यमानोऽप्यसुरः पुनः पुनः ।
यथा मदान्धो न गतान्न्यवर्ततामवरात्तदाभून्मरुतां सरस्वती ॥३२॥

Though time and again, impeded by such evil portents, the Asura did not retreat from marching forth; there was heard from the sky, the voice of gods. (32).

मदान्ध मा गा भुजदंडचण्डिमावलेपतो मन्मथहन्तृसूनुना ।
सुरैः सनाथेन पुरंदरादिभिः समं समन्तात्समरं विजित्वरैः ॥३३॥

"Oh, thou, blinded by conceit, do not proceed to fight with the all-conquering gods, Indra and others, led by the son of the destroyer of Manmatha, (thou) actuated by the overweening pride of thy puissant arms. (33).

गुहोऽसुरैः षड्दिनजातमात्रको निदाघधामेव निशातमोभरैः ।
विषह्यते नाभिमुखो हि सङ्गरे कुतस्त्वया तस्य समं विरोधिता ॥३४॥

Guha, who was born only six days ago, will not tolerate you confronting him in battle, like the sun, the inspissated darkness of the night; whence can there be your hostility towards him? (34).

अभ्रंलिहैः शृङ्गशतैः समंततो दिक्चक्रवालैः स्थगितस्य भूभृतः ।
क्रौञ्चस्य रंध्रं विशिखेन निर्ममे येनाहवस्तस्य सह त्वया कुतः ॥३५॥

लब्ध्वा धनुर्वेदमनङ्गविद्विषस्त्रिःसप्तकृत्वः समरे महीभुजाम् ।
कृत्वाभिषेकं रुधिरांबुभिर्घनैः स्वक्रोधवह्निं शमयांबभूव यः ॥३६॥

How do you think of fighting one, who bored with his arrows a hole in the Krauñca mountain that was hidden by sky-scouring peaks, and by the circle of quarters, and who learnt the archer's craft from the enemy of Ananga, and who quenched the fire of his wrath by bathing the battle-field with the thick blood of Kṣatriyas, thrice-seven times. (35-36).

न जामदग्न्यः क्षयकालरात्रिकृत्स क्षत्रियाणां समराय वल्गति ।
येन त्रिलोकीसुभटेन तेन कुतोऽवकाशः सह विग्रहग्रहे ॥३७॥

Since even Jāmadagnya, the dread night of death to the Kṣatriyas, dare not move to fight this one warrior in the three worlds, whence can there be any occasion for them to fight him? (37).

त्यजाशु गर्वं मदमूढ मा स्म गाः स्मरारिसूनोर्वरशक्तिगोचरम् ।
तमेव नूनं शरणं व्रजाधुना जगत्सुवीरं स चिराय जीव तत् ॥३८॥

Oh, thou inebriated through pride, do not fall under the strong power of the son of the enemy of Smara; go and throw thyself on the protection of that one great warrior in the world, so that thou mayest live long." (38).

श्रुत्वेति वाचं वियतो गरीयसीं क्रोधादहंकारपरो महासुरः ।
प्रकम्पिताशेषजगत्त्रयोऽपि सन्नकम्पतोच्चैर्वियदभ्यधाच्च सः ॥३९॥

Having heard these weighty words of the gods from heaven, the great Asura, bloated with pride, who made even all the three worlds tremble through fear, himself trembled and in anger loudly addressed the gods in heaven thus: (39).

किं ब्रूथ रे व्योमचरा महासुराः स्मरारिसूनुप्रतिपक्षवर्तिनः ।
मदीयबाणव्रणवेदना हि साऽधुना कथं विस्मृतिगोचरीकृता ॥४०॥

"What say you? Ye gods, taking sides with the son of the enemy of Smara; how dare you forget now the pain of the wounds caused by my shafts? (40).

कटुस्वरैः प्रालपथाम्बरस्थिताः शिशोर्बलात्षड्दिनजातकस्य किम् ।
श्वानः प्रमत्ता इव कार्त्तिके निशि स्वरं वनान्ते मृगधूर्तका इव ॥४१॥

Oh ye, gods, why do you prattle with a bitter voice on account of the prowess of a child, born only six days ago, like maddened hounds of a Kārttika night, or like wily deer barking in the forest? (41).

सङ्गेन वो गर्भतपस्विनः शिशुर्वराक एषोऽन्तमवाप्स्यति ध्रुवम् ।
अतस्करस्तस्करसङ्गतो यथा तद्वो निहन्मि प्रथमं ततोऽप्यमुम् ॥४२॥

By association with you, the child pitiable from birth, will surely meet its death, as an innocent person in association with thieves; so I will kill you first and then this child. (42).

इतीरयत्युग्रतरं महासुरे महाकृपाणं कलयत्यलं क्रुधा ।
परस्परोत्पीडितजानवो भयान्नभश्चरा दूरतरं विदुद्रुवुः ॥४३॥

When the great Asura had spoken thus in a very gruff voice and vigorously flourished his big sword in anger, the gods took to their heels, and mutually bruising their knees quickly ran a great distance. (43).

ततोऽवलेपाद्विकटं विहस्य स व्यधत्त कोशादसिमुत्तमं बहिः ।
रथं द्रुतं प्रापय वासवान्तिकं नन्वित्यवोचन्निजसारथिं रथी ॥४४॥

Then seated in his chariot, he laughed rancorously, and then unleashed his good sword from its scabbard, and then asked his charioteer to drive his chariot to where Vāsava was. (44).

मनोतिवेगेन रथेन सारथिप्रणोदितेन प्रचलन्महासुरः ।
ततः प्रपेदे सुरसैन्यसागरं भयंकराकारमपारमग्रतः ॥४५॥

Then the great Asura, driving in his chariot, steered by his charioteer, reached ahead the ocean of the godly hosts of frightening dimensions. (45).

पुरः सुराणां पृतनां प्रथीयसीं विलोक्य वीरः पुलकं प्रमोदजम् ।
बभार भूम्नाथ स बाहुदण्डयोः प्रचण्डयोः संगरकेलिकौतुकी ॥४६॥

Seeing before him the great army of the gods, the warrior bore upon his mighty arms, thrills of pleasure, being eager for battle. (46).

ततो महेन्द्रस्य चराश्चमूचरा रणान्तलीलारभसेन भूयसा ।
पुरः प्रचेलुर्मनसोऽतिवेगिनो युयुत्सुभिः किं समरे विलम्ब्यते ॥४७॥

Then the emissaries of Indra, moving in the army, impelled by the impetuousity of sporting on the battle-field, moved forward with a speed, exceeding that of the mind; will they who desire to fight dilly-dally ? (47).

पुरःस्थितं देवरिपोश्चमूचरा बलद्विषः सैन्यसमुद्रमभ्ययुः ।
भुजं समुत्क्षिप्य परेभ्य आत्मनोऽभिधानमुच्चैरभितो न्यवेदयन् ॥४८॥

The emissaries of the enemy of the gods advanced to the ocean of Indra's army, and lifting up their arms, loudly announced their names to the enemies. (48).

पुरोगतं दैत्यचमूमहार्णवं दृष्ट्वा परं चुक्षुभिरे महासुराः ।
पुरारिसूनोर्नयनैककोणके ययुर्भटास्तस्य रणेऽवहेलया ॥४९॥

The great gods were greatly agitated on seeing the demon's army, and through scorn of battle, the hostile warriors were comfortably contained in a corner of the eye of Kumāra, the son of the enemy of the cities, out of utter contempt for the battle. (49).

द्विषद्बलत्रासविभीषिताश्चमूर्दिवौकसामन्धकशत्रुनन्दनः ।
अपश्यदुद्दिश्य महारणोत्सवं प्रसादपीयूषधरेण चक्षुषा ॥५०॥

The son of the enemy of Andhaka cheered with an ambrosial glance of his eye, with a view to encouraging for the great struggle, the godly hosts who were frightened by the army of the great Asura, as it worried them. (50).

उत्साहिताः शक्तिधरस्य दर्शनान्मृधे महेन्द्रप्रमुखा मखाशनाः ।
अहं मृधे जेतुमरीनरीरमन्न कस्य वीर्याय वरस्य संगतिः ॥५१॥

The gods, the eaters of oblations offered in sacrifices, were emboldened in battle at the sight of the wielder of Śakti, enjoyed saying "I shall fight the enemy in battle". Whose spirit is not cheered in the company of the great ? (51).

परस्परं वज्रधरस्य सैनिका द्विषोऽपि योद्धुं स्वकरोद्धृतायुधाः ।
वैतालिकश्रावितताराविक्रमाभिधानमीयुर्विजयैषिणो रणे ॥५२॥

The soldiers of Indra and his enemy, wielding weapons to conquer their enemies, clashed together, their names and exploits being loudly announced by heralds. (52).

संग्रामं प्रलयाय संनिपततो वेलामतिक्रामतो
वृन्दारासुरसैन्यसागरयुगस्याशेषदिग्व्यापिनः ।
कालातिथ्यभुजो बभूव बहलः कोलाहलः क्रोषणः
शैलोत्तालतटीविघट्टनपटुर्ब्रह्माण्डकुक्षिंभरिः ॥५३॥

The two armies of the gods and the Asuras respectively, transgressing all limits, sought to annihilate each other in battle; they had pervaded all the quarters; a great outcry was raised by them adept in rending the high sides of mountains and the hollows of Brahmā's creation, as they enjoyed the hospitality of the god of death. (53.)

षोडशः सर्गः

अथान्योन्यं विमुक्तास्त्रशस्त्रजालैर्भयंकरैः
युद्धमासीत्सुनासीरसुरारिबलयोर्महत् ॥१॥

And a great battle ensued between the hosts of the gods and the demons, as they hurled terrific missiles and weapons against one another. (1).

पत्तिः पत्तिमभीयाय रथाय रथिनं रथी ।
तुरंगस्थं तुरंगस्थो दन्तिस्थं दन्तिनि स्थितः ॥२॥

An infantry-man attacked an infantry-man, a warrior in a chariot another of his kind, a horseman another horseman, and one mounted on an elephant another of his kind. (2).

युद्धाय धावतां धीरं वीराणामितरेतरम् ।
वैतालिकाः कुलाधीशा नामान्यलमुदाहरन् ॥३॥

As the warriors solemnly advanced to meet their rivals, the bards, the ornaments of their race, announced their names so as to laud them. (3).

पठतां बन्दिवृन्दानां प्रवीरा विक्रमावलीम् ।
क्षणं विलम्ब्य चित्तानि ददुर्युद्धोत्सुकाः पुरः ॥४॥

As the bards sang the series of exploits of the warriors, they hung awhile, and gave ear to the songs, although they were to fight. (4).

संग्रामानन्दवर्धिष्णौ विग्रहे पुलकाञ्चिते ।
आसीत्कवचविच्छेदो वीराणां मिलतां मिथः ॥५॥

As the warriors encountered one another, their coats of mail burst open as their bodies expanded through joy of battle as they were covered with horripilation. (5).

निर्दयं खड्गभिन्नेभ्यः कवचेभ्यः समुत्थितैः ।
आसन्व्योमदिशस्तूलैः पलितैरिव पाण्डुराः ॥६॥

As the coats of mail were cruelly torn to shreds by swords, there flew out of them balls of cotton, which made the quarters of the sky grey, as with white hair. (6).

खड्गा रुधिरसंलिप्ताश्चण्डांशुकरभासुराः ।
इतस्ततोऽपि वीराणां विद्युतां वैभवं दधुः ॥७॥

The swords of the warriors smeared with blood, shone

like the rays of the sun, and flashed about like lightning streaks. (7).

विसृजन्तो मुखैर्ज्वाला भीमा इव भुजंगमाः ।
विसृष्टाः सुभटै रुष्टैर्व्योम व्यानशिरे शराः ॥८॥

Discharged by good warriors who were angry, the arrows, which seemed to hurl forth blazing meteors like terrific serpents, pervaded the quarters. (8).

बाढं वपूंषि निर्भिद्य धन्विनां निघ्नतां मिथः ।
अशोणितमुखा भूमिं प्राविशन्दूरमाशुगाः ॥९॥

As the archers killed one another, their arrows, penetrating their bodies, had their tips, unsmeared by blood, and penetrated the earth to a great depth. (9).

निर्भिद्य दन्तिनः पूर्वं पातयामासुराशुगाः ।
पेतुः प्रवरयोधानां प्रीतानामाहवोत्सवे ॥१०॥

In that festival of battle, the arrows of great warriors penetrated the tuskers and filled them and then fell to earth themselves. (10).

ज्वलदग्निमुखैर्बाणैर्नीरन्ध्रैरितरेतरम् ।
उच्चैर्वैमानिका व्योम्नि कीर्णे दूरमपासरन् ॥११॥

When dense volleys of arrows had covered the sky thickly, the gods quickly receded from it. (11).

विभिन्नं धन्विनां बाणैर्व्यथार्तमिव विह्वलम् ।
ररास विरसं व्योम श्येनप्रतिरवच्छलात् ॥१२॥

Riddled with the shafts of archers, the sky was as if overwhelmed with misery, and, as it were, bellowed viciously through the cries of hawks. (12).

चापैराकर्णमाकृष्टैर्विमुक्ता दूरमाशुगाः ।
प्रधावन्रुधिरास्वादलुब्धा इव रणैषिणाम् ॥१३॥

The arrows, discharged by archers from bows, drawn back to the ends of their ears, discharged to a great distance, ran as if thirsty for blood of the fighters. (13).

गृहीताः पाणिभिर्वीरैर्विकोशाः खड्गराजयः ।
कान्तिजालच्छलादाजौ व्यहसन्संमदादिव ॥१४॥

The series of scabbardless swords, flourished by warriors, seemed to laugh, through great joy under the guise of a network of their splendour on the field of battle. (14)

खड्गाः शोणितसंदिग्धा नृत्यन्तो वीरपाणिषु ।
रजोघने रणेऽनन्ते विद्युतां वैभवं दधुः ॥१५॥

Swords, dancing in the hands of warriors, and smeared with blood on that ample battle-field filled with dust, bore the splendour of lightning. (15).

कुन्ताग्रकाशिरे चण्डमुल्लसन्तो रणार्थिनाम् ।
जिह्वाभीमा यमस्येव लेलिहाना रणाङ्गणे ॥१६॥

The lances of warriors flashing fiercely, shone on the battle-field, like the lolling tongues of the god of death. (16).

प्रज्वलत्कान्तिचक्राणि चक्राणि वरचक्रिणाम् ।
चण्डांशुमण्डलश्रीणि रणव्योमनि बभ्रमुः ॥१७॥

The wheels of the chariots of great warriors, which flashed with flaming circle of light, and having the splendour of the sun's sphere, whirled on the battlefield of the sky. (17).

केचिद्वीरैः प्रणादैश्च वीराणामभ्युपेयुषाम् ।
निपेतुः क्षोभतो वाहादपरे मुमुहुर्मदात् ॥१८॥

Some warriors were thrown off their mounts, by the agitation caused by the deep outcries of charging warriors, and others, through intoxication. (18).

कश्चिदभ्यागते वीरे जिघांसौ मुदमावधौ ।
परावृत्य गते क्षुब्धे विषमादाहवप्रियः ॥१९॥

A certain warrior was overjoyed to find another come to kill him, and agitated at sight of him, felt sad to find him slink away from him, fond of battle, as he was. (19).

बहुभिः सह युद्ध्वा वा परिभ्रम्य रणोल्बणाः ।
उद्दिश्य तानुपेयुः केऽपि ये पूर्ववृता रणे ॥२०॥

Warriors, bold in battle, having engaged many in fight, turning round, approached those again, whom they had fought before. (20).

अभितोऽभ्यागतान्योद्धुं वीरान्रणमदोद्धतान् ।
प्रत्यनन्दन्भुजादण्डरोमोद्गमभृतो भटाः ॥२१॥

Warriors, bearing horripilation on their puissant arms, met in battle all those who came from all sides to encounter them,—warriors, who were maddened by pride for battle. (21).

शस्त्रभिन्नेभकुम्भेभ्यो मौक्तिकानि च्युतान्यधः ।
अध्याहवक्षेत्रमुप्तकीर्तिबीजांकुरश्रियम् ॥२२॥

The pearls that had dropped down from the temples of elephants riven with swords fell on the field of battle; both were like the sprouts of the seeds of glory, sown in that field. (22).

वीराणां विषमैर्घोषैर्विद्रुता वारणा रणे ।
शास्यमाना अपि त्रासाद्दुद्रुवुर्धूतांकुशा दिशः ॥२३॥

The elephants that ran amuck on the battle-field, though controlled by their mahouts, frightened by the wild cries of the fighters, ran to the ends of quarters, despite the goads. (23).

रणे बाणगणैर्भिन्ना भ्रमन्तो भिन्नयोधिनः ।
निममज्जुर्मिलद्रक्तनिम्नगासु महागजाः ॥२४॥

The great elephants, riddled by volleys of shafts, wandering without their mahouts who had been killed, dived into rivers of blood commingling. (24).

अपारेऽसृक्सरित्पूरे रथेषूच्चैस्तरेष्वपि ।
रथिनोऽभिरिपुं क्रुद्धा हुंकृतैर्व्यसृजञ्छरान् ॥२५॥

Even the high chariots, as they were immersed in very

deep rivers of blood, the warriors inside them, angrily and with deep grunts, discharged arrows against their enemies. (25).

खड्गनिलूनमूर्धानो व्यापतन्तोऽपि वाजिनः।
प्रथमं पाययामासुरसिना दारितानरीन् ॥२६॥

The warriors whose heads were lopped [off by swords, although they fell from horses felled the enemies, quartered by swords. (26).

वीराणां शस्त्रभिन्नानि शिरांसि निपतन्त्यपि ।
अधावन्दन्तदष्टोष्ठभीमान्यभिरिपुं क्रुधा ॥२७॥

The heads of warriors, cut off by weapons, even though they fell, pursued the enemy, looking fierce as they bit the lower lip with the teeth. (27).

शिरांसि वरयोधानामर्धचन्द्रहृतान्यलम्।
आददाना भृशं पादैः श्येना व्यानशिरे नभः ॥२८॥

And hawks, holding in their claws, the heads of warriors cut by crescent-head arrows, pervaded the skies. (28).

क्रोधादभ्यापतद्दन्तिदन्तारूढाः पदातयः।
अश्वारोहा गजारोहप्राणान्प्रासैरपाहरन् ॥२९॥

The infantry soldiers and horsemen, angrily climbed the tusks of elephants, who were attacking them and smote their mahouts with Prāsas. (29).

शस्त्रच्छिन्नगजारोहा विभ्रमन्त इतस्ततः।
युगान्तवातचलिताः शैला इव गजा बभुः ॥३०॥

The elephants, whose mahouts were killed by weapons, wanderirg about, appeared like mountains, shaken by winds of aeon. (30).

मिलितेषु मिथो योद्धुं दन्तिषु प्रसभं भटाः।
अगृह्णन्रुध्यमानाश्च शस्त्रैः प्राणान्परस्परम् ॥३१॥

Warriors mounted on elephants encountered others, and forcibly as they fought, took each other's life with their weapons. (31).

रुषा मिथो मिलद्दन्तिदन्तसंघर्षजोऽनलः।
योधाञ्शस्त्रहृतप्राणानदहत्सहसाऽरिभिः ॥३२॥

The fire which was caused by the mutual clashing of the tusks of elephants, who angrily encountered one another, burnt down warriors all of a sudden, killed by their weapons, by their enemies. (32).

आक्षिप्ता अपि दन्तीन्द्रैः कोपनैः पत्तयः परम्।
तदसूनहरन्खड्गघातैः स्वस्य पुरः प्रभोः ॥३३॥

The infantry-men, who were hurled with their trunks by great and angry elephants, killed them by strokes of swords, before their masters. (33).

उत्क्षिप्य करिभिर्दूरान्मुक्तानां योधिनां दिवि।
प्रापि जीवात्मभिर्दिव्या गतिर्वा विग्रहैर्मही ॥३४॥

The souls of warriors, flung up far into the sky, attained heaven, while their bodies fell to the earth. (34).

खड्गैर्धवलधारालैर्निहत्य करिणां करान् ।
तैर्भुवापि समं विद्धान्संतोषं न भटा ययुः ॥३५॥

The warriors were not satisfied by only lopping the trunks of elephants with swords with their white edges, although they were felled to the ground. (35).

आक्षिप्याभिदिवं नीताः पत्तयः करिभिः करैः ।
दिव्याङ्गनाभिरादातुं रक्ताभिद्रुतमीषिरे ॥३६॥

The infantry-soldiers, that were snatched up by the elephants with their trunks, and flung towards the heaven were quickly sought after by the nymphs of heaven, that were smitten with love. (36).

धन्विनस्तुरगारूढा गजारोहाञ्शरैः क्षतान् ।
प्रत्यैच्छन्मूर्च्छितान्भूयो योद्धुमाश्वसतश्चिरम् ॥३७॥

Archers, mounted on horses desired the warriors, wounded by arrows, and fainted, to revive, and waited for them. (37).

क्रुद्धस्य दन्तिनः पत्तिर्जिघृक्षोरसिना करम् ।
निर्भिद्य दन्तमुसलावारुरोह जिघृक्षया ॥३८॥

An infantry-soldier, who desired to cut the lower part of the tusks of an attacking elephant, ascended his pestle-like tusk, with a view to taking it. (38).

खड्गेन मूलतो हृत्वा दन्तिनो रदनद्वयम् ।
प्रातिपक्ष्ये प्रविष्टोऽपि पदातिर्निरगाद्द्रुतम् ॥३९॥

An infantry-soldier, who had penetrated the ranks of the enemy, having cut from the very root, the two tusks of an elephant, quickly withdrew from those ranks. (39).

करेण करिणा वीरः सुगृहीतोऽपि कोपिना ।
असिनाऽसूञ्जहाराशु तस्यैव स्वयमक्षतः ॥४०॥

A warrior, although seized by an infuriated elephant with his trunk, quickly killed him with his sword, himself remaining unwounded. (40).

तुरंगी तुरगारूढं प्रासेनाहत्य वक्षसि ।
पततस्तस्य नाज्ञासीत्प्रासघातं स्वके हृदि ॥४१॥

A warrior, mounted on the horse of a horseman, who was struck with Prāsa, struck him in the breast and did not realise that he himself was struck in the breast by that warrior, as he fell. (41).

द्विषा प्रासहृतप्राणो वाजिपृष्ठदृढासनः ।
हस्तोद्धृतमहाप्रासो भुवि जीवन्निवाभ्रमत् ॥४२॥

A certain warrior, though killed by his foe with his Prāsa, keeping firmly to his seat, on his horse, wielding a big Prāsa in his hand, wandered over the earth, as if he was alive. (42).

तुरंगसादिनं शस्त्रहृतप्राणं गतं भुवि ।
अबद्धोऽपि महावाजी न साश्रुनयनोऽत्यजत् ॥४३॥

A big horse with tears in its eyes, although free, waited for his rider, felled dead on the ground, to revive: (43).

भल्लेन शितधारेण भिन्नोऽपि रिपुणाश्वगः ।
नामूर्च्छत्कोपतो हन्तुमियेष प्रपतन्नपि ॥४४॥

A horseman, although pierced by his enemy, with a sharpedged lance, did not fall into a swoon, and although falling down, desired to kill his foe. (44).

मिथः प्रासाहतौ वाजिच्युतौ भूमिगतौ रुषा ।
क्षस्त्र्या युयुधतुः कौचित्केशाकेशि भुजाभुजि ॥४५॥

The warriors, struck mutually by Prāsa, and felled to the earth, fought angrily with daggers, by pulling each other by the hair, and by fighting one another with bare arms. (45).

रथिनो रथिभिर्बाणैर्हृतप्राणा दृढासनाः ।
क्षतकार्मुकसंधानाः सप्राणा इव मेनिरे ॥४६॥

The warriors in chariots killed their rivals in chariots with arrows but who, keeping firm in their seats, and losing their hold on their bows, were thought by them to be alive. (46).

न रथी रथिनं भूयः प्राहरच्छस्त्रमूर्च्छितम् ।
प्रत्याश्वसन्तमन्विच्छन्नातिष्ठद्युधि लोभतः ॥४७॥

A warrior in a chariot, did not strike another, swooning under a blow from a weapon, but out of itching for fight, waited for him to revive. (47).

अन्योन्यं रथिनौ कौचिद्गतप्राणौ दिवं गतौ ।
एकामप्सरसं प्राप्य युयुधाते वरायुधौ ॥४८॥

Two other warriors in chariots, who killed one another, armed as they were with goodly weapons, ascended to the heavens, and there had altercations for the hand of the self-same nymph. (48).

मिथोऽर्धचन्द्रनिर्लूनमूर्धानौ रथिनौ रुचा ।
खेचरौ भुवि नृत्यन्तौ स्वकबन्धावपश्यताम् ॥४९॥

Two warriors in chariots, who had cut each other's heads with crescent-tipped arrows, shining brightly, saw their torsos, falling to the earth while they themselves were wandering in the sky. (49).

रणाङ्गणे शोणितपङ्कपिच्छिले कथं कथंचिन्ननृतुर्धृतायुधाः ।
नदत्सु तूर्येषु परेतयोषितां गणेषु गायत्सु कबन्धराजयः ॥५०॥

Lines of headless trunks, wielding weapons in their hands, danced somehow on the battle-field which was clammy with blood-wetted mud, while musical instruments were sounding and a multitude of the wives of ghouls were singing. (50).

इति सुररिपुवृत्ते युद्धे सुरासुरसैन्ययोः
रुधिरसरितां मज्जद्दन्तिव्रजेषु तटेष्वलम् ।
अरुणनयनः क्रोधाद्भीमभ्रमद्भ्रुकुटीमुखः
सपदिककुभामीशानभ्यागमत्स युयुत्सया ॥५१॥

While thus the godly and Asura hosts clashed, and

while on the banks of rivers of blood, elephants were sunk deep, Tāraka, the enemy of the gods, his eyes red through anger, and his eye-brows moving threateningly, immediately advanced to the guardian of the quarters and others, to fight with them. (51).

सप्तदशः सर्गः

दृष्ट्वाभ्युपेतमथ दैत्यपतिं पुरस्ता-
त्संग्रामकेलिकुतुकेन घनप्रमोदम् ।
योद्धुं मदेन मिमिलुः ककुभामधीशा
बाणान्धकारितदिगम्बरगर्भमेत्य ॥१॥

Seeing before them the Lord of demons advancing, greatly rejoicing through delight in the sport of battle, and who darkered the sky with volleys of arrows, the guardians of the quarters, proudly came together for fighting the demonlord, who had advanced to them. (1).

देवद्विषां परिवृढो विकटं विहस्य
बाणावलीभिरमरान्विकटान्ववर्ष ।
शैलानिव प्रवरवारिधरो गरिष्ठा-
नद्भिः पराभिरथ गाढमनारताभिः ॥२॥

The leader of the enemies of the gods laughed rancorously and showered the gods with dreadful volleys of arrows, like a great cloud, mountains, with profuse unremitting and excellent showers. (2).

जम्भद्विषत्प्रभृतिविश्पतिचापमुक्ता
बाणाः शिता दनुजनायकबाणसङ्घान् ।
अह्नाय तार्क्ष्यनिवहा इव नागपूगान्
सद्यो विचिच्छिदुरलं कणशो रणान्ते ॥३॥

The volleys of the sharp arrows of the gods shot from their bows, snapped to smithereens the volleys of arrows of the leader of demons, like flights of Garuḍa, immediately snapping into bits groups of snakes. (3).

तान्प्रज्वलत्फलमुखैर्विषमैः सुरारि-
नामाङ्कितैः पिहितदिग्गगनान्तरालैः ।
आच्छादितस्तृणचयानिव हव्यवाह-
श्चिच्छेद सोऽपि सुरसैन्यशराञ्शरौघैः ॥४॥

The enemy of the gods, snapped to bits, the volleys of arrows of the army of the gods, with his arrows tipped with flaming iron points and with his name inscribed on them, and that covered the spaces between quarters, like unto fire, sheaves of grass, that cover them. (4).

दैत्येश्वरो ज्वलितरोषविशेषभीमः
सद्यो मुमोच युधि यान्विशिखान्सहेलः ।
ते प्रापुरुद्भटभुजंगमभीमभावं
गाढं बबन्धुरपि तांस्त्रिदशेन्द्रमुख्यान् ॥५॥

The arrows which the Lord of the demons, looking terrific with flaming anger, shot with ease, immediately turned into frightful serpents, and firmly bound the principal gods. (5).

ते नागपाशविशिखैरसुरेण बद्धाः
श्वासानिलाकुलमुखा विमुखा रणस्य ।
दिङ्नायका बलरिपुप्रमुखाः स्मरारि-
सूनोः समीपमगमन्विपदन्तहेतोः ॥६॥

The guardians of the qnarters, of whom Indra was the principal, averse to fighting, were bound by the Asura with arrows, which were of the nature of nooses of serpents with their mouths full of the wind of breath, that stifled them, approached Kumāra, the son of Śiva, for ending their misery. (6).

दृष्टिप्रपातवशतोऽपि पुरारिसूनो-
स्ते नागपाशघनबन्धविपत्तिदुःखात् ।
इन्द्रादयो मुमुचिरे स्वयमस्य देवाः
सेवां व्यधुर्निकटमेत्य महाजिगीषोः ॥७॥

Indra and others, who were relieved of the intense pains, caused by the misery of being tightly bound by the nooses of serpents, by Kumāra, by a mere glance at them, advanced to that great conqueror, and extolled him with words of praise. (7).

उद्दीप्तकोपदहनोऽथ सुरेन्द्रशत्रु-
रह्नाय सारथिमवोचत चण्डबाहुः ।
बद्धा मया सुरपतिप्रमुखाः प्रसह्य
बालस्य धूर्जटिसुतस्य निरीक्षणेन ॥८॥

मुक्ता बभूवुरधुना तदिमान्विहाय
कर्तास्म्यमुं समरभूमिपशूपहारम् ।

तत्स्यन्दनं सपदि वाहय शंभुसूनुं
द्रष्टास्मि दर्पितभुजाबलमाहवाय ॥९॥

The enemy of Indra, with the flame of the fire of anger enkindled immediately, spoke to his charioteer, "The gods with Indra as their principal, bound by me, have been instantly released by the infant son of Dhūrjaṭi, with a mere glance; so leaving these, I will offer him to the battle-ground, as a beast is offered in sacrifice; so immediately drive the chariot where the son of Śambhu is; I will encounter him who is proud of the strength of his arms in battle." (8-9).

तत्स्यन्दनः सपदि सारथिसंप्रणुन्नः
प्रक्षुब्धवारिधरघोरगभीरघोषः ।
चण्डश्चचाल बलिताखिलशत्रुसैन्य-
मांसास्थिशोणितविपङ्कविलुप्तचक्रः ॥१०॥

His chariot, immediately driven by his charioteer, while it produced a deep and solemn sound, as that of the ocean in agitation, moved frighteningly, its wheels lost in the gory mud, caused by the flesh and bones of the troopers in the hostile army, struck down in battle. (10).

दृष्ट्वा रथं प्रलयवातचलद्गिरीन्द्र-
कल्पं दलद्बलविरावविशेषरौद्रम् ।
अभ्यागतं सुररिपोः सुरराजसैन्यं
क्षोभं जगाम परमं भयवेपमानम् ॥११॥

The army of Indra, trembling through fear, was

greatly agitated at sight of the chariot, looking the mountain Himālaya, shaken by the winds of dissolution, and looking especially terrific owing to the hubbub of his enemy's army, that was being killed. (11).

प्रक्षुभ्यमाणमवलोक्य दिगीशसैन्यं
शंभोः सुतं कलहकेलिकुतूहलोत्कम् ।
उद्दामदोःकलितकार्मुकदण्डचण्डः
प्रोवाच वाचमुपगम्य स कार्तिकेयम् ॥१२॥

Seeing that the army of the guardians of the quarters was agitated, the Asura, fierce-looking with his puissant arms, wielding the heavy bow-staff, advanced to Kārttikeya, the son of Śiva, spoiling for the sport of war, and addressed him thus :— (12).

रे शंभुतापसशिशो बत मुञ्च मुञ्च
दोर्दर्पमत्र विरम त्रिदिवेन्द्रकार्यात् ।
शस्त्रैः किमत्र भवतोऽनुचितैरतीव
बालत्वकोमलभुजातुलभारभूतैः ॥१३॥

"Oh, the son of the anchorite Śiva, give up the pride of arms in respect of me; cease from doing this good office to Indra; what could your weapons avail here, which are improper for your very delicate infant hands and a burden unto them ? (13).

एवं त्वमेव तनयोऽसि गिरीशगौर्योः
किं यासि कालविषयं विषमैः शरैर्मे ।
संग्रामतोऽपसर जीव पितुर्जनन्या-
स्तूर्णं प्रविश्य वरमङ्कतलं विधेहि ॥१४॥

Thus, you are the only son of Giriśa and Gaurī, why do you fall into the domain of death, by my arrows; withdraw from the battle-field; sit in the lap of thy father and mother and make them feel blessed. (14).

सम्यक्स्वयं किल विमृश्य गिरीशपुत्र
जम्भद्विषोऽस्य जहिहि प्रतिपक्षमाशु ।
एष स्वयं पयसि मज्जति दुर्विगाह्ये
पाषाणनौरिव निमज्जयते पुरा त्वाम् ॥१५॥

Oh, son of Giriśa, think well for thyself, and quickly leave the side of Indra, the enemy of Jambha; he is sinking himself in waters unfordable like a boat, fashioned out of stones, and will draw thee along with himself." (15).

इत्थं निशम्य वचनं युधि तारकस्य
कम्पाधरो विकचकोकनदारुणाक्षः ।
क्षोभात्त्रिलोचनसुतो धनुरीक्षमाणः
प्रोवाच वाचमुचितां परिमृश्य शक्तिम् ॥१६॥

Having heard the words of Tāraka on the battle-field, Kumāra with his lips quivering, and his eyes red like a blooming red lotus, looked in agitation at his bow, and reflecting upon his own strength, addressed him in proper words :— (16).

दैत्याधिराज भवता यदवादि गर्वा-
त्तत्सर्वमप्युचितमेव तवैव किं तु ।
द्रष्टाऽस्मि ते प्रवर बाहुबलं वरिष्ठं
शस्त्रं गृहाण कुरु कार्मुकमाततज्यम् ॥१७॥

"Oh, sovereign Lord of Asuras, what thou didst say last in thy pride, is, indeed proper for thee; I shall (soon) feel the superior strength of thy arms; take up thy weapon, and put the string upon thy bow". (17).

इत्युक्तवन्तमवदत्त्रिपुरारिपुत्रं
दैत्यः क्रुधोष्ठमधरं किल निर्विभिद्य ।
युद्धार्थमुद्भटभुजाबलदर्पितोऽसि
बाणान्सहस्व मम सावितशत्रुपृष्ठान् ॥१८॥

The Asura, in anger, bit his lower lip, spoke to Kumāra, "You are conceited with the strength of your arms, and urged to fight; bear to be riddled by my arrows, that have struck the backs of my enemies." (18).

दुःप्रेक्षणीयमरिभिर्धनुराततज्यं
सद्यो विधाय विषमान्विशिखं न्यधत्त ।
स क्रोधभीमभुजगेन्द्रनिभं स्वचापं
चण्डं प्रपञ्चयति जैत्रशरैः कुमारे ॥१९॥

Stringing his bow, dreadful to the eyes of his enemies, he immediately placed upon that bow, dreadful arrows which were frightful like an infuriated lord of serpents, and he aimed arrows, calculated to conquer, at Kumāra. (19).

कर्णान्तमेत्य दितिजेन विकृष्यमाणं
कोदण्डमेतदभितः सुषुवे शरौघान् ।
व्योमाङ्गणे लिपिकरान्किरणप्ररोहैः
सान्द्रैरशेषककुभां पलितंकरिष्णून् ॥२०॥

The bow, stretched to the tip of the ear, sent forth volleys of arrows around him, strewing the courtyard of the sky, which made all the quarters white, as with grey hair. (20).

बाणैः सुरारिधनुषः प्रसृतैरनन्तै-
निर्घोषभीषितभटो लसदंशुजालैः ।
अन्धीकृताखिलसुरेश्वरसैन्य ईश-
सूनुः कुतोऽपि विषयं न जगाम दृष्टेः ॥२१॥

By the innumerable arrows, shot from the bow of the enemy (arrows) of the end shining with numerous rays, which by their terrific whipping sound, had struck fear in the hearts of warriors and which veiled the hosts of the gods in darkness, the son of Īśa was nowhere to be seen by the eyes. (21).

देवेन मन्मथरिपोस्तनयेन गाढ-
माकर्णकृष्टमभितो धनुराततज्यम् ।
बाणानसूत निशितान्युधि यान्सुजैत्रां-
स्तैः सायका बिभिदिरे सहसा सुरारेः ॥२२॥

The bow, stretched to the tips of the ears, after it was strung, by the son of Śiva, delivered sharp and conquering arrows in the battle which instantly snapped the arrows of the Asura. (22).

रेजे सुरारिशरदुर्दिनके निरस्ते
संध्यस्तरां निखिलखेचरखेदहेतौ ।

देवः प्रभाप्रभुरिव स्मरशत्रुसूनुः
प्रद्योतनः सुघनदुर्धरधामधामा ॥२३॥

When the cloudy day, caused by volleys of the arrows of the Asura, was dissipated instantly, which was the cause of the misery of all the gods, lord Kārttikeya, the abode of dazzling refulgence shone like the very resplendent sun. (23).

तत्राथ दुःसहतरं समरे तरस्वी
धामाधिकं वहति धीरतरं कुमारे ।
मायामयं समरमाशु महासुरेन्द्रो
मायाप्रचारचतुरो रचयांचकार ॥२४॥

There, in the battle, as Kumāra shone with a deeper splendour, the king of the Asuras, swift in fight, took to magical strategy in the battle, adept that he was in magical devices. (24).

अह्नाय कोपकलुषो विकटं विहस्य
व्यर्थं समर्थ्यं वरशस्त्रयुधं कुमारे ।
जिष्णुर्जगद्विजयदुर्ललितः सहेलं
वायव्यमस्त्रमसुरो धनुषि न्यधत्त ॥२५॥

The Asura, excited instantly with anger, laughing rancorously, and thinking that fighting with Kumāra with excellent weapons was futile, conceited by his conquest of the world, the conqueror, fixed with ease upon his bow an arrow, presided over by the god of wind. (25).

संधानमात्रमपि यस्य युगान्तकाल-
भूतभ्रमं पवनभीषणघोरघोषः ।

उद्धूतधूलिपटलैः पिहिताम्बराशः
प्रच्छन्नचण्डकिरणो व्यसरत्समीरः ॥२६॥

The very fixing of which on the bow caused in all beings great delirium and as a consequence of this, the wind howling in wild rage so as to frighten men, which veiled the quarters of the sky with clouds of dust blown up and which concealed the hot-rayed one (the sun), began to blow. (26).

कुन्दोज्ज्वलानि सकलातपवारणानि
धूतानि तेन मरुता सुरसैनिकानाम् ।
उड्डीयमानकलहंसकुलोपमानि
मेघाभधूलिमलिने नभसि प्रसस्रुः ॥२७॥

That wind blew up the umbrellas white like Kunda flowers, of men-at-arms in the godly host, umbrellas resembled flights of swans, and floated upwards in the sky, which was dark with cloud like dust. (27).

विध्वस्य तेन सुरसैन्यमहापताका
नीता नभस्तलमलं नवमल्लिकाभाः ।
स्वर्गापगाजलमहौघसहस्रलीलां
व्यातेनिरे दिवि सिताम्बरकैतवेन ॥२८॥

The huge flags of the godly host, shining like fresh jasmine flowers, had the grace of thousands of spurting tiny streams, of the river of heaven, under the guise of their white streamers. (28).

धूतानि तेन सुरसैन्यमहागजानां
[illegible] शतशो[illegible] चित्रुराणि वलत्कुथानि ।

पेतुः क्षितौ कुपितवासववज्रलून-
पक्षस्य भूधरकुलस्य तुलां वहन्ति ॥२९॥

Herds of big elephants in the godly hosts, hundreds of them instantly distressed, were hurled by that wind, and fell to the earth, with their housings torn, resembling mountains, whose wings were lopped. (29).

तास्ताः खरेण मरुता रथराजयोऽपि
दोधूयमाननिपतिष्णुतुरंगमाश्च ।
वित्रस्तसारथिकुलप्रवराः समन्ता-
द्व्यावृत्य पेतुरवनौ सुरवाहिनीनाम् ॥३०॥

And those various lines of chariots in the armies of the gods, being shaken by that violent wind, had their horses coming a-cropper and fell down on the earth, after having wandered all round, whose charioteers, the leaders of their families, also fell down. (30).

हित्वाऽऽयुधानि सुरसैन्यतुरंगवाहा
वातेन तेन विधुराः सुरसैन्यमध्ये ।
शस्त्राभिघातमनवाप्य निपेतुरुर्व्यां
स्वीयेषु वाहनवरेषु पतत्सु सत्सु ॥३१॥

The horsemen in the armies of the gods, giving up their weapons, troubled by the wind as they were, came a-cropper to the earth, without being struck by weapons as their good mounts fell to the earth. (31).

तेनाहतास्त्रिदशसैन्यपदातयोऽपि
स्रस्तायुधाः सुविधुराः परुषं रसन्तः ।

वात्याविवर्तदलवद्भ्रममेत्य दूरं
निष्पेतुरम्बरतलाद्वसुधातलेऽस्मिन् ॥३२॥

Struck by that wind, the infantrymen in the godly hosts dropped their weapons, were greatly distressed and wept bitterly and were whirled up in the sky a great distance, like a leaf going up in the eddying whirlwind, and fell from the sky to the earth. (32).

इत्थं विलोक्य सुरसैन्यमथो अशेषं
दैत्येश्वरेण विधुरीकृतमस्त्रयोगात् ।
स्वर्लोकनाथकमलाकुशलैकहेतु-
र्दिव्यं प्रभावमतनोदतनुः स देवः ॥३३॥

Seeing the entire armies of the gods, thus distressed by the missile of the Lord of the Asuras, for the purpose of securing the welfare of the royal fortune of Indra, Kārttikeya manifested great divine power. (33).

तेनोज्झितं सकलमेव सुरेन्द्रसैन्यं
स्वास्थ्यं प्रपद्य पुनरेव युधि प्रवृत्तम् ।
दृष्ट्वाऽसृजद्दहनदैवतमस्त्रमिद्ध-
मुद्दीप्तकोपदहनः सहसा सुरारिः ॥३४॥

The entire army of Indra, felt relieved through it, and prepared themselves for the battle, and seeing it, the enemy of the gods, his anger inflamed, instantly released the flaming missile, presided over by the firegod. (34).

वर्षातिकालजलदद्युतयो नभोऽन्ते
गाढान्धकारितदिशो घनधूमसंघाः ।

सद्यः प्रसस्रुरसितोत्पलदामभासो
दृग्गोचरत्वमखिलं न हि सन्नयन्तः ॥३५॥

Thick masses of smoke, shining like the very clouds of the rainy season at the skirts of the sky, that had darkened the quarters, instantly spread about—of the colour of a garland of blue lotuses, making all existing things invisible to the eye. (35).

विश्वचक्रवालमिलनैर्मलिनैस्तमोभि-
र्लिप्तं नभःस्थलमलं घनवृन्दसान्द्रैः ।
धूमैर्विलोक्य मुदिताः खलु राजहंसा
गन्तुं सरः सपदि मानसमीषुरुच्चैः ॥३६॥

The sky was pervaded by smoke, dark like the rows of clouds, dark for having swallowed the circle of the quarters, and at the sight of it, the swans were greatly delighted, and filled with a deep yearning for going to the Mānasa lake. (36).

जज्वाल वह्निरतुलः सुरसैनिकेषु
कल्पान्तकालदहनप्रतिमः समन्तात् ।
आशामुखानि विमलान्यखिलानि कीला-
जालैरलं कपिलयन्सकलं नभोऽपि ॥३७॥

A great fire blazed around the army of gods, which was like the fire of a cataclysm, making the bright mouths of the quarters and the entire sky tawny with innumerable flames. (37).

उज्जागरस्य दहनस्य निरर्गलस्य
ज्वालावलीभिरतुलाभिरनारताभिः ।
कीर्णं पयोदनिवहैरिव धूमसंघै-
र्व्योमाप्यलक्ष्यत कुलैस्तडितामिवोच्चैः ॥३८॥

By the numerous flames of the blazing fire, which knew no let or hindrance, and were unremitting, the sky was covered by the columns of smoke, which were like the rows of clouds, and looked as if it was thickly covered by shimmery lightning streaks. (38).

गाढाद्भयाद्वियति विद्रुतखेचरेण
दीप्तेन तेन दहनेन सुदुःसहेन ।
दन्दह्यमानमखिलं सुरराजसैन्य-
मत्याकुलं शिवसुतस्य समीपमाप ॥३९॥

By that blazing, unbearable fire, the luminaries of the sky were made to fly; the entire godly host being frightfully singed and greatly disturbed, advanced to the son of god Śiva. (39).

इत्यग्निना घनतरेण ततोऽभिभूतं
तद्देवसैन्यमखिलं विकलं विलोक्य ।
सस्मेरवक्त्रकमलोऽन्धकशत्रुसूनु-
र्बाणासनेन समधत्त स वारुणास्त्रम् ॥४०॥

Then Kumāra, seeing that entire godly host, overpowered by that dense fire, and distressed, with a smiling face, fixed upon his bow, the missile, presided over by Varuṇa. (40).

घोरान्धकारनिकरप्रतिमो युगान्त-
कालानलप्रबलधूमनिभो नभोऽन्ते ।
गर्जारवैर्विघटयन्नवनीधराणां
शृङ्गाणि मेघनिवहो घनमुज्जगाम ॥४१॥

There floated high up in the sky, a dense mass of clouds, like clouds of inspissated smoke, and like the smoke of the fire of world-cataclysm, rending by its loud bellowing the peaks of mountains. (41).

विद्युल्लता वियति वारिदवृन्दमध्ये
गम्भीरभीष्मरवैः कपिशीकृताशा ।
घोरा युगान्तचलितस्य भयंकराऽथ
कालस्य लोलरसनेव चमच्चकार ॥४२॥

Streaks of lightning flashed among the rows of clouds, making a deep and frightening roar and rendering the quarters tawny, caused wonder like the dread, frightening and lolling tongue of the god of Death. (42).

कादम्बिनी विरुरुचे विषकण्ठिकाभि-
रुत्तालकालरजनीजलदावलीभिः ।
व्योम्न्युच्चकैरचिररुक्परिदीपिताशा-
दृष्टिच्छदा विषमघोषविभीषणा च ॥४३॥

There shone a line of clouds, full of waters, like the dread night of cataclysm, that illumined in the sky on high the various quarters, veiling the eyes and threatening by its dread roar. (43).

व्योम्नस्तलं पिदधतां ककुभां मुखानि
गर्जारवैरविरतैस्तुदतां मनांसि ।
अम्भोभृतामतितरामनणीयसीभि-
र्धारावलीभिरभितो ववृषे समूहैः ॥४४॥

Multitude of clouds sent down big and unremitting showers all round, veiling the sky and the mouths of quarters and distressing the mind by their incessant roar. (44).

घोरान्धकारपटलैः पिहिताम्बराणां
गम्भीरगर्जनरवैर्व्यथितासुराणाम् ।
वृष्ट्या तया जलमुचां वरुणास्त्रभाजां
विश्वोदरंभरिरपि प्रशशाम वह्निः ॥४५॥

The clouds born of the Varuṇa missile, veiling the skies by formidable darkness, by their deep rumble, distressed the enemies of gods, and poured showers that quenched the fire, which filled the hollows of the universe. (45).

दैत्योऽपि रोषकलुषो निशितैः क्षुरप्रै-
राकर्णकृष्टधनुरुत्पतितैः स भीमैः ।
तद्भीतिविद्रुतसमस्तसुरेन्द्रसैन्यो
गाढं जघान मकरध्वजशत्रुसूनुम् ॥४६॥

The Asura, too, excited by anger, struck deeply the son of the enemy of Makaradhvaja, (Kāma), with terrible Ksurapra arrows, flying from his bow stretched back to the tips of his ears, through fear of which the entire godly host took to its heels. (46).

देवोऽपि दैत्यविशिखप्रकरं सचापं
बाणैश्चकर्त कणशो रणकेलिकारी ।
योगीव योगविधिशुष्कमना यमाद्यैः
सांसारिकं विषयसंघममोघवीर्यम् ॥४७॥

God Kumāra, too, indulging in the sport of war, snapped into bits the arrows and the bow of the Asura, just as a Yogī, himself dry as dust, by his yaugic practices, snaps the infallible bonds of Saṁsāra. (47).

भ्रूभङ्गभीषणमुखोऽसुरचक्रवर्ती
संदीप्तकोपवहनोऽथ रथं विहाय ।
क्रीडत्करालकरवालकरोऽसुरेन्द्र-
स्तं प्रत्यधावदभितस्त्रिपुरारिसूनुम् ॥४८॥

The sovereign lord of the Asuras, his face dreadful with its knitted eyebrows, with the fire of anger flaming in his face, left his chariot, and flourishing his dreadful scimitar flew to meet him. (48).

अभ्यापतन्तमसुराधिपमीशपुत्रो
दुर्वारबाहुविभवं सुरसैनिकैस्तम् ।
दृष्ट्वा युगान्तदहनप्रतिमां मुमोच
शक्तिं प्रमोदविकसद्वदनारविन्दः ॥४९॥

The son of Īśa, Kumāra, his face beaming with joy, released his Śakti, that resembled the fire, that consumed the world at the end of an aeon,—against the sovereign lord of the Asuras, who rushed to meet him and the prowess of whose arms was irresistible to the soldiers of the godly host. (49).

उद्द्योतिताम्बरदिगन्तरमंशुजालैः
शक्तिः पपात हृदि तस्य महासुरस्य ।
हर्षाश्रुभिः सह समस्तदिगीश्वराणां
शोकोष्णबाष्पसलिलैः सह दानवानाम् ॥५०॥

The Śakti, illumining all the quarters with its circle of rays, struck the heart of the great Asura together with the tears of joy of the guardians of the quarters and the tears of grief of the demons. (50).

शक्त्या हृतासुमसुरेश्वरमापतन्तं
कल्पान्तवातहतभिन्नमिवाद्रिशृङ्गम् ।
दृष्ट्वा प्ररूढपुलकाञ्चितचारुदेहा
देवाः प्रमोदमगमंस्त्रिदशेन्द्रमुख्याः ॥५१॥

The gods, headed by Indra, seeing the lord of the Asuras struck down by the Śakti, like a mountain-peak blasted by a blast of the wind of cataclysm, had fine horripilation breaking on their bodies and were filled with great delight. (51).

यत्रापतत्स दनुजाधिपतिः परासुः
संवर्तकालनिपतच्छिखरीन्द्रतुल्यः ।
तत्रादधात्फणिपतिर्धरणीं फणाभि-
स्तद्भूरिभारविधुराभिरधो व्रजन्तीम् ॥५२॥

There where fell the lord of the Asuras, dead, comparable to a great mountain, falling down at the end of an aeon, there, sinking down, the lord of serpents bore the earth on his hoods which were distressed by his heavy weight. (52).

स्वर्गापगासलिलसीकरिणी समन्ता-
त्सौरभ्यलुब्धमधुपावलिसेव्यमाना ।
कल्पद्रुमप्रसववृष्टिरभून्नभस्तः
शंभोः सुतस्य शिरसि त्रिदशारिशत्रोः ॥५३॥

There fell all round upon the head of Kumāra, the enemy of the gods, a shower of Kalpa flowers from the heavens saturated with the spray of the waters of the heavenly river—flowers surrounded by swarms of bees, attracted by their fragrance. (53).

पुलकभरविभिन्नवारबाणा भुजविभवं बहु तारकस्य शत्रोः ।
सकलसुरगणा महेन्द्रमुख्याः प्रमदमुखच्छविसंपदोऽभ्यनन्दन् ॥५४॥

The gods with Indra as their leader, whose armours had burst by thick horripilation that broke out upon their bodies, their faces beaming with a richness of joyful comlexion, congratulated the might of the arms of Tāraka's foe. (54).

इति विषमशरारेः सूनुना जिष्णुनाजौ
त्रिभुवनवरशल्ये प्रोद्धृते दानवेन्द्रे ।
बलरिपुरथ नाकस्याधिपत्यं प्रपद्य
व्यजयत सुरचूडारत्नघृष्टाग्रपादः ॥५५॥

When the lord of Asuras (i.e. Tāraka), the incomparable warrior in the three worlds (lit. the great tormentor of the three worlds), was thus killed (lit. laid low) in battle by Kumāra, the victorious son of god Śiva, Indra, the enemy of Asura Bala who had acquired the sovereignty of heaven, had his feet rubbed by gems in the chest of gods and was all triumphant (55).